W9-AQE-719

CURRICULUM LABORATORY

Teaching Grammar in Context

Teaching Grammar in Context

Constance Weaver
Department of English
Western Michigan University

Andrew Carnegie Library
Livingstone College
701 W. Monroe St.
Salisbury, NC 28144

Boynton/Cook Publishers
HEINEMANN
Portsmouth, NH

Boynton/Cook Publishers, Inc.
A subsidiary of Reed Elsevier Inc.
361 Hanover Street
Portsmouth, NH 03801-3912
Offices and agents throughout the world

Copyright © 1996 by Constance Weaver. All rights reserved. No part of this book may be reproduced in any form or by any electronic or mechanical means, including information storage and retrieval systems, without permission in writing from the publisher, except by a reviewer, who may quote brief passages in a review.

Acknowledgments for borrowed material begin on page 287.

Library of Congress Cataloging-in-Publication Data

Weaver, Constance.
  Teaching grammar in context / Constance Weaver.
    p.   cm.
  Includes bibliographical references and index.
  ISBN 0-86709-375-7 (acid-free paper)
  1. English language—Grammar—Study and teaching. 2. English language—Grammar—Study and teaching (Secondary)   I. Title.
PE1065.W345   1996
428'.007—dc20   95-50512
                                                                 CIP

Editor: Scott Mahler
Production: Melissa L. Inglis
Cover design: Jenny Jensen Greenleaf

Printed in the United States of America on acid-free paper
99 98 97 96 RRD 1 2 3 4 5 6 7 8 9

Andrew Carnegie Library
Livingstone College
701 W. Monroe St.
Salisbury, NC 28144

CONTENTS

List of Illustrations

PREFACE

More than fifteen years ago, the National Council of Teachers of English published my *Grammar for Teachers* (1979). In the intervening years, this book has been one of NCTE's bestsellers, attesting to the widespread concern about teaching grammar but also reflecting the book's congruence with the writing process movement of the 1980s and 1990s. While suggesting that teachers need to know grammar in order to teach writing more effectively, I also argued that students mainly need to be guided in learning and applying certain grammatical concepts as they revise and edit their writing.

For a long while I had nothing new to say on the topic of teaching grammar. Indeed, I was no longer teaching courses in grammar, but instead teaching courses in the reading and writing processes and whole language education. My books have reflected that thrust: for example, *Reading Process and Practice: From Socio-psycholinguistics to Whole Language* (1994) and *Understanding Whole Language* (1990). But for the past seven or eight years, I have also been teaching, once a year, a graduate/undergraduate course on grammar and the teaching of grammar. Teaching this course has forced me to reread and update myself on the relevant research, naturally, but also to reexamine, refine, and expand my thinking about what aspects of grammar need to be taught to writers, along with the related questions of why, when, and how.

The present book derives, then, not only from my original background in grammar and linguistics, language acquisition, the writing process, and the teaching of writing, but from more recent forays into learning theory and the acquisition of literacy. As much as anything else, the book is informed by my experiences as a teacher/researcher, always taking new risks and trying to figure out why something has or hasn't worked. Thus, what I currently think about teaching grammar in the context of writing reflects an amalgam of research and experience, which is always to some degree in flux. It is this evolving theory that I invite you to explore in these pages, and to which I urge you to contribute as a teacher/researcher yourself. The book is intended for teachers at all levels, but especially the junior high and high school levels, where grammar has been taught most intensively.

Chapter 1 introduces some common meanings of *grammar* and provides a historical overview of traditional school grammar books and grammar teaching. Chapter 2 examines reasons commonly given for teaching grammar as a school subject and calls these reasons into question by describing decades of research that show the teaching of grammar in isolation to have little, if any, effect on the writing of most students. What might be more effective? To lay the groundwork for exploration of this topic, Chapter 3 considers how preschoolers acquire the basic structures of their native language and how the basic grammar of a second language may likewise be acquired. Developing an important point from that discussion, Chapter 4 suggests a research-based perspective on the concept of error itself and on the "errors" our students make as writers, then concludes with practical alternatives to what Lois Rosen (1987) has dubbed "the error hunt." Chapter 5 draws upon the preceding chapters and further research in suggesting what aspects of grammar we might focus on, as we guide our students in becoming more effective in writing and revising sentences and in editing their writing. Finally, Chapter 6 addresses the teaching of grammar from the perspective of learning theory.

Originally, these six chapters were to be followed by chapters dealing with teaching different grammatical concepts in the context of writing. But as I met with teachers interested in sharing more effective ways of teaching useful aspects of grammar, we realized that it would be good to have these chapters written by various teachers who have tried different things in their classrooms. Before long, we concluded that I should publish the more theoretical, research-derived chapters as a separate book and that together we should work toward a sequel in which we will share some of the lessons we've learned, through experience, about teaching grammar in the context of writing.

The Appendix, with sample lessons from my own teaching, looks forward to the future book. These lessons illustrate the kinds recommended in Chapter 6: incidental teaching, inductive learning, mini-lessons, and extended mini-lessons. They also illustrate the five broad topics for grammar lessons suggested in Chapter 5: (1) teaching concepts of subject, verb, clause, sentence, and related concepts for editing; (2) teaching style through sentence combining and sentence generating; (3) teaching sentence sense and style through the manipulation of syntactic elements; (4) teaching the power of dialects and dialects of power; and (5) teaching punctuation and mechanics for convention, clarity, and style.

While this list sounds fairly comprehensive, the book does not actually cover everything you might have wanted to know about grammar and the teaching of it. First, the book does not deal much with linguistic theories; rather, I have mostly drawn upon such theories without discussing them in detail. Second, the book does not include much of the descriptive/prescriptive grammar found in the grammar handbooks. Third, the samples in the Appendix reflect my own teaching situations and therefore do not deal with the particular needs of so-called basic writers, or with the needs of and issues involved in teaching students for whom English is not the native language, or for whom a so-called standard dialect is not the dialect of their nurture or community (but see Chapter 3 and the Appendix). Most of these issues will be treated more thoroughly in the forthcoming sequel, tentatively titled *Lessons to Share: Teaching Grammar in Context.*

In writing this text, I originally thought that whenever I used grammatical terms, I would define them and give examples. Thus, for instance, Chapter 3 includes definitions of the terms I think most important to teach, and Chapter 5 includes some terms used in the examples to clarify research studies described. However, defining or exemplifying every term proved impractical, so I settled for defining a few in the text itself and, in the Glossary, defining and illustrating these terms and others that were used prominently in the book. Fortunately, though, I don't think readers of this book need to have a strong background in grammar to grasp my major points. While a strong grammar background will enable readers to follow the details of an argument, the essence of the arguments should typically be clear without that background.

Thanks go to those in my Grammar and Teaching Grammar class who have shared their work and their ideas, particularly Dan Baker, Dan Cupery, and Jane Kiel; to classroom teachers who have shared materials, particularly Amy Berryhill, Lisbeth Bond, Renée Callies, Scott Peterson, Christina Travis, Susie Veeder, Sarah Woltjer-Bollow, and Grace Vento-Zogby; to Dorothy Strickland of Rutgers University for her contribution to Chapter 6; and to my longtime friend Rosemary Monkhouse Beamand, for her prompt help with research. In general, I want to thank those in the Grammar and Teaching Grammar class who have forced me to rethink issues and thereby taught me as much as I have taught them. Thanks go especially to all of those who have contributed samples of their drawing and/or writing, from kindergartners to adults. I am particularly indebted also to my colleague and friend Ellen Brinkley for reading and commenting on most of the chapters herein—though of course the book's shortcomings remain my responsibility.

Scott Mahler, Associate Editorial Director of Heinemann–Boynton/Cook, has been invaluable as a critic and supporter in the final stages of preparing the manuscript. Thanks go also to Alice Cheyer for her dedication and thoroughness in editing the manuscript and to Melissa Inglis for her expert handling of the book's production.

As always, though, my greatest appreciation goes to my son, John, and to my partner, Rolland. They offer unfailing support for my work and bring joy to my daily life.

1

Grammar and the Teaching of Grammar

An Introduction

At the outset it seems sensible to consider various meanings attached to the term *grammar* and something of the history of grammar texts and the teaching of grammar. That is the purpose of this introductory chapter.

The Meanings of *Grammar*

When teachers are invited to brainstorm what the term *grammar* means to them, they commonly produce a list such as this:

- Parts of speech (elements or categories)
- Syntactic structures (phrases, clauses, sentence types; roles of elements within larger structures)
- "Correct" sentence structure (subject-verb agreement and such)
- "Correct" punctuation and other aspects of mechanics
- Appropriate usage (often thought of as "standard" or educated forms)
- Sentence sense; style (appropriate and effective use of syntactic options; ability to manipulate syntactic elements)

The first two of these, parts of speech and syntactic structures, are part of what one might call a description of how different kinds of words in a language combine into grammatical structures, or *syntax*. Thus one definition of *grammar* would be "a description of the syntax of a language," or an explanation of its syntax (a theory of language structure). The next three items, dealing with correctness and appropriateness, clearly involve prescriptions of how to use language. Thus another meaning of *grammar* is "a set of prescriptions or rules for using language." Still another meaning deals with sentence sense and style: for instance, the construction of clear, readable sentences, and the deliberate use of syntactic constructions for particular effects. The latter might be defined as "the rhetorically effective use of syntactic structures," or in other words suiting syntax to such things as the meaning, audience, genre, voice, and intended pace of a text. All three kinds of *grammar*—but especially the descriptive and prescriptive—are commonly found in the grammar books used in schools, such as *Warriner's High School Handbook* (1992), an offspring of the long-lived *Warriner's English Grammar and Composition* series (1986; first edition, 1951). For related treatments of the various meanings of grammar, see Hartwell (1985) and Francis (1954).

Most teachers conceptualize grammar as descriptions of the structure of a language, prescriptions for its use, perhaps as sentence sense or style, and as the kind of books designed for teaching all these. However, relatively few teachers have realized that underlying these four senses of *grammar* is a more fundamental one: the unconscious command of syntax that enables us to understand and speak the language. Even toddlers use grammatical constructions that are reductions and precursors of the mature syntax they will gradually acquire. In this most fundamental sense, then, we do not need to teach grammar at all: the grammar of our native language is part of what we learn in acquiring that language. Furthermore, non-native speakers of a language can acquire the language in much the same way as native speakers, given similar kinds of opportunities to hear, use, read, and write the language. These topics are addressed in subsequent chapters.

For now, suffice it to say that there are four major senses of *grammar* that will concern us in this book:

- Grammar as a description of syntactic structure
- Grammar as prescriptions for how to use structures and words
- Grammar as rhetorically effective use of syntactic structures
- Grammar as the functional command of sentence structure that enables us to comprehend and produce language

Chapter 2 introduces some of the reasons commonly given for direct teaching of grammar as a system and a set of rules for language use: the descriptions and prescriptions found in school grammar texts. First, however, we consider the historical context from which these reasons have arisen.

Traditional School Grammar in a Historical Perspective

During previous centuries, traditional school grammar seems to have had two primary aims: (1) disciplining and training the mind (and sometimes the soul); and (2) teaching grammatical forms and word usages that were considered correct or socially prestigious. Ostensibly the socially prestigious forms were taught to enable the lower classes to move more readily into the middle class (or the middle classes into the upper class), but one suspects that in effect if not intent, the result has more often been to offer the middle and upper classes an excuse for considering themselves superior to others (e.g., Noguchi, 1991, p. 114).

In any case, the teaching of grammar to schoolboys dates back to Greece in the second century B.C. Prior to that, Aristotle and the Stoics regarded grammar as a means of understanding language, but language as a product of humans' nature and therefore, "like man's other attributes, subject to anomalies inexplicable within any strict system of grammar" (Huntsman, 1983, p. 61). However, the Alexandrian grammarians seem to have assumed that language once reflected reality. In a sense, their early grammars were attempts to recover that reality by imposing order on language, especially the language of the centuries-old texts they were trying to understand (Huntsman, p. 61). In our schools, the Alexandrian tradition has dominated the study of grammar for more than two thousand years.

The first grammar text, published by Dionysios of Thrace late in the second century B.C., became the standard for Greek schoolboys until the twelfth century A.D. It also became the basis for Latin grammars, such as the grammars of Donatus in the fourth century A.D. and of Priscian in the sixth century. Their works "dominated school grammar study throughout the Middle Ages to the Renaissance" (Hillocks and Smith, 1991, p. 592).

During the Middle Ages, the concept of grammar as training the mind reached a peak. Grammar became the chief subject of the trivium (grammar, rhetoric, and logic), studied intensively because it was considered the foundation of all knowledge. Indeed, grammar was considered the gateway to sacred knowledge as well as secular; it was the prerequisite for understanding theology and philosophy as well as literature. Considered the basis for all liberal learning, "grammar was thought to discipline the mind and the soul at the same time" (Huntsman, 1983, p. 59). At that time, the major task of the religious cleric (clergyman) was to use the arts, especially grammar, "to disclose the hidden mysteries of Scripture." Also, Christians thought that grammar would enable them to examine "valid processes of reasoning, the operations of the mind itself" (Morrison, 1983, p. 39). Perhaps it is no wonder that until the late 1960s and early 1970s, Great Britain had what they called "grammar" schools for the highest achieving secondary-level students. Indeed, such elitist schools still survive in a few school districts, even today.

In the eighteenth century, as the Industrial Revolution created a new middle class, traditional school grammar books of English became more numerous and more important. Mastering the grammar books' prescriptions helped the nouveau riche gain social acceptance. But even more than before, the eighteenth-century English grammar books were based upon the early Latin grammars and the structure of Latin. For example, English nouns were described as having the same cases as Latin nouns, though in fact English had already lost most of its distinctive inflectional endings for nouns and verbs. Users of the language were admonished to avoid splitting an infinitive (e.g., to avoid saying "to boldly go") because infinitives are single words in Latin. In other words, the eighteenth-century English grammarians concluded that because Latin infinitives cannot be split (e.g., *amare*, 'to love'), English infinitives should not be split. Their prescriptions for English were based on descriptions of Latin, even where these were irrelevant to English. So it was, too, with the prescription against ending a sentence with a preposition: this literally *can't* be done in Latin so, the eighteenth-century grammarians reasoned, it *shouldn't* be done in English. This recourse to the structure of Latin reflected the belief that languages like English and German and French and Spanish were "corruptions" of Latin, which was thought to provide a purer standard, a more accurate reflection of thought and reality.

There were, of course, dissenting voices, even in ancient Rome, such as that of the orator and rhetorician Quintilian. True, in support of tradition, Quintilian did describe in his *Institutes of Oratory* essentially the same parts of speech named by the earlier Greek grammarians, and Quintilian did believe that one major concern of the grammarian should be "rules for correctness" (*Institutes*, I.v.1). However, he also believed that standards for usage should be based upon the current usage of the educated, not upon ancient authority that has ceased to govern the speech of learned individuals (I.vi.43–45).

This insight from the first century A.D. remains unappreciated even today, because the explanations and prescriptions of the eighteenth-century English grammarians (and the Latin grammarians before them) continue to form the backbone of grammar texts. In the last hundred years, the structure of the English language has come to be much better understood by scholarly grammarians and by linguists—that is, by scholars who have attempted to study language scientifically, and to study how language is actually used by people. But the grammar textbooks have not changed much to reflect this new knowledge about the language itself and how it is used. Indeed, grammar texts still include attention to spelling and to word meanings and choices, as did the texts of the classical grammarians (Huntsman, 1983, pp. 58–59).

An excursion into the nature and rationale of grammar texts and teaching in the United States sheds further light not only on the purposes but on the methods of instruction.

From relatively early times, English grammar has been one of the "basics" taught in U.S. schools. For instance, the Massachusetts legislature passed in 1789 a law requiring schools to provide instruction in "orthography [spelling], reading, writing, grammar, English language, arithmetic, and decent behavior" (Woods, 1986, p. 5).

During the first half of the nineteenth century, what counted as learning grammar was mainly the memorization and recitation of "definitions, rules, paradigms, examples, and other grammatical features" (Woods, p. 7). Once these were committed to memory, supposedly the student would then be able to apply them. Theoretically, students would learn to apply the rules with ease by parsing sentences: identifying the parts of speech of the words "and specifying their case, gender, number, tense, or person in a given sentence" (Woods, p. 18, fn. 2). In addition to promoting application of grammatical concepts, the activities of memorizing, reciting, and parsing were thought to train the mind, to promote mental discipline. Until the period from 1825 to 1830, grammarians of English gave little or no evidence of being concerned that students actually *understand* the grammatical information they were required to memorize and recite (Woods, p. 8).

The latter half of the nineteenth century saw the introduction of exercises into the grammar texts, on the grounds that students needed to be active in their own learning. These exercises included activities like answering questions, writing sentences to exemplify certain kinds of grammatical functions and constructions, and sometimes rearranging or combining sentences. Indeed, descriptions of the contents of such grammar texts sound very much like what we find offered as learning aids in the grammar texts of today. That is, the texts allowed for limited production of language, in addition to requiring analysis.

The emphasis on grammar as a reflection of thought took on renewed importance in the later 1800s. Woods (1986, p. 18) nicely summarizes this trend as follows:

> [Samuel] Greene's [1874] intricate sentence analysis had been meant as a way of showing students how "to look directly through the expression to the thought" (as a logician must). Similarly, the pedagogy of diagramming, which characterized the next generation of texts after Greene's, is defended by Reed and Kellogg (*Higher Lessons in English*, 1872) as a method that teaches students "to look through the literary order and discover the logical order" for "[i]t is only by the aid of such a map, or picture, that the pupil can, at a single view, see the sentence as an organic whole" [Reed and Kellogg, 1909, p. 8]. Naturally, the exercises in diagramming, like those in analysis and construction, were validated by that noblest stamp of nineteenth-century theory, mental discipline: "To study thought through its outward form, the sentence, and to discover the fitness of the different parts of the expression to the different parts of the thought is to learn to think" [Reed and Kellogg, p. 7].

By the end of the nineteenth century, grammar came to be considered a means of improving writing. Even in that context, however, grammar was considered a form of mental discipline and a means of social refinement (Woods, 1986, p. 18).

Recently the twentieth century has seen a shift away from the emphasis on grammar as mental discipline and a shift toward even more emphasis on grammar as a means of improving writing. However, the descriptions of the eighteenth-century grammarians and the teaching methods of the latter half of the nineteenth century persisted into the twentieth century (H. L. Smith, 1946) and are still very much with us. Indeed, Thomas and Kintgen (1974) note with dismay that "The school-grammars totally ignore many of the important facts that we have learned about language in the last 150 years" (p. 13), and Hillocks and Smith (1991) note that today's school grammars still reflect the early Greeks' emphasis on grammatical paradigms and their belief that "right" grammatical forms are discoverable. "Over two thousand years later these are still with us," they lament (p. 591).

In Chapter 2, we consider some of the reasons commonly offered today for teaching grammar as a formal discipline, a system of descriptions and prescriptive rules that, in fact, are not always accurate or helpful. We then consider the research evidence that militates against the pragmatic justification for teaching grammar. After considering other relevant kinds of research in Chapters 3–5, we consider in Chapter 6 an emerging research base that points toward more fruitful ways of teaching selected aspects of grammar.

2

Teaching Grammar
Reasons for, Evidence Against

When people talk about "teaching grammar," what they usually mean is teaching descriptive and prescriptive grammar: that is, teaching sentence elements and structure, usage, sentence revision, and punctuation and mechanics via a grammar book or workbook, or perhaps a computer program. They mean teaching grammar as a system, and teaching it directly and systematically, usually in isolation from writing or the study of literature. They mean studying parts of speech and their functions in sentences, various types of phrases and clauses, and different sentence types, perhaps accompanied by sentence diagraming and usually followed by a study of such concepts as subject-verb agreement and pronoun reference. Since this is what people typically mean by "teaching formal grammar" or "the traditional teaching of grammar," it is also what we shall mean in this chapter as we discuss reasons for and evidence against the practice.

The articles listed in Figure 2.1 articulate some of these reasons and describe some of the research.

Why Teach Grammar?

Over the centuries, various reasons have been offered for teaching formal grammar, among them these:

1. The study of grammar is important simply because language is a supreme human achievement that deserves to be studied as such.
2. The study of grammar can be an important vehicle for learning to study something the way a scientist does.
3. The study of grammar will help form the mind by promoting "mental discipline."

FIGURE 2.1 References for and against the teaching of formal grammar.

deBeaugrande, R. (1984). Forward to the basics: Getting down to grammar. *College Composition and Communication, 35,* 358–367.

d'Eloia, S. (1977). The uses—and limits—of grammar. *Journal of Basic Writing, 1* (Spring/Summer), 1–20.

Hartwell, P. (1985). Grammar, grammars, and the teaching of grammar. *College English, 47,* 105–127.

Hillocks, G., Jr. (1986). Grammar and the manipulation of syntax. In *Research on written composition* (pp. 133–151). Urbana, IL: ERIC/RCS and NCRE. Distributed by the National Council of Teachers of English.

Hillocks, G., Jr., & Smith, M. W. (1991). Grammar and usage. In J. Flood, J. M. Jensen, D. Lapp, & J. R. Squire (Eds.), *Handbook of research on teaching the English language arts* (pp. 591–603). New York: Macmillan.

Kolln, M. (1986). Closing the books on alchemy. *College Composition and Communication, 32,* 139–151.

McQuade, F. (1980). Examining a grammar course: The rationale and the result. *English Journal, 69,* 26–30.

Sanborn, J. (1986). Grammar: Good wine before its time. *English Journal, 75,* 72–80.

Sedgwick, E. (1989). Alternatives to teaching formal, analytical grammar. *Journal of Developmental Education, 12* (3), 8–10, 12, 14, 20.

4. The study of grammar will help students score better on standardized tests that include grammar, usage, and punctuation.

5. The study of grammar will help people master another language more readily.

6. The study of grammar will help people master the socially prestigious conventions of spoken and/or written usage.

7. The study of grammar will help people become better users of the language, that is, more effective as listeners and speakers, and especially as readers and writers.

One can hardly quarrel with the idea that language is intrinsically interesting and worthy of study, except to point out that grammar books rarely make it so, and that students are less likely to be interested in the grammar of their language per se than in various appealing aspects of language *use*, such as the language of advertising, the "double-speak" of government, the language of sexism, and various ethnic and community dialects. And the study of grammar *can* help students learn to work like scientists, provided the teacher approaches it that way instead of the way it is traditionally taught (see Postman and Weingartner, 1966).

But what of the other reasons for teaching grammar? They reflect the assumption that studying grammar in itself, apart from reading and writing, or speaking and listening, will automatically produce desirable effects such as improved mental ability, higher scores on standardized tests, mastery of another language or of socially prestigious grammatical forms, and greater effectiveness as users of the language.

Logically, we need to consult the research evidence.

Early Research Summaries

As long ago as 1936, the Curriculum Commission of the National Council of Teachers of English recommended that "'all teaching of grammar separate from the manipulation of sentences be discontinued . . . since every scientific attempt to prove that knowledge of grammar is useful has failed . . .'" (as quoted in H. A. Greene, 1950, p. 392).

About fifteen years later, an article in the *Encyclopedia of Educational Research* (1950) summarized the available research on the teaching of grammar as a system and a subject, with the comment that these summary statements were warranted by "the best opinion, practice, and experimental evidence" (H. A. Greene, 1950, p. 393). The 1960 edition of the *Encyclopedia of Educational Research* includes similar summary statements (Searles and Carlson, 1960, p. 461), so I have combined some of them here, indicating only the year of each statement as it is quoted or closely paraphrased:

1. "The disciplinary value which may be attributed to formal grammar is negligible" (1950). That is, research does not support the contention that the study of grammar brings about mental discipline (1960).
2. "No more relation exists between knowledge of grammar and the application of the knowledge in a functional language situation than exists between any two totally different and unrelated school subjects" (1950). In fact, one investigator found a higher correlation between achievement in grammar and mathematics than between achievement in grammar and composition or oral language abilities (1960).
3. "In spite of the fact that the contribution of the knowledge of English grammar to achievement in foreign language has been its chief justification in the past, the experimental evidence does not support this conclusion" (1950). It appears that "knowledge of grammar does not materially affect a student's ability to learn a foreign language" (1960).

4. "The study of grammar has been justified because of its possible contribution to reading skills, but the evidence does not support this conclusion" (1950).
5. "The contribution of grammar to the formation of sentences in speech and in writing has doubtless been exaggerated" (1950).
6. "Diagraming sentences does not carry over to expressional problems [actual writing]." Indeed, "it teaches students nothing beyond the ability to diagram" (1960).

In short, the research apparently gave no support to the idea that teaching grammar would help students develop mental discipline, master another language, or become better users of their native language. Indeed, further evidence indicated that training in formal grammar did not transfer to any significant extent to writing "correct" English or even to recognizing it.

In 1963, Richard Braddock, Richard Lloyd-Jones, and Lowell Schoer wrote an NCTE report titled *Research in Written Composition*. For three decades, scholars have been quoting the statement that concludes their discussion of research on the teaching of grammar:

> In view of the widespread agreement of research studies based upon many types of students and teachers, the conclusion can be stated in strong and unqualified terms: the teaching of formal grammar has a negligible or, because it usually displaces some instruction and practice in actual composition, even a harmful effect on the improvement of writing. (pp. 37–38)

This bold statement seemed only a logical extension of DeBoer's conclusion from the available research four years before. DeBoer (1959) had written:

> The impressive fact is . . . that in all these studies, carried out in places and at times far removed from each other, often by highly experienced and disinterested investigators, the results have been consistently negative so far as the value of grammar in the improvement of language expression is concerned. Surely there is no justification in the available evidence for the great expenditure of time and effort still being devoted to formal grammar in American schools. (p. 417)

These strong indictments from the late 1950s and early 1960s clearly echo the NCTE's 1936 summary statement in its resolution against the teaching of grammar: "every scientific attempt to prove that knowledge of grammar is useful has failed." Of course, this conclusion will be no surprise to teachers who have observed that many students are unable or unwilling to analyze and label the parts of sentences or to apply the grammatical "rules" they have been taught.

Research on the Effects of Structural and Transformational Grammar

The 1950s and early 1960s saw the rise of structural linguistics, which attempted to describe languages more consistently, without recourse to meaning or to previous grammars, and therefore more objectively and "scientifically" than traditional grammarians had done. Structural linguists based their grammatical descriptions on careful analysis of English as it was actually spoken in their time, not on hand-me-down rules from Latin and from English grammars of earlier centuries. Therefore, some investigators hypothesized that a study of grammar from the viewpoint of structural linguistics might prove more valuable to writers than a study of traditional grammar, with its inconsistencies and unabashed use of meaning in determining the functions of grammatical elements. George Hillocks's 1986 review (with Michael W. Smith) of the research indicates, however, that overall the research comparing the effects of teaching structural grammar does not demonstrate that it is appreciably superior to the teaching of traditional grammar, with regard to its effects on writing (Hillocks, 1986, pp. 134–135).

The rise of transformational grammar in the 1960s and 1970s generated a similar optimism regarding the practical value of studying grammar through that approach. It emphasized how surface structures can be generated from hypothesized deep, underlying structures, and how underlying structures can be transformed into different stylistic variants. For instance, *The woman is tired* might be derived linguistically from a deep structure like "Something + tired + the + woman," thus validating many native speakers' sense that *tired* in the original sentence is a verb, though it functions as an adjective in the surface sentence. Similarly, a deep structure like "A + new + surgeon + performed + the + operation" might surface as either *A new surgeon performed the operation* or *The operation was performed by a new surgeon*, thus demonstrating the relationship between stylistic variants that mean essentially the same thing.

Bateman and Zidonis (1966) were perhaps the first researchers to investigate the effect that studying transformational grammar might have upon students' writing. The experimental group that studied transformational grammar during their ninth- and tenth-grade years wrote with a lower incidence of errors than the control group that studied no grammar. The transformational group also used more mature sentence structures (the kinds of structures that characterize older writers), though this difference was largely due to four students (about a fifth of the experimental group) and was not statistically significant.

In 1969, John Mellon reported a study in which he had hypothesized that a knowledge of transformational grammar in combination with practice in sentence combining would result in greater syntactic fluency in students' writing. The students in five experimental classes were exposed to terminology and grammatical explanations reflective of transformational theory, though actual practice in sentence combining seems to have been the major focus of the experimental treatment. The students in five control classes studied a course in traditional grammar. The two placebo classes that studied no grammar at all had additional lessons in literature and composition, but no additional writing assignments. During a one-year period, the experimental group significantly increased its syntactic fluency on all twelve of the factors analyzed. The control and placebo groups increased on only three of the factors at the same level of significance. The absolute growth in the experimental group was approximately double the growth in the control and placebo groups (Mellon, 1969, p. v). However, there were no appreciable differences in the overall quality of students' writing (p. 69).

In the wake of Mellon's study, Frank O'Hare (1973) reasoned that the greater syntactic maturity of Mellon's transformational group might have been due to their practice in sentence combining alone, rather than to their study of transformational grammar in conjunction with sentence combining. Indeed, Mellon (1969) himself had written, "Clearly, it was the sentence-combining practice associated with the grammar study, not the grammar study itself, that influenced the syntactic fluency growth rate" (p. 74).

Thus O'Hare hypothesized that sentence combining by itself might produce the same kinds of results, without the formal study of grammar or the use of technical terminology. Using nontechnical terms to describe different structures, O'Hare had his experimental group do sentence-combining exercises, while the control group studied no grammar but spent more time in the regular language arts curriculum. The result? The sentence-combining group made significant gains over the control group, in terms of syntactic maturity—which O'Hare (1973) defined as the range of sentence types used (p. 19). In fact, his seventh-grade sentence combiners wrote well beyond the syntactic maturity level typical of eighth graders, and in many respects very similar to that of the twelfth graders in a study by Kellogg Hunt (1965a), which had provided the benchmark data on syntactic maturity at different grade levels, compared with that of adults. Students in the experimental group also "wrote compositions that were significantly better in overall quality than the control group's compositions" (O'Hare, 1973, pp. 67–68). Thus O'Hare's research suggested that sentence-combining practice alone can enhance syntactic maturity and writing quality, without grammatical terminology or the study of grammar.

A substantial number of studies have supported this conclusion. Hillocks (1986) reports:

> These [sentence-combining] studies have led to a number of sentence combining texts and a host of dissertations from 1973 to the present. The overwhelming majority of these studies have been positive, with about 60 percent of them reporting that work in sentence combining, from as low as grade 2 through the adult level, results in significant advances (at least $p < .05$) on measures of syntactic maturity. Thirty percent of the reports have recorded some improvement at a nonsignificant level or at a level which was not tested for significance. Only 10 percent of the reports have been negative, showing either no significant differences or mixed results. (pp. 142–143)

In their summaries of research on the teaching of grammar, Hillocks (1986) and Hillocks and Smith (1991) present a thorough review of the relevant research since the early 1960s, including studies comparing the effects of teaching traditional or structural or transformational grammar with the effects of teaching no grammar, and studies comparing the effects of teaching structural or transformational grammar with the effects of teaching traditional grammar. After discussing these various studies, including the Elley study described in detail in a later section, Hillocks (1986) concludes:

> None of the studies reviewed for the present report provides any support for teaching grammar as a means of improving composition skills. If schools insist upon teaching the identification of parts of speech, the parsing or diagramming of sentences, or other concepts of traditional grammar (as many still do), they cannot defend it as a means of improving the quality of writing. (p. 138)

Little research on the teaching of mechanics has been done, but the available evidence does not offer much reason to be optimistic about teaching grammar as an aid to avoiding or correcting errors, either (Hillocks, 1986, p. 139; and see Chapter 6 of the present book for a discussion of Calkins, 1980, and DiStefano and Killion, 1984). In fact, as we shall see, the three-year Elley study showed that the writing of students studying transformational or traditional grammar was not significantly different from the no-grammar group, *even on the mechanics of writing*. Thus Hillocks

(1986) issues a strong indictment against the formal teaching of traditional grammar: "School boards, administrators and teachers who impose the systematic study of traditional school grammar on their students over lengthy periods of time in the name of teaching writing do them a gross disservice" (p. 248).

A Note on Functional Grammar

In Australia especially, the functional grammar of British linguists Halliday and Hasan has gained increasing influence in the schools (Halliday, 1985; Halliday and Hasan, 1976). Grammarians in this linguistic tradition claim that functional grammar is more relevant to writing because it emphasizes the functions or uses of grammatical constructions. Here are some ways in which functional grammar differs from traditional grammar (Collerson, 1994, pp. 142–144):

- It is primarily concerned with how the language works to achieve various purposes.
- It focuses first on larger grammatical components (clauses and sentences) and their functions within texts, not on parts of speech. Units at the clause and sentence level are considered most important because of their relationship to rhetorical and stylistic effectiveness.
- It is more concerned with effectiveness than with prescribing adherence to "rules"—that is, to particular conventions of language use.

As far as I know, research has not been conducted to determine the effects on student writing of teaching functional grammar in isolation, as a system for understanding the language. Indeed, the idea of teaching functional grammar in isolation from writing and speaking would seem contrary to the whole notion of focusing on the functional aspects of language structure.

A Dissenting Voice

In light of this overwhelming body of evidence, it may seem surprising that there is any dissenting voice among scholars. But in 1981, before the Elley study and before the Hillocks and Smith summaries, Martha Kolln wrote an article critiquing some earlier research summaries, describing some other relevant research, and articulating her own conviction—without offering any research support—that it should be helpful for students in their writing to bring their unconscious grammatical knowledge to conscious awareness, through the study of the categories and structures and labels of grammar.

One significant contribution is her critique of the research underlying the widely cited research summaries of Braddock, Lloyd-Jones, and Schoer (1963) and of Dean Memering (1978). For example, she points out weaknesses in the design and implementation of some of the studies summarized by Braddock et al.—weaknesses of which the authors apparently were aware (Braddock, Lloyd-Jones, and Schoer, 1963, p. 37). And indeed, just preceding DeBoer's (1959) decisive summary of the research, he had written that "a close examination of some of the reports of investigations of the effectiveness of grammar instruction might reveal flaws in research design or conclusions not fully warranted by the evidence" (p. 417). Since Braddock, Lloyd-Jones, and Schoer also noted weaknesses in methodology and interpretation in the studies from which they generalized, one wonders why these hints of flawed research studies did not inspire more scepticism about their conclusions.

Kolln points out that in the same year as the Braddock report was published (1963), Henry C. Meckel described in the *Handbook of Research on Teaching* many of the same studies as Braddock and colleagues had done. However, his conclusions were rather different. Meckel's conclusions that can be directly compared with those of Braddock et al. are as follows:

1. There is no research evidence that grammar as traditionally taught in the schools has any appreciable effect on the improvement of writing skill.
2. The training periods involved in transfer studies have been comparatively short, and the amount of grammar instruction has frequently been small.
3. There is no conclusive research evidence, however, that grammar has *no* transfer value in developing composition skill.
4. More research is needed on the kind of grammatical knowledge that may reasonably be expected to transfer to writing.
5. Research does not justify the conclusion that grammar should not be taught systematically.
6. There are more efficient methods of securing *immediate* improvement in the writing of pupils, both in sentence structure and usage, than systematic grammatical instruction.

The major points on which Meckel differs from Braddock et al. are items 4 and 5. He explains item 4 by indicating that research in which students are led to apply the grammatical principles taught may produce more positive results than research in which grammar is studied in and by itself. Similarly, he explains item 5 by saying that the systematic teaching of grammar does not preclude explicit attention also to the application of the grammar taught. That is, the formal study of grammar does not have to be the isolated or unapplied study of grammar.

Thus while Kolln points out that the research showing the ineffectiveness of teaching grammar for improving writing is not completely valid, her major contribution lies in pointing out that grammar study in conjunction with explicit application may have more promise than grammar study alone (her 1991 book *Rhetorical Grammar* reflects this conviction). However, it is still by no means clear that "application" cannot be done just as effectively, and a lot more efficiently, without detailed, explicit grammar study. Witness, for example, O'Hare's (1973) research on sentence combining.

Three Studies in Detail

By far the most impressive research on the effects of grammar study is that conducted by Elley, Barham, Lamb, and Wyllie (1976). Equally interesting, however, are an earlier study by Macauley in Scotland (1947), who focused on the degree to which grammar is actually learned, and a study undertaken by a secondary school teacher, Finlay McQuade (1980), who focused on the practical effects of grammar study. All of these studies were reported before the publication of Kolln's article.

The Study by Macauley (1947)

Macauley's study—or rather, his series of studies—strongly suggests that despite years of grammar study, students do not achieve much ability to identify even the basic parts of speech as these function in sentences.

Macauley reports that grammar is (or was in the 1940s) extensively taught in both the primary (elementary) and secondary schools of Scotland, for an average of about thirty minutes a day at both levels. He further explains:

> Formal grammar has to begin at 7½ years of age with lessons on the noun, singular and plural number, and the verb; at 8, is added the study of

adjectives; at 8½, personal pronouns and the tenses of verbs; at 9, analysis of simple sentences, conjugation of verbs, kinds of nouns and case of nouns; at 9½, particular analysis, tenses of auxiliary verbs, adverbs; at 10, adverb, preposition and conjunction, the relative pronoun, interchange of phrases and clauses; and so on till in the top primary class at age 11½ to 12 the course to be covered includes complete revision of all the parts of speech with declensions and conjugations, and written exercises involving analysis and parsing of easy, simple, complex, and compound sentences. (p. 153)

In short, the teaching of grammar in the elementary grades emphasizes parts of speech and their functions.

With such extensive and intensive teaching of these aspects of grammar, one might assume that the grammar would be well learned. Not so, according to Macauley's research.

A number of tests were used, similar to the one in Figure 2.2. This test consists of fifty sentences in which the student is to indicate the part of speech of the underlined word, given the choices of noun, pronoun, verb, adjective, or adverb. The student needs to understand that the *function* of a word determines the part of speech in a given context.

Macauley explains that given the method of scoring, students could have gotten about 11 percent of the answers right simply by guessing. Nevertheless, he and his scorers decided to use a 50 percent correct score as a standard of success—not a very demanding standard, given the years of intensive teaching of grammar. For all the test items, the average (mean) score for the 131 students was an incredibly low 27.9 percent. The scores ranged from 35.5 percent at one school to 21.8 percent at another (without knowing Scottish geography, the reader cannot relate these scores to the kind of school, whether city, town, or rural).

For each part of speech, there were ten items. For the five parts of speech, the rate of successful identification was as shown in Figure 2.3. Out of the 131 students, only one scored 50 percent or better on all five parts of speech.

To corroborate or challenge these results, Macauley administered the same test to a group of (average) students entering a junior secondary school. The students were approximately the same age (twelve), but the scores were even lower. Macauley explains that this is probably because the best students had already been siphoned off to a senior secondary school.

Macauley went on to determine the results for students who had spent two years in a junior secondary school, during which they continued to receive instruction in grammar. Their scores did rise steadily from an overall

FIGURE 2.2 Macauley's grammar test (1947). Apparently Macauley expected students to focus on how the word *functions* in the sentence. Since this expectation is not clear in the directions, the lack of clarity must surely have affected the results.

INSTRUCTIONS: Here are fifty sentences. In each sentence, there is a word underlined. On your answer sheet, you have to indicate what part of speech you think the underlined word is. Do so by putting a ring round N or V or P or A or J, according as you think the word is a Noun, Verb, Pronoun, Adverb, or Adjective.

1. His new <u>cycle</u> was stolen.
2. He <u>cycled</u> from the farm to the hostel.
3. <u>You</u> must visit us soon.
4. Meet me <u>here</u> in an hour.
5. The <u>daily</u> paper peeped out of his pocket.
6. The shopkeeper promised to send fresh milk <u>daily.</u>
7. What have I done to deserve <u>this?</u>
8. A haircut <u>lasts</u> him a month.
9. The cobbler put the boot on the <u>last.</u>
10. Lightning was the <u>last</u> horse to pass the post.
11. The steamer touched in at <u>Rothesay.</u>
12. <u>Who</u> stole my heart away?
13. He seems a nice, <u>friendly</u> dog.
14. The dog watched his master <u>hopefully.</u>
15. Are you going to <u>dance</u> tonight?
16. It <u>was</u> shortly after midnight.
17. He looked <u>very</u> worried.
18. <u>It</u> never rains but it pours.
19. The letter was delivered by the first <u>post.</u>
20. You must be <u>patient</u> with me.
21. My <u>watch</u> seems to be slow.
22. Are you going to the <u>dance,</u> to-night?
23. Give me <u>my</u> money and let me go.
24. The day will probably be <u>cool.</u>
25. I will keep what is <u>mine.</u>
26. He was <u>cooling</u> off after the game.
27. The tide was ebbing <u>fast.</u>
28. The child was knocked <u>over</u> in the rush.
29. We <u>watch</u> the progress of our team.
30. Those <u>who</u> can find the time, should visit the exhibition.
31. I should like <u>some</u> to take home.
32. You should <u>post</u> early in the day.
33. <u>Why</u> did he do it?
34. The doctor visited his <u>patients.</u>
35. The <u>fastest</u> runner does not always win.
36. I <u>suffer</u> from nerves.
37. Which <u>team</u> do you support?
38. I might have believed you <u>earlier.</u>
39. I should like <u>some</u> fruit to take home.
40. <u>What</u> have I done to deserve this?
41. He used a stop watch to <u>time</u> the runners.
42. <u>Where</u> shall we meet?
43. Have <u>patience</u> and I will pay thee all.
44. It is the early bird <u>that</u> gets the worm.
45. <u>Which</u> team do you support?
46. It was <u>shortly</u> after midnight.
47. It is not so long since we saw <u>them.</u>
48. I <u>might</u> have believed you earlier.
49. He was well-known for his <u>friendliness.</u>
50. We hope to encourage the <u>team</u> spirit.

FIGURE 2.3 Macauley's results (1947).

PART OF SPEECH	MEAN SCORE ON THOSE 5 ITEMS	PERCENT OF STUDENTS SCORING 50% OR BETTER
Noun	43.3	36.6
Verb	30.5	20.6
Pronoun	28.5	16.0
Adverb	19.8	3.8
Adjective	17.8	5.3

mean of 26.3 percent to a mean of 35.4 percent of items correct. Obviously, however, few students achieved the minimally acceptable standard of 50 percent. Out of the 397 students, only four scored at least 50 percent on all five parts of speech.

Finally, Macauley used the same test with students in a senior secondary school for the academic elite, wherein there are nevertheless technical and domestic tracks for "early leavers." Despite continued intensive teaching of grammar throughout three years of secondary school, Macauley found, there was still relatively little improvement:

- No domestic or technical class scored above 40 percent on the whole test.
- The only classes scoring 50 percent or above on all five parts of speech were the two classes studying a foreign language.
- The overall mean for the top boys' class and the top girls' class increased from 46.5 percent in the first year to 62 percent in the third year.
- By the third year, when more than half the senior secondary students had left school, still only 41.5 percent of all the remaining students scored 50 percent or higher on the total test.

In trying to interpret the results, Macauley first hypothesized that the students in the elementary grades did so poorly because "a certain stage of mental maturity appears to be required for the understanding of grammatical function" (p. 159). However, the results for the students in junior and senior secondary schools are not a lot more impressive.

On the one hand, we cannot consider Macauley's results entirely reliable, since his directions did not make it clear that students were to determine the word's part of speech by its function. Particularly troublesome in this regard are the items where the underlined word is a pronoun in form but an adjective in function; however, the lack of clarity in the directions could certainly have affected responses to some other items, too.

On the other hand, even assuming that students understood the parts of speech somewhat better than their scores suggested, one can hardly escape the conclusion that extensive and intensive teaching of grammar may not be warranted—even if the mastery of grammar itself were our primary or sole aim, rather than the learning of grammar for some other purpose such as mental discipline, learning a second language, or the improvement of writing.

The Study by Elley et al. (1976)

This three-year longitudinal study in New Zealand began when students were in their third-form year, at age thirteen. The study involved 248 students in eight matched classes of average ability; one "bright" and three "slow-learning" classes were deliberately excluded so as to make any observed differences more likely the result of the approach itself rather than of the differences among students. To control for teacher differences, the three teachers each taught each program to each class part of the time.

A transformational (TG) group studied the grammar, rhetoric, and literature strands of the Oregon Curriculum (Kitzhaber, 1970). The transformational grammar strand focused on explaining the rules of grammar that a native speaker naturally uses; the aim of the strand was simply to teach students about the syntax of English, not to teach grammar for any utilitarian purpose. The reading-writing course (RW) included the rhetoric and literature strands of the Oregon Curriculum, but substituted extra reading and creative writing (mostly reading) for the transformational grammar strand. The third group studied from a *Let's Learn English* (LLE) program (Smart, 1969), wherein the grammar taught is largely traditional, and more functional than the grammar taught in the Oregon Curriculum. It also included many applications. The teachers consulted regularly in order to maintain similar emphases in those aspects of the English curriculum that were not being compared.

Various language tests were used to ascertain any differences that might arise from the differing approaches. These included (but were not limited to) the *PAT Reading Comprehension and Reading Vocabulary Tests* (1969), a test of sentence combining, and a test of English usage that required students to correct "errors" in specially prepared short sentences and continuous prose. At the end of each year of the study, all students wrote a set of essays on various topics. Four essays were assessed for each student in the first year of the study, with three essays being assessed in the two subsequent years. The essays were assessed by carefully trained groups of English teachers from nearby high schools.

During the first year of the study, none of the three programs showed a significant superiority on any of the twelve variables assessed. The only significant difference was in attitudes: the TG group liked writing less than the other groups. Only one of the possible language test comparisons proved significant the second year, though the two groups using the Oregon Curriculum showed significantly more positive attitudes toward literature and toward explanatory and persuasive writing. However, the TG group found English more difficult than the other groups, and claimed to read less than they used to. However, none of these differences was dramatic.

At the end of the third year, both the TG and RW groups scored significantly better than the LLE (traditional grammar) group on sentence-combining exercises. On the English usage test, both grammar groups produced means significantly higher than the reading-writing group. For the TG group, the discrepancy was at least 10 percent on 16 of the 38 items; the traditional grammar group showed a similar superiority over the reading-writing group. However, "what slight superiority there was in the two grammar groups was dispersed over a wide range of mechanical conventions, and was not clearly associated with sentence structure" (Elley et al., 1976, p. 15).

On the essays, there were no significant differences among groups in overall quality. In light of earlier studies of the effect on writing of studying transformational grammar, the syntactic structures of the essays were analyzed in detail. However, only one difference proved significant out of a possible 36 comparisons: the TG group did not use as many participles as the other two groups. Thus "there is no support in these results for the hypothesis that a special study of any kind of transformation increases the propensity to use them" (p. 17).

The authors conclude that transformational grammar study has a negligible effect on the language growth of secondary school students, and that traditional grammar also shows no measurable benefits. The slight advantage of the TG group in mastering some minor conventions of usage were "more than offset by the less positive attitudes which they showed towards their English studies" (p. 18). Nor were any significant differences found in the School Certificate English results of the three groups, nor in a follow-up writing assessment a year later. The authors indicate, "It is difficult to escape the conclusion that English grammar, whether traditional or transformational, has virtually no influence on the language growth of typical secondary school students" (p. 18).

The Study by McQuade (1980)

In contrast to the exceptionally detailed three-year study of Elley et al., Finlay McQuade's study involved a more modest investigation of the effect that his Editorial Skills class had on high school students.

Aware that research on the teaching of grammar did not support teaching grammar on the grounds that it would improve writing, he nevertheless thought that the Editorial Skills course might enhance students' performance on the College Entrance Examination Board's Achievement Test in Composition, since it included questions dealing with correctness in grammar as well as punctuation, usage, and diction. Since the eleventh and twelfth graders who took the Editorial Skills course chose it as an elective, they were highly motivated to succeed.

The course itself reviewed parts of speech and basic sentence structure, then dealt with application of such principles as "agreement, reference, parallel construction, tense, case, subordination" to the task of finding errors in sentences written expressly for that purpose. A similar approach was taken to punctuation, diction, and—if time permitted—to spelling. Students completed dozens of exercises and five mastery tests; there were also interim and final exams, each testing everything previously studied "and, presumably, mastered." The course was popular, with students signing up for it semester after semester, claiming to have learned a lot, and insisting that it helped on the SAT tests as well as on the CEEB's Achievement Test in Composition.

In short, everyone seemed happy with the course, until failures began to appear. The English faculty developed tests to identify students below a certain level of competence in reading, writing, mechanics, and vocabulary, and some students who had passed the Editorial Skills class were assigned to the mechanics competence course on the basis of that assessment. This unexpected turn of events led McQuade to actually investigate the effects of the Editorial Skills course, instead of merely assuming that it succeeded in its aim because everyone seemed to think so.

Much to McQuade's surprise and chagrin, the results of his investigation did not bear out even the modest claim that the Editorial Skills test might improve scores on the Achievement Test. Here is what he found:

- Overall, students showed as much gain on their Cooperative English Tests in years that they *hadn't* taken the Editorial Skills class as in the year that they had (p. 28).
- The Editorial Skills class seems to have made no difference in

preparation for the CEEB Achievement Test: students who hadn't taken the course showed just as much difference between the SAT and the later Achievement Test as students who had taken the course (p. 29).

- The class average on the pre-test was actually higher than the average on the post-test (p. 28).
- Though there were fewer errors per T-unit (a grammatical sentence) on the post-test essays (about half as many errors, in fact), it turned out that most of this reduction in errors was a reduction in relatively simple errors (mainly capitalization) by just a few of the students (pp. 29–30).
- Furthermore, though "the essays in the first set are not spectacular . . . the essays in the second set . . . are miserable." The students' sentences were "awkwardly and I believe self-consciously constructed to honor correctness above all other virtues, including sense" (p. 29).

McQuade concludes, "No reduction of the number of errors could be significant, I reasoned, when the post-course essays are inferior in every other way to the pre-course essays" (p. 29).

In short, these three studies as well as numerous others during the twentieth century indicate that there is little pragmatic justification for systematically teaching a descriptive or explanatory grammar of the language, whether that grammar be traditional, structural, transformational, or any other kind.

Why Teachers Continue to Teach Grammar

There are, of course, a number of reasons why teachers continue to teach grammar despite the research demonstrating its lack of practical value. Among such reasons are the following, some of which are articulated especially well by d'Eloia (1981):

1. Unaware of the research, they may simply assume that "of course" teaching grammar improves reading and writing—or at least the ability to edit written work or to do better on standardized tests that include grammar, usage, and punctuation. This assumption is sometimes promoted by articles

in professional journals where authors may have a deep and often unexamined commitment to a behaviorist concept of learning: that practice and more practice equals learning, and that what is learned will automatically be applied in appropriate situations.

2. They simply do not believe the research, but assume that the research studies must be faulty: "If only the teachers in the research studies had taught grammar the way I do, they would surely have been more successful." Or, if only the study had been designed differently, it would have demonstrated the value of teaching grammar. The most common argument is that surely formal grammar is valuable when applied to writing (e.g., Kolln, 1981). Those who make this argument seem not to consider that most concepts useful to writing can be taught without recourse to the formal study of grammar: in other words, it's the guided application that is valuable, not the formal study of grammar itself.

3. They believe that grammar is interesting in and of itself and teach it primarily for that reason. Such teachers include those who make grammar study a genuine inquiry and a process of discovery for their students.

4. They assume that what writers and readers need to know about grammar in order to comprehend texts and to write effectively must be known *consciously*. Typically these teachers have never thought about the fact that babies and toddlers learn the basics of grammar before entering school, and without direct instruction. Nor have they thought about the fact that most published creative writers seem to have little conscious understanding of grammar as a system.

5. They are aware that some students who are good readers and writers also find grammar study easy. This correlation encourages faulty cause-effect reasoning: students can read/write well because they know grammar; therefore, teaching grammar will make students better readers and writers.

6. They teach grammar because it's easier to assign exercises and grade them according to the answer key (or have a student grade them) than to lead students through the process of producing effective pieces of writing.

7. They believe that grammar study at least does no harm. Therefore, they feel justified in taking the easy way out and teaching grammar according to the book.

8. They are required by their school or school system to teach grammar, and they may have neither the energy to try to change the system nor the

knowledge to teach selected aspects of grammar in less traditional and possibly more effective ways. They may simply not know what else to do to help students with the grammar-related aspects of their writing. Or, they may not be confident enough in their own knowledge of grammar to feel comfortable abandoning the grammar book and answer key.

9. They fear that if they don't teach grammar, students might miss out on something for which they—both teachers and students—will be held accountable. This fear may make them feel guilty at the mere thought of not teaching grammar formally and systematically.

10. They bow to pressure from parents and other community members who are unaware of the research but naively think that teaching grammar will improve their children's use of English. Clearly the idea that grammar is good for a person has become a hallowed part of our cultural mythology, a legacy from the Middle Ages, when the study of grammar was considered vital for disciplining the mind and soul.

11. They believe that the research is valid in general, or for groups of students "on the average," but are still convinced that the writing of some students will benefit from the explicit study of grammar. Perhaps they remember learning ways of varying and manipulating sentence elements through their own study of grammar in school. They may remember learning the conventions of punctuation and grammar through formal study and realize that they themselves were able to apply, in their own writing, the more practical aspects of what they were taught. Often, therefore, teachers think, "Grammar helped me, so it's bound to help some of my students, too." They are willing to teach grammar to entire classes for the benefit of at least a few students.

12. They believe that grammar is valuable when it is applied to writing, and perhaps are not aware of—or do not believe—the research demonstrating that grammatical concepts can be applied without formal study of grammar as a system.

In most of these instances, what teachers may not have fully considered or understood is the point just mentioned: that students can learn and apply many grammatical concepts without learning to analyze and label the parts of speech and various other grammatical constructions. While this recognition does not solve all our problems in teaching grammar, it can certainly be a starting point for experimenting with other approaches to teaching those aspects of grammar that are most relevant to writing.

Toward Other Alternatives

There are, then, many reasons why teachers continue to teach formal grammar as a system. However, teachers and administrators knowledgeable about the previously discussed research should find that research difficult to ignore. Despite concerns about methodology, implementation, and interpretation in some of the studies, a preponderance of the evidence points in one direction. Especially impressive is the scrupulously rigorous three-year study by Elley et al.; indeed, even the study by Finlay McQuade is impressive, given the various kinds of data he examined. Overall, *it is difficult to escape the conclusion that teaching formal, isolated grammar to average or heterogenous classes, perhaps even to highly motivated students in elective classes, makes no appreciable difference in their ability to write, to edit, or to score better on standardized tests.* Departures from such results seem to be the exception rather than the rule.

What, then, are teachers to do? The following are some specific suggestions, most of which will receive further consideration in following chapters.

1. Restrict the teaching of grammar as a system to elective classes and units, offered with no pragmatic justification as an incentive, but only for the pleasure and challenge of studying the language. Emphasize inquiry and discovery more than, or rather than, mastery of all the major elements, functions, and constructions of the grammar (Postman and Weingartner, 1966).

2. Promote the acquisition and use of grammatical constructions through reading, and even by reading to students various works that are more sophisticated in grammatical structures than the writing that most of the students do (see Chapter 3).

3. When explaining various aspects of grammar, usage, and punctuation to help students with their writing, minimize the use of grammatical terminology and maximize the use of examples. Teach the minimal terminology primarily by using it in a functional context and through brief lessons as necessary, rather than through memorization of definitions and the analysis of sentences (see Chapters 4–6).

4. Emphasize the production of effective sentences rather than their analysis (see Chapter 5 and several lessons in the Appendix).

5. Teach not only "correct" punctuation, according to the handbooks, but effective punctuation, perhaps based upon classroom examination of published texts (see several lessons in the Appendix).

6. Lead students in discussing and investigating questions of usage, not in doing usage exercises from a grammar book. Similarly, lead students in exploring the power of dialects through literature and film. Contrast the grammatical constructions of different ethnic and community dialects with each other and with the Language of Wider Communication (so-called standard English), and consider the different effects that differing dialects have in different circumstances in the real world (see several lessons in the Appendix).

7. Engage non-native speakers of English in using the language as best they can, knowing that social interaction, reading, and writing to share ideas will promote the functional acquisition of English more than will grammatical study (see Chapter 3).

Of course, these suggestions do not exhaust the possibilities for language study in the classroom; they merely include several that focus on grammar and its relationship to conventions and choices in usage and punctuation, felicity and appropriateness in sentence structure and style, the power of dialects and dialects of power, the acquisition of grammatical constructions, and the potential excitement and challenge of investigating selected aspects of the grammatical system. Notice that none of these suggestions requires studying grammar as an interlocking system of elements, structures, and rules; even elective classes for the study of grammar can focus on selected aspects that are especially intriguing, if the students and teacher so desire.

Much of our time-honored grammar study has been undertaken in the name of improving writing, but "maximizing the benefits of grammar instruction requires teaching less, not more, grammar" (Noguchi, 1991, p. 16). This is true in part because the teaching of grammar is thereby more focused, but also because less grammar instruction means more time for writing itself, including the revision and editing phases wherein assistance with specific aspects of grammar becomes particularly valuable. Noguchi (1991) explains in his final summary:

> Less time spent on formal grammar instruction will mean more time to spend on the frequent and most serious kinds of stylistic problems [including mechanics], more time to examine the various social uses and users of English, and more time to explore the power, the responsibilities, and the social ramifications accompanying the written word. It will also mean more

time . . . to teach and engage students in the writing process, and, of course, more time for actual writing. Less formal instruction in grammar will, furthermore, mean more time for students to find out how language makes them uniquely human, how language not only divides human beings but also unites them. In general, less formal instruction in grammar will mean more time to develop in students a healthy awareness and appreciation of language and its uses, not just of limits but also of possibilities. (p. 121)

We should ponder, consider or reconsider the experimental research evidence, and rethink the what, why, and how of our teaching of grammar. "In the end," Noguchi says, "less is more."

It is time we tried teaching less grammar in the name of good writing, and undertook more research to determine the effectiveness of that general strategy. Toward these goals, I have included some of my own teaching experiments in the Appendix. Other teachers will describe their experiments, too, in the forthcoming companion volume.

3

Acquiring Grammatical Competence

This chapter focuses on how speakers acquire grammatical competence in their native language, with some attention to how grammatical competence can be acquired in another language as well. We focus on the acquisition of oral language in this chapter, leaving written language to Chapter 5.

Since the more recent and insightful analyses of language acquisition have drawn upon modern linguistics, we first introduce some principles, concepts, and terminology based upon transformational linguistics and its immediate predecessor, structural linguistics.

Linguistic Tools for Understanding and Analysis

The beginnings of structural linguistics are often traced to Leonard Bloomfield's landmark work *Language*, published in 1933. But it was not until the 1950s that structural linguistics began to attract the attention of teachers, with such texts as Charles Fries's *The Structure of English* (1952), Paul Roberts' *Patterns of English* (1956), W. Nelson Francis's *The Structure of American English* (1958), and James Sledd's *A Short Introduction to English Grammar* (1959).

In sharp contrast to traditional school grammarians and their grammars, the structuralists were determined to base their grammars on an analysis of the structures of a language as actually spoken by native speakers. They focused on oral language—that is, on actual language use, or *perform-*

FIGURE 3.1 Example of structuralists' Immediate Constituent Analysis (adapted from Francis, 1958).

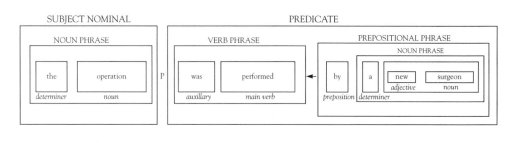

ance. And in so doing, they also focused on what we later came to call *surface structure*. In analyzing the surface structure of a sentence, they typically used Immediate Constituent Analysis, or ICA (Francis, 1958). That is, they analyzed sentences into increasingly smaller constituents. Figure 3.1 offers an example, based on the procedures of W. Nelson Francis (1958).

The person who introduced a distinction between *surface structure* and *deep structure* was the linguist Noam Chomsky, the originator of transformational-generative linguistics, or transformational linguistics for short (see Chomsky, 1957, 1965, 1968a; and early popularizations of transformational grammar by Thomas, 1965, and Malmstrom and Weaver, 1973). In his *Syntactic Structures* (1957), Chomsky suggested that what a grammar really ought to do is account for native speakers' intuitive understanding of language structure. That is, a grammar ought to explain the unconscious but functional knowledge of grammar that enables all of us to comprehend and produce language, rather than analyze the language actually produced. In other words, Chomsky was interested in accounting for native speakers' language *competence*.

It was his attempt to account for speakers' intuitive knowledge of grammar that led Chomsky to distinguish between deep structure and surface structure. Take, for instance, the following sentences:

The operation was performed by a new surgeon.

The operation was performed by a new technique.

On the surface, these sentences have the same structure: noun phrase, verb phrase, prepositional phrase. Nevertheless, our intuitive sense of the deep structure tells us that the superficially parallel phrases *by a new surgeon* and *by a new technique* work differently in their respective sentences.

In the first sentence, *a new surgeon* is the deep or underlying subject of *performed*: a new surgeon performed the operation. But in the second sentence, we know that *a new technique* cannot perform an operation and that *technique* therefore cannot be the deep or underlying subject of *performed*.

Chomsky thought of deep structure as being grammatical in nature, but such examples as this suggested to other linguists that deep structure was even deeper: that it involved meaning or semantics, rather than just structure or syntax. Thus other linguists developed the concept of *propositions* (e.g., Fillmore, 1968). A proposition expresses a state or action and the entities involved in that state or action. Thus in propositional terms, a simplified deep structure of the two example sentences might be as follows, with the terms in square brackets indicating the semantic relationships between each entity and the verb:

SENTENCE	PROPOSITION
The operation was performed by a new surgeon.	Perform (surgeon, operation) [agent, object]
The operation was performed by a new technique.	Perform (*someone*, technique) [agent, means]

Notice that, as Chomsky had noted, the agent or doer of an action does not necessarily occur in subject position within a sentence. It's the subject in *A new surgeon performed the operation*, but it's the object of the preposition *by* in *The operation was performed by a new surgeon*.

An article of Chomsky's, "Language and the Mind" (1968b), provides an introduction to the philosophical differences between structural and transformational linguistics, as well as to what Chomsky thought a linguistic grammar should do (see also Katz, 1964, and Hillocks and Smith, 1991).

Part of what interested Chomsky was the fact that the same deep structure could have more than one surface structure. Because deep structures were not to be thought of as actual sentences but only as elements and structures underlying them, Chomsky chose to depict deep structure words and other elements as joined by plus symbols. He called the basic structures of the language *kernel* structures and showed how more complex sentences could be derived from underlying kernels, with a single set of deep structures often generating more than one surface structure. Take, for example, the following deep structure kernels, which can be combined in more than one way in the surface structure:

DEEP STRUCTURE KERNEL	SURFACE SENTENCE
a + new + surgeon + performed + the + operation my + uncle + had + the + operation	A new surgeon performed the operation that my uncle had. A new surgeon performed the operation my uncle had. A new surgeon performed my uncle's operation. The operation that my uncle had was performed by a new surgeon. The operation my uncle had was performed by a new surgeon. My uncle's operation was performed by a new surgeon.

Let us recapitulate, then, some of the concepts and terms that are often used in grammatical descriptions and in the research on the acquisition of grammar, while also adding some new terms or explanations. In some instances, these definitions reflect my attempt to clarify through simplification.

SURFACE STRUCTURE   The linear sequence of words, phrases, clauses, and sentences, as they are uttered or written.

One important measure of surface structure is what is commonly called a minimum terminable unit, or T-unit, after the research of Kellogg Hunt (1965a). A *T-unit* consists of an independent clause plus the dependent clause(s) or phrase(s) (if any) that are attached to it or embedded within it. In this book, a *grammatical sentence* is the same as a T-unit. However, a T-unit (grammatical sentence) is not necessarily the same as a *punctuated sentence*, which consists of whatever occurs between the initial capital letter and the end punctuation (period, question mark, exclamation point). In fact, a punctuated sentence may consist of one T-unit, more than one T-unit, or less than a T-unit; in the last instance, the punctuated sentence would be called a fragment, or a minor sentence (Kline and Memering, 1977). The possible relationships between grammatical sentences (T-units) and punctuated sentences are further clarified in Chapter 5, where these terms become more important (p. 125). See also the Glossary's entries for **T-unit** and **punctuated sentence.**

DEEP STRUCTURE   One or more basic, or kernel, structures that underlie the structure of actual spoken or written sentences, according to transformational grammar. Often, there is no one-to-one correspondence between deep (kernel) structures, on the one hand, and grammatical or punctuated

FIGURE 3.2 Surface and deep(er) structures.

Surface structures	The operation was performed by a new surgeon.
	or
	A new surgeon performed the operation.
	The deep structure is modified by transformations to produce either surface structure.
Deep structure	A + surgeon + performed + the + operation
	The + surgeon + was + new
	Semantic relationships in the deeper structure underlie the deep structure.
Deeper structure (propositions)	Perform [agent, object] + New [agent, attribution]

sentences, on the other hand. The deep structure of a sentence is what we understand about structural relationships among the words, even when these relationships are not clearly signaled by the surface structure.

PROPOSITIONS   These are what we might call deeper structures: the semantic relationships among the words in a kernel structure and the meaningful elements that signal those relationships.

The surface structure of sentences, the linear order of words, phrases, and clauses, is something like the tip of an iceberg: the part we actually see or hear. The deep and deeper structure is like the submerged part: the part we do not see. Figure 3.2 is an attempt to represent, in nontechnical terms, the relationships between two alternative surface structures and their underlying deep and deeper structure. As we shall see in Chapter 5, a major hallmark of increasing grammatical competence is the ability to incorporate more deep(er) structures into a single T-unit, or grammatical sentence.

Grammatical Competence and Its Acquisition

Before they even enter school, children have acquired a complex set of grammatical structures and a complex set of rules for combining elements into such structures. To gain an appreciation for the elegance and subtlety of the grammatical system that is internalized, it often helps to try to verbalize some of the rules that we all use quite unconsciously in our speaking and writing. Therefore, without making any claim as to exactly when such knowledge is acquired, I invite you to try to formulate rules, or generalizations, that account for the following phenomena.

Invitation 1

Part of what native speakers have learned about English is the proper order of any auxiliary ("helper") verbs that may come before a main verb (when the sentence is "active," not "passive"). Below is a list of the major kinds of auxiliary verbs, followed by some sample combinations. In addition to examining these, you might try other combinations of your own to see what sounds grammatical and what doesn't. Then try to formulate the basic rule that governs the ordering of auxiliaries. In what order must these three major kinds of auxiliaries occur?

- Modal auxiliaries: *will, can, shall, may, must* ("present tense" forms); *would, could, should, might* ("past tense" forms)
- HAVE verb: *have* and *has* (present tense); *had* (past tense and past participle); *having* (present participle)
- BE verb: *am, is, are* (present tense); *was, were* (past tense); *being* (present participle); *been* (past participle)

In the following example sentences, the main verb and all preceding auxiliaries are italicized:

Sharon *is leaving* at noon today.

She *has left* instructions.

Jerry *will be taking* over her job. [*Take over* seems to function as a two-word or *phrasal* verb.]

He *must try* to figure out what to do.

Carla *might have written* that memo.

Sharon *must have been eating* ketchup on her hot dog.

Invitation 2

Something else native speakers have learned about English is when *any* (or *anyone, anything,* etc.) is required in a sentence, when *some* (or *someone, something,* etc.) is required, and when either word may be used. Supply the appropriate choice or choices in each blank, without taking time to agonize over which response seems natural. Then consider: how might we formulate the rule that apparently governs our use of *any* and *some* and their compound forms?

I don't want ——— dessert.

The weather forecaster doubts that we'll have ——— rain today.

He'll never agree to ——— kind of settlement.

We don't have ——— thing to worry about.

I can't imagine ——— one doing that.

I can't think of ——— thing else, can you?

I'd like ——— ice cream, please.

We're supposed to have ——— rain today.

I'd appreciate it if ——— one could help.

She might agree to ——— kind of settlement.

I just thought of ——— thing else.

Does ——— one have another question?

Is there ——— thing else you need?

I wonder if she'd like ——— new magazines.

Let's ask whether they have ——— candy.

Discussion of Invitations 1 and 2

Regarding the major kinds of auxiliaries, we might adopt a simplification of the transformationalists' concise rule:

Aux → (Modal) (HAVE) (BE)

What this says is that an auxiliary consists of an optional modal, followed by an optional form of HAVE, followed by an optional form of BE. That is, we don't have to use an auxiliary at all: it is entirely optional. But if we have more than one of them, they have to occur in this order (unless the sentence is passive). The examples also demonstrate other interesting rules about the structure of verb phrases, as long as the sentence is active rather than passive. Namely, a HAVE auxiliary is always followed by a past participle form, and a BE auxiliary is always followed by a verb in the present participle form. Transformationalists captured these insights in a slightly more complex rule, Aux → (M) (HAVE + EN) (BE + ING). The EN means that the following word will be in the past participle form; likewise, the ING means that the following word will be in the present participle form. A sentence with all these elements is *Sharon* **must have been** *eating ketchup on her hot dog.*

This one rule covers a complex variety of examples. But how did we learn to use it? Clearly not through direct instruction: most parents and, for that matter, most teachers, don't know this rule. But we do not have to know it consciously. This is part of what we unconsciously learn as we acquire the grammatical structure of English. (See the Appendix for a sample lesson that elicits this structure, and for the additional point that the first word in a verb phrase carries the tense marker.)

In Invitation 2, what we find is that sentences with a negative element in them seem to require *any* rather than *some;* most native speakers will agree that this rule accounts for all or most of the sentences in the left-hand column. The first five in the second column imply certainty and seem to require *some.* The last four in that column suggest uncertainty and seem to take either *any* or *some.* This is an example of the kinds of insights that transformationalists have captured in their descriptive "rules." This particular concept comes from William Rutherford's *Sentence Sense* (1973), a text designed to lead students to discover some of these insights for themselves.

We don't know, of course, how young children acquire such "rules." What we do know is that such rules are not directly taught to children, and that children show evidence of beginning to acquire them by about the age of two or three, when they typically begin using auxiliary verbs and modifiers like *any* and *some.*

In one experimental study, for instance, three-year-olds were shown pictures of a tool, a substance, and an action. When asked which one was "a sib," they typically chose the tool. When asked which was "some sib," they typically chose the substance. When asked which one showed "sibbing," they typically chose the action (Brown, 1957, as cited in De Villiers and De Villiers, 1979). The children's incipient understanding of this use of *some* must surely be one of the prerequisites to their coming to understand subtle distinctions in the use of *some* and *any.*

Invitations 3 and 4 are designed to inspire insight not only into the nature of the structure that is acquired, but into the process of language acquisition and how linguists have come to understand it.

Invitation 3

This invitation involves a phenomenon that is not strictly grammatical: it involves an intersection of the sound, or phonological, system with the grammatical system. Specifically, it involves the pronunciation of the regular past tense ending. Consider what sound(s) we add in making the following regular verbs past tense. What seems to determine which sound or sounds we add? Try to determine one or more rules to account for our automatic choices.

stop	stab	slam	play	wait
lick	plug	sin	tee	wade
laugh	love	clang	sigh	
unearth	writhe		slow	
kiss	fizz		cue	
wish			try	
lurch	judge			

Invitation 4

Often by the age of four, young children have developed several increasingly sophisticated rules for making sentences negative. For each group of sentences, try to decide what that rule must be.

a. No money.
   No a boy bed.
   No fall!
   No singing song.
   No the sun shining.
   No sit there.

b. That no Mommy.
   He no bite you.
   There no squirrels.
   I no want envelope.
   I no taste them.
   That no fish school.

   This not ice cream.
   They not hot.
   Paul not tired.
   I not crying.
   He not taking the
     walls down.

c. I didn't did it.
   You didn't caught me.
   I didn't caught it.

d. I don't sit on Cromer coffee.
   I don't want it.
   I don't like him.
   I don't know his name.

These examples are from Klima and Bellugi-Klima (1966, pp. 192–196), with the stages simplified somewhat for the sake of the adults trying to determine the rules that characterize each set.

Discussion of Invitations 3 and 4

Like the rule that accounts for the ordering of auxiliary verbs, the rule that accounts for the regular past tense endings is elegant and simple. To make a regular verb past tense, we add a / t / sound if the verb ends in an unvoiced consonant (one with the vocal cords not vibrating), and we add a / d / sound if the verb ends in a voiced sound, whether consonant or vowel; however, if the verb ends in a / t / or a / d / sound, we add a schwa-like vowel, plus / d /. How do children learn this rule? Again, it certainly isn't by direct teaching! Nevertheless, children give evidence of learning this as a rule around the age of two or three.

The way we know children are learning this rule is by observing what they do with the past tenses of irregular verbs—the ones that don't follow the rule. Initially, they seem to imitate adult forms: they may say "went" or "bought," for example. But as they learn the regular rule for past tense (around age two or three), they begin saying "goed" and "buyed" (or, less often, "wented" and "boughted"). Indeed, this is how we know they have learned the rule for making verbs past tense, and not just a lot of separate past tense forms. The same thing happens with irregular plurals: children will at first say "men" and "feet," then switch to "mans" and "foots" (usually) when they have learned the rule for making regular nouns plural. Before long, in each case, the children learn the irregular forms of the adult language community in which they are immersed. Unconsciously, perhaps, they learn these forms as exceptions to the regular rules they have unconsciously learned.

Rules to account for the negative sentences in Invitation 4 can be formulated as follows, for the groups (a)–(d):

a. Put *no* or *not* at the beginning of the entire utterance.
b. Put *no* or *not* between the subject and predicate parts of the sentence.
c. When the verb does not already have an auxiliary verb, add the appropriate present or past tense form of *do* to carry the negative *n't*, and put this before the main verb. (This is described in transformational terms as changing an underlying positive kernel structure to a negative surface structure.)
d. Add the appropriate present or past form of *do* to carry the negative marker and simultaneously remove the tense marker associated with the main verb. (Again, this is explained as a transformation from a positive deep structure to a negative surface structure.)

If these rules sound complicated, that's part of the point: that the child develops an increasingly sophisticated set of rules for making sentences negative, all without direct instruction or intervention from adults. (Indeed, when adults try to hasten the process, they typically do not succeed.)

Taken together, these four invitations and the discussion of them should make clear several points:

- The grammatical system children learn is complex and abstract; it can be captured in sometimes elegant rules, but these are not rules that adults typically know or could teach.
- Children develop increasingly sophisticated hypotheses about the structure of their language—hypotheses that can be expressed in the form of rules that explain their grammatical competence and are responsible for their actual language performance.
- Errors are necessary concomitants of growth in language acquisition.
- Children acquire the grammar of their language without direct instruction.

The next section elaborates on these critical observations about language acquisition, specifically the acquisition of grammatical competence.

The Process of Language Acquisition

Of course, we don't really know how children acquire grammatical competence in their native language. We can only extract the patterns from recorded utterances and formulate rules that would account for those utterances, consider what the environment contributes to language acquisition, and speculate about the contributions that are made by the human mind. Other methods of investigation are used too (Ingram, 1989), but no investigative method can actually get inside the learner's mind.

The first evidence of children's beginning to learn grammar comes when they begin to put two words together to form sentences, that is, utterances that have the intonation patterns of a sentence. Such utterances can be called *meaning units* or *M-units* (McCaig, 1972), since they express basic elements of propositions. Examples of some of the earliest kinds of semantic relationships, taken from various published sources, are illustrated in Figure 3.3. These examples are labeled with terms common in language acquisition studies rather than with strict propositional notations. Notice that in the examples of nonexistence (De Villiers and De Villiers, 1979), "all gone" and "no more" may function as single words. These examples do not illustrate all of the semantic relationships evident in children's two-word sentences, but they illustrate most of them.

Several interesting observations can be made regarding such early utterances:

1. They express a variety of semantic relationships.
2. At first, only two words of a proposition can be uttered at a time. So, for instance, if a child wanted to convey the proposition that "Daddy is moving the TV," she might say "Daddy move" (agent/action), "Move TV" (action/object), "Daddy TV" (agent/object), or perhaps two of these in sequence: "Daddy move, move TV." But the child just beginning to put two words together in M-units would not yet be able to put three words together in a single utterance (R. W. Brown, 1973). This, indeed, seems to be a universal fact of language acquisition: no matter what language is being acquired, children typically go through a stage wherein they can put two words together to form a sentence, but not three or more (Slobin, 1972).
3. These two-word sentences do not include grammatical markers, such

FIGURE 3.3 Semantic relationships in early utterances.

AGENT/ACTION	ACTION/OBJECT	AGENT/OBJECT
Mommy read.	Hit ball.	Snoopy bone. [watching
Sarah write.	Pick flower.	Snoopy bury it]
I sit.	Push cat.	Daddy TV. [watching
Doggie bite.	Eat cookie.	Daddy move the TV]

ATTRIBUTION	POSSESSION	NOMINATION (LABELING)
Big dog.	Mommy sock. [holding	That car.
Dirty pillow.	up her sock]	That baby.
Spoon sticky.	My ball.	Here baby.
	Ursula nose. [putting a	
	finger on her nose]	

RECURRENCE	ENTITY/LOCATION	ACTION/LOCATION
'Nother cookie.	Cookie here.	Sit chair.
More milk.	Sweater chair.	Play outside.
Tickle again.	Mouse cup.	Walk street.

NONEXISTENCE	REJECTION	DENIAL
No money.	No wash. [to mean	No wet. [meaning "I am
Beads all gone.	"Don't wash me"]	not wet"]
No more soup.		

as plural or past tense endings, or function words like *a/an* or *the; and* or *but; with* or *to* or *in*. Emergent speakers first use nouns, then add verbs, adjectives, and adverbs in creating two-word sentences.

4. The grammar of such utterances, then, consists entirely of word order. Such word order follows the word order of adult utterances. Note, for instance, that an adult model for "Big dog" might be "It's a big dog," while an adult model for "Spoon sticky" might be "The spoon is sticky." In other words, adult language includes instances in which an adjective precedes a noun, but also instances in which the adjective follows the noun and a linking verb. Thus the differing patterns confirm rather than contradict the generalization that children's early utterances follow the word order of adult utterances.

Representing More of the Surface Structure

Gradually a child becomes able to produce longer and more complex utterances, making the propositions and deep structure more and more explicit in the surface structure. Let us take, as an example, a child who has been wrongly accused of having eaten the last cookie in the cookie jar

(Weaver, 1979). The father, poor suspicious soul, has just accusingly asked his daughter Sally, "Did you eat the cookie?" The child might merely shake her head from side to side or say "no" to express the proposition False (Eat [Sally, cookie]), that is, "It is false that Sally ate the cookie." However, if she is about two years old (give or take a little), she might say "no eat" or "no cookie" or "Sally no," using sentences of no more than two words. As the child grows in language acquisition, she will be able to express more and more of the underlying deep structure in the surface structure of her reply. One might predict the following sequence of increasingly mature surface structures (with other alternatives being possible, but perhaps less likely):

UTTERANCE	INCREASING COMPLEXITY
"No." (Obviously this answer is common at any age because, in context, it is adequate to express the underlying proposition.)	One morpheme. (The child is able to express just one *morpheme* per utterance—just one minimal unit of meaning.)
"No eat. No cookie." (The child may produce either utterance or both in sequence, with an intonation break between.)	Two morphemes, or a sequence of two two-morpheme utterances.
"No eat cookie. Me no eat." (Either, or both in sequence.)	Three morphemes, or a sequence of two three-morpheme utterances.
"Me no ate cookie."	Four morphemes. (At this point, "ate" may still be a single morpheme for the child, not a combination of "eat" + past tense.)
"Me no ate the cookie."	Five morphemes. (The definite article "the" is added.)
"Me didn't ate the cookie."	Six morphemes, assuming that both "did" and "ate" are still one-morpheme units for the child.
"Me didn't eat the cookie."	Seven morphemes. (The tense marker is removed from the main verb, indicating that past is now a separate morpheme.)
"I didn't eat the cookie."	Seven morphemes. (The pronoun is in the subject form.)

This hypothetical sequence is based partly on my own observations but mainly on inferences from Klima and Bellugi-Klima (1966), Dale (1976, p. 107), Cazden (1972, p. 54), and R. W. Brown (1973, p. 274). The details of increasingly complex surface structure may not be entirely correct for any individual child (in particular, the use of *I* is likely to be acquired earlier). Nevertheless, the general pattern of development seems universal. As their linguistic abilities mature, young children seem to go through at least the following overlapping stages or phases in learning to make their utterances conform to adult norms:

1. They express more and more of the nouns or "arguments" that are involved in a proposition. For example, once the child can utter three-word sentences, she can express both the agent (using the pronoun *me*) and the object *(cookie)*, while still specifying the action, *eat*.

2. They express more and more of the grammatical markers, beginning with those that are the least complex but convey the most important meanings. For instance, the progressive *-ing* on verbs, the plural *-s* on nouns, and the prepositions *in* and *on* are among the first grammatical markers to appear. The articles *a* and *the* appear noticeably later, while the verb third person singular (as in "It looks funny") usually appears still later (R. W. Brown, 1973; De Villiers and De Villiers, 1973). It is logical that the third person singular should be a relatively late acquisition, since word order alone will make the meaning clear.

3. As children are beginning to express more and more of the grammatical markers, they are also beginning to combine propositions. For example, Sally might say "Me no ate Daddy cookie" if she thought the cookie belonged to her father. One underlying proposition is that Sally did not eat the cookie, and another is that the cookie belonged to Daddy.

4. They make requisite alterations in the surface structure. For instance, *didn't ate* becomes *didn't eat*, and the pronoun *I* replaces *me* or *my* in subject position.

As this discussion indicates, the first aspect of grammar to emerge is an incipient command of *word order*, which can be seen even in the child's two-word utterances. *Word endings* and *function words* follow, as the child's command of syntactic structures continues to increase.

Perhaps the most important generalization we can make is that in acquiring grammatical competence, children increasingly express more of the deeper propositional structures in their surface structures. Considering just the surface structure, such learning might appear to proceed from part to whole. But viewed from the point of the deeper, underlying structure, it is just the opposite: first comes the whole, the underlying propositions, and then gradually comes an ability to represent the parts that reflect and convey that whole.

What Is Acquired

Considering some of the research into the syntax of kindergartners gives an even greater appreciation of the complexity of the grammatical system children acquire before they enter first grade.

In 1967, O'Donnell, Griffin, and Norris reported the results of a massive study of the syntax of elementary school children. They compared the use of syntactic constructions in the spoken language of kindergartners and students in grades 1, 2, 3, 5, and 7, and in the writings of students in grades 3, 5, and 7.

In oral language, there was significant growth in the use of syntactic structures between the end of the kindergarten year and the end of the first-grade year; as the investigators put it, "The first-grade year was one of rapid and extensive development in exploiting language structures" (p. 99). What may seem more surprising, however, is the fact that the kindergartners used almost all the constructions used orally by the older students. The following are some of the investigators' observations:

1. The eleven basic sentence patterns of main clauses that were tabulated in the study "were all used in the speech of kindergarten children, although six of them occurred very infrequently" (p. 88). Indeed, four of these six patterns were not used much more often by the older students—not even by the seventh graders (p. 72). Figure 3.4 includes simple examples to illustrate these patterns, as well as the other constructions and functions analyzed. However, the investigators seldom included speech samples to illustrate them, so most of the examples are mine.

2. Of the thirty-nine specific structures and functions analyzed for this study, the three completely missing from kindergartners' speech were not much used by older children either (p. 91). Those three were noun + adverb constructions (**man outside**), indirect objects (*Give **the dog** a bone*), and objective complements (*We elected him **secretary***). On the other hand, some items seem clearly to be early acquisitions, well used by the kindergartners (p. 92).

FIGURE 3.4 Grammatical constructions and patterns, other than coordinate constructions, analyzed by O'Donnell, Griffin, and Norris (1967).

STRUCTURAL PATTERNS OF THE MAIN CLAUSES ANALYZED
Subject-verb: *The baby cried.*
Subject-verb-object: *He took my pencil.*
Subject-verb–predicate nominal: *Our dog is a German shepherd.*
Subject-verb–predicate adjectival: *Our dog is big.*
Subject-verb–indirect object–direct object: *I gave the dog a bone.*
Subject-verb-object–object complement (nominal): *We elected Candace president.*
Subject-verb-object–adjectival complement: *Our teacher considers her responsible.*
Adverbial-verb-subject: *Slowly ticked the clock.*
There-verb-subject: *There were lots of kids at the party.*
It-verb-subject: *It would be easy to blame him.*
Passive constructions: *Our garden was eaten by rabbits.*

HEADED NOMINAL CONSTRUCTIONS
[Each of these constructions consists of a noun, the "head" of the construction, preceded or followed by something that modifies it and is therefore functioning like an adjective, regardless of its internal structure.]
Noun + noun: *barn door*
Noun + adjective: *cold rain; time in immemorial*
Noun + genitive [possessive] form: *man's coat; children's boots*
Noun + relative [adjectival] clause: *boy who was riding his bike*
Noun + prepositional phrase: *bird in a tree*
Noun + infinitive phrase: *food to eat*
Noun + participle or participial phrase: *falling leaves; woman washing her car*
Noun + adverb: *man outside*

NONHEADED NOMINAL CONSTRUCTIONS
[These are all nominal constructions if and when they function like nouns.]
Noun clause: *I know **that it costs a lot.***
Infinitive phrase: ***To leave early** would be sensible.*
Infinitive with subject: *I want **you to go with Michael.***
Gerund phrase: ***Watching TV** is Greg's favorite sport.*

ADVERBIAL CONSTRUCTIONS
Adverbial clauses: ***Since the rates went up,** I canceled our cable TV service. Let me know **if you lower the rates again.***
Sentence adverbials: ***Nevertheless,** it's true. You, **I think,** might become a writer. **The store being closed,** I can't, **unfortunately,** get you more paper right now.*
Adverbial infinitives: *He saved up his money **to buy a new computer.***

3. All three major kinds of subordinate clauses—nominal, adjectival, and adverbial—were used quite often by kindergarten children: "relative [adjectival] clauses, in fact, were used most frequently in kindergarten" (p. 98).

We shall see in a later chapter that low-achieving students typically do not demonstrate as good a command of the syntactic resources of our language as the children whose speech and writing were analyzed by O'Donnell, Griffin, and Norris. However, even the low-achieving students' command of syntax is impressive (Loban, 1976). And surely even this chapter's brief introduction to language acquisition gives the lie to statements like "He doesn't even know what a sentence is." Except, perhaps, for children with severe language disorders, this simply is not true. Of course, none of us speak exclusively in grammatically complete sentences, and in fact, the sentences of middle-class, educated adults are often the most convoluted and the least grammatical (Labov, 1969). It is also true that children and adults may not always write in grammatically complete or coherent sentences, and we do not always punctuate our writing in units that correspond precisely to grammatical sentences. However, even the youngest schoolchildren have already acquired a functional command of the grammar of their language and their community dialect, including most of its sentence structures, clauses, and various kinds of phrases. Youngsters entering school are already proficient language users who demonstrate that they have acquired most of the grammatical resources of their native language.

Two particularly good discussions of child language acquisition are Lindfors (1987) and Genishi and Dyson (1984). An especially readable introduction to language acquisition is De Villiers and De Villiers, *Early Language* (1979).

Evidence from Reading Miscues

In addition to direct evidence of grammar acquisition through oral and written use, we have indirect evidence from reading miscues. Coined by Kenneth Goodman (1965), the term *miscue* refers to any departure the reader makes from the actual words of the text. Miscues not only provide insight into the reading process but also demonstrate that readers have an intuitive sense of the grammar of the language that they draw upon while reading. This holds true for most of the youngest and least proficient readers as well as for good readers.

To illustrate, let us first examine some of the miscues made by an exceptionally good reader, Jay. At the time he read the O. Henry story "Jimmy Hayes and Muriel" (Porter, 1936), Jay was in the sixth grade. Here are some sentences in which Jay made one miscue and then restructured the rest of the sentence so that it would be grammatical.

JAY: *"Ain't heard much about her beauty. . . ."*
TEXT: "Ain't ever heard anybody call her a beauty. . . ."

JAY: *"This here's Muriel," said Hayes, with an oratorical wave of his hand. "She's got qualities."*
TEXT: "This here Muriel," said Hayes, with an oratorical wave of his hand, "has got qualities."

These restructurings make it clear that Jay has a strong intuitive grasp of the structure of English.

But even most younger and less proficient readers demonstrate an intuitive awareness of the grammar of English through the miscues they make. For example, Karl, a first grader, was enrolled in the Reading Recovery program for children deemed at risk of failure in learning to read. (Thanks to Grace Vento-Zogby for these examples. The books Karl was reading from are *Look* [Cutting, 1988]; *Huggles Goes Away* [Cowley, 1986]; *The Bicycle* [Cowley, 1983] *Ratty-tatty* [Cowley, 1987]; *Mom's Haircut* [Semple and Tuer, 1987].) Even in October, during his first lesson, Karl was making miscues that fit the grammar of the sentence. Indeed, his miscues showed him attentive to grammar and meaning, but not always to the actual letters of the word. For instance, with the following miscues, Karl read the actual words of the text except where indicated:

KARL: *bird   Food!*
TEXT: "Look," said the birds. /"Bread!"

Here are some other examples from early lessons:

KARL: *food,*
TEXT: some sandwiches,
      [The picture shows a stack of sandwiches.]
KARL: *Huggles goes away.*
TEXT: Goodbye!

During his nineteenth lesson, Karl made three interrelated miscues, showing that, like Jay, he could draw upon his intuitive knowledge of grammar to restructure text and maintain grammaticality. For example:

KARL: *bear   goes   splat*
TEXT: and the bicycle got . . . / squashed.
        [The bear was riding the bicycle and indeed
        went splat, on top of the bicycle.]

By March, Karl was beginning to make miscues that cannot be viewed as logical substitutions for the words in the text. However, these miscues almost always fit with the preceding grammar, suggesting that Karl was using grammar to predict what was coming next. When his predictions were not grammatical with the following text, Karl typically corrected them. For example:

KARL: *wasn't*
TEXT: It went off **snap!**
        [The miscue *wasn't* fits with *off*, but not with *off* **snap!** Karl
        corrected it, making the sentence grammatical.]
KARL: *the*
TEXT: Mom needed a haircut, so she decided . . .
        [The miscue *the* fits with the preceding grammar, but not
        with the following grammar. Karl corrected it.]

Miscue patterns like Karl's are not unusual. Rather, they are quite common among even the first graders in the Reading Recovery program. Such miscue patterns show that these children have a strong intuitive sense of grammar, which they use in their reading.

Further evidence that even the less proficient readers have a strong sense of grammar comes from Jaime, a child who was nine at the time her reading was recorded for a miscue analysis (Weaver, 1996). Although she seldom corrected miscues that failed to go with the *following* grammar or meaning, she made effective use of grammar (and usually meaning) to predict what was coming next. Of the 75 consecutive miscues that were analyzed, 73 percent went with the grammar and meaning of the preceding context, and another 7 percent went with the preceding grammar *or* meaning, but not both. The following examples are from Jaime's reading of *Clifford Takes a Trip* (Bridwell, 1966). Except as indicated, Jaime read the actual words of the text:

JAIME: *he didn't*
TEXT: but it did hurt his feelings
        [Jaime read "but he didn't," then omitted the rest of the
        sentence.]

JAIME:	*take*　*a*
TEXT:	The little old man gave Clifford a little lunch, to thank him for his help.
	[Both miscues go with the grammar of the preceding part of the sentence. The first miscue, *take*, also goes grammatically with the next word in the text.]
JAIME:	*every car*
TEXT:	Clifford just tip-toed over the cars.
JAIME:	*He don't*　*had come*
TEXT:	We didn't know Clifford was coming.
	[Jaime commonly says "he don't" in normal speech.]
JAIME:	*look*　*their mother*
TEXT:	Good old Clifford / took the baby bears / back to Mama Bear.
	[Each of the miscues fits with the grammar of what comes before.]

Thus Jaime's miscues lend further evidence to the argument that we use our intuitive knowledge of grammar in reading as well as in speaking and writing, even though we may be completely unable to explain grammatical patterns and rules, and may even be unaware that we unconsciously know the grammar of our native language.

Second Language Acquisition

Those unfamiliar with second language acquisition research may be surprised to learn of the substantive evidence demonstrating that a second or additional language may be most readily acquired in much the same way as one's native language: through immersion in oral and written language—that is, through immersion in situations where one needs and wants to listen, speak, read, and write in order to understand and be understood. This is true for adults as well as children. Indeed, even when second language learners are taught the grammatical structure and rules of the second language, they may acquire these in a different way or a different order—or not acquire some of them at all (Terrell, 1991).

Stephen Krashen's model of second language acquisition has been especially influential, providing a theoretical explanation for why this should be so. Krashen (1981, 1982, 1985) contrasts *language learning* with *language acquisition*. "Learning" another language is what many of us have done in school. We have memorized vocabulary, studied grammar, translated passages, perhaps rehearsed conversational phrases (all depending upon the instructional approach). In short, we have studied the language, but we may never have achieved much facility in listening to or speaking the language, or in reading or writing it for any authentic purpose outside of class. Such language learning involves "knowing about" a language, but it doesn't necessarily lead to knowing the language in the same sense as if it were truly acquired. Or to put it differently, many of us have studied a language in school, but few have acquired genuine competence in the language through that process.

As we have seen with children learning their native language, language acquisition is a subconscious process that leads to functional command of the rules of a language, though not necessarily to conscious knowledge about the language or its rules. Krashen has pointed out that what is minimally required for first or second language acquisition is *comprehensible input* from others in the environment: language that is comprehensible enough that the language learner can unconsciously abstract the patterns and rules from the language heard and/or read. Thus someone acquiring a second language entirely through exposure to it might, even as an adult, go through some of the same stages as a child learning that language natively. For example, Puerto Rican teenagers suddenly transplanted to New York City typically go through the same sequence of rules for negation as do young children learning English as their native language. Several studies show that adults acquiring a second language will acquire the grammatical markers of that language in a fairly predictable order, even if the grammar has been explicitly taught to them in a different order (Terrell, 1991, p. 55). And pidgin languages that arise when speakers of mutually unintelligible languages need to communicate bear striking resemblance to the early sentences and structures of young children (e.g., compare child language with the structure of pidgins, as in Schumann, 1974).

To be comprehensible, language input must be rich enough to provide raw data for the abstraction of patterns and the construction of rules. On the other hand, the language input must be sufficiently comprehensible for the language learner to connect meaning with form (Snow, 1986). In addition to the concept of comprehensible input, two other hypotheses in Krashen's theory of second language acquisition are especially relevant here. One is his hypothesis that a *low affective filter* is necessary for language acquisition to take place. Briefly put, a low affective filter means that the person is relatively open to learning from the comprehensible input, which includes being relatively unafraid of taking risks and making mistakes. This is obviously the situation with young children learning their native language, but it may also be a necessary condition for adults to truly acquire a language. When speakers and writers edit their language production by drawing upon their conscious understanding of the forms of the language, they are using their language *monitor*. Continual use of the monitor may result in somewhat more "correct" language production, but it can also raise the affective filter—one's mental block against learning from the comprehensible input and taking risks in speaking and/or writing (Krashen, 1985; I have gone somewhat beyond Krashen in emphasizing the importance of taking risks).

In *The Input Hypothesis* (1985), Krashen discusses some of the evidence for his theory of second language acquisition. What I would like to do here is review some of the evidence from studies in which the acquisition of English through reading is contrasted with the learning or acquisition of English through more direct means.

Elley's Review of Nine Studies

In "Acquiring Literacy in a Second Language: The Effect of Book-Based Programs," Warwick Elley (1991) reviews nine studies of the acquisition of English as a second language, most of which were undertaken in the South Pacific and Southeast Asia. Most notable among these is his own earlier study (Elley & Mangubhai, 1983). Typically these studies compared the results of programs based on structured systematic instruction in English with "book flood" programs, which exposed children to large numbers of high-interest storybooks. In other words, the studies compared the effects of a direct instruction approach with an indirect instruction approach designed simply to provide children with comprehensible input, through books.

The direct instruction approach typically was based upon the principles articulated by structural linguists (e.g., Bloomfield, 1942) and audiolingual methodology: practice on a carefully sequenced set of grammatical structures, through imitation, repetition, and reinforcement. In contrast, the book flood approaches reflected "natural" or whole language learning principles. They usually involved sustained silent reading of an extensive number of picture books; the Shared Book Experience (Holdaway, 1979), which included not only reading but related discussion and activities; or a combination of Sustained Silent Reading and the Shared Book Experience. In one instance, these two procedures were supplemented by a modified language experience approach involving children in reading material they had dictated.

From these combined studies, the following patterns emerged:

1. Students in the book flood programs did better on almost all standardized measures of reading, including not only comprehension skills but also word identification and phonics skills.

2. Usually favoring the book flood students were differences in measures of oral and written language and vocabulary (e.g., listening comprehension, written story completion), and sometimes differences in other aspects of school achievement as well (see also Elley, 1989).

3. Among the book flood students, those in Shared Book Experience programs typically showed greater gains on various tests than those in silent reading programs. (Probably this result suggests the value of reading and discussing the text together.)

4. Students in the book flood programs generally had a more positive attitude toward books and reading. (One wonders if these programs also affected children's attitudes toward English as a second language.)

5. *Students in the book flood programs often did better on tests of the grammatical structures explicitly taught in the audiolingual programs*. Elley notes that this interpretation "was [also] supported by an incidental study in which knowledge and use of English in natural settings was found to be largely unaffected by deliberate instruction in them" (1991, p. 389). (This correlates, too, with the research that grammatical markers tend to be learned in a consistent order, regardless of the order in which they are taught.)

Elley summarizes, in part, as follows: "That pupils showed equally large gains in the discrete-point tests of grammatical structures and vocabulary as they did in the more integrative measures of reading, listening, and writing is particularly damaging for those who argue that structures and vocabulary should be deliberately taught" (1991, p. 402).

In short, Elley's summary of these nine studies provides strong evidence for the hypothesis that comprehensible input and a low affective filter facilitate language acquisition more readily than direct teaching of grammar and vocabulary. This is not to say that the direct teaching of grammar plays no role at all in the acquisition of a second language, especially for adults and adolescents. But the research evidence *does* suggest that direct teaching of grammar is not necessary for acquiring the basic structure of a second language, anymore than for acquiring one's native language.

The CUNY Experiment

In "Fluency First: Reversing the Traditional ESL Sequence" (1991b) and "Fluency Before Correctness: A Whole Language Experiment in College ESL" (1991a), Adele MacGowan-Gilhooly describes an interesting experiment in teaching English as a Second Language to students wanting to enter the City University of New York (CUNY). While the initial experiments at CUNY did not include a control group, the instructors did have data available for comparing their experimental approach with the approach they had used previously.

Basing their approach on already existing research into the acquisition of a second language, they decided to emphasize first fluency, then clarity, and to work explicitly on correctness only after the first two goals had been achieved. (See 1991a, pp. 39–40, for their working definitions of fluency and clarity.) Essentially the fluency-to-clarity-to-correctness sequence parallels the stages of first language acquisition; it is in effect a whole-to-part approach, wherein communication is the first goal. The teachers adopted these and other principles of whole language learning and teaching, including the idea that emergent speakers of a language must be immersed in using it. Because the students had to pass tests in reading and writing in order to be admitted to regular courses at the university, the revised sequence of three courses emphasized wide reading and extensive writing, but discussion of the readings and the students' writings also involved the language learners in a substantial amount of speaking and listening as well.

A description of the three courses will help clarify how these principles were realized in practice.

ESL 10 The students read 1,000 pages of popular fiction, along with autobiographical and biographical works. They had to read about 70 pages a week, plus copy passages that struck them and respond to those passages in a double-entry journal. They also worked on a writing project that had to total 10,000 words by the end of the semester (about 40 to 50 typewritten pages). Most of the ESL students wrote autobiographical pieces or family histories. Their partners helped the students make the pieces more comprehensible, logical, and interesting; teachers then gave more of this kind of feedback for the writers to consider for final revisions. "By semester's end, most [students] were reading and writing fluently and even more correctly than in the beginning, without having received any corrections or grammar instruction" (1991b, p. 80). (For the text developed for this class, see MacGowan-Gilhooly, 1993.)

ESL 20 This course focused on clarity in organizing and developing expository papers. But the teachers eased the students into expository writing by beginning with the reading of historical fiction or nonfiction having to do with the United States. Again, the students responded to the readings in double-entry journals and discussed their readings in small groups. They also wrote a 10,000-word, semester-long project on some aspect of the United States—its people, history, culture, or problems. Various kinds of writing were included. By the end of the term, most students were writing clearly enough to pass the course. (For the text developed for this class, see MacGowan-Gilhooly, 1995).

ESL 30 This course focused on the elimination of the most serious and most frequently occurring errors, and on looking just for these errors while editing. "This eliminates the bulk of students' errors without the cognitive overburden of trying to correct every error" (1991b, p. 81). The other major focus was preparing for the test that the university requires of ESL students before they can take most of their regular courses. In ESL 30, students read and wrote argumentative prose, often real-world prose like letters to newspapers or public officials. Again, they received help in revising, but in this course they also received help in editing to eliminate errors. They kept individualized study lists of spelling words, new vocabulary, useful facts, grammar points they needed to focus on, mechanics issues, and style issues. (MacGowan-Gilhooly notes her disappointment that this course had to be narrowed to a test-preparation course and indicates that some students who were writing well at the end of ESL 20 do not progress in ESL 30, and a few even seem to regress under the pressure of preparing for the university's writing assessment test; see 1991a, p. 45.)

MacGowan-Gilhooly reports that since CUNY implemented this whole language approach, the passing rate on the reading assessment test has almost doubled (1991a, p. 45). The writing test passing rate increased from 35 to 56 percent (1991b, p. 83). Fewer students were repeating ESL 10, 20, or 30, and the external readers of the writing test commented on what good writers the ESL students had become (1991a, p. 45). Furthermore, these improvements occurred even though only about two-thirds of the faculty were using the new whole language approach (1991b, p. 74). However, the most compelling evidence, MacGowan-Gilhooly believes, is qualitative rather than quantitative. In comparison with previous classes, the teachers of the new whole language–oriented classes reported such changes as these in their students and their classes (1991b, pp. 83–84):

- More confidence, better ability to work in groups, more tolerance for divergent views
- More daring in their use of new vocabulary
- Greater ability to write interesting pieces
- Essays of greater depth and richness, more fluency, and better grammar
- Better reading comprehension and speed
- Greater enjoyment of reading than in previous ESL courses
- Better discussions of readings
- Better analytical thinking, much greater intellectual curiosity
- Improvement in speaking (according to many students)
- Students were more serious, concentrated, self-reliant, and open to others

While these are only impressions, many of them are obviously worth researching to document in more rigorous fashion. MacGowan-Gilhooly (1991b) also reports:

> Traditional approaches seemed to inhibit experimentation and exaggerate the importance of errors. Before the course, students could not apply rules they had learned to their writing; but after it, it seemed they could. Yet the only grammar instruction they had had was in the context of questions about their own writing as they revised it. (p. 84)

On a personal note, I was so impressed with the results of the early CUNY experiments that I incorporated a literature-and-response element into my graduate course in the reading process, which at that time enrolled mostly students in a master's degree program in teaching English as a second language. Many of the students were themselves non-native speakers of English; several had already taught English in their home countries. In addition to extensive professional reading in journals, I required students to read about 75 pages of literature (usually fiction) per week, and to respond with dialogue journal entries. Often, they wrote a typewritten page or two of response, though I didn't really expect that much. After I incorporated this requirement, one of the students wrote at the end of the semester that at first she could only read three or four pages at a time in English and write a few sentences, but by the end of the semester she could read a hundred pages and write several pages of her own. Other students likewise made major leaps in fluency.

Obviously the students had achieved greater fluency through immersion in reading and writing, but what of their acquisition of grammar? Dan Cupery (1992) reports the results of research he conducted for his final paper in that class. In brief, those international students who had the most limited command of the syntactic resources of English at the beginning of the term made noticeable syntactic progress by the end of the term. Compared with their pre-test stories, the post-test stories generally showed noticeable syntactic growth in words per T-unit, clauses per T-unit, free modifiers per T-unit, and especially in embeddings per T-unit (embeddings include subordinate clauses, free modifiers, and a few other constructions). The writers who were originally most proficient showed little change in their use of grammatical elements. The study was much too small (eight subjects) to achieve statistical significance, but it suggests a direction for further research.

The studies discussed reflect the range of research bearing on the question of how learners can most readily acquire the grammar of a second or other language. While they vary from rigorously conducted research (e.g., Elley and Mangubhai, 1983) to noncomparative teacher research among a small group of students in a single classroom (Cupery, 1992), they all exemplify a recent interest in investigating whether a second language is best acquired through immersion in the language itself, or through direct instruction in the structures and vocabulary of the language, or through some combination of both. Substantive evidence suggests that basic grammatical competence is best developed through exposure to comprehensible input and through attempting to communicate in the target language, relatively unhampered by initial concerns about correctness. In second language acquisition as well as in first language acquisition, grammatical correctness may be best achieved by focusing on fluency first, rather than on grammar itself. Furthermore, the evidence from the studies summarized by Elley (1991), from other studies of learning English as a second language (e.g., Gradman and Hanania, 1991), and from a comprehensive summary by Krashen (1993) strongly suggests that reading, reading, and more reading may be critical for first *and* second language learners, both in developing fluency and in expanding their command of the syntactic resources of the language (e.g., Perera, 1984). Krashen's *The Power of Reading* (1993) summarizes a considerable body of research, but we may have only just begun to document the powerful effects of reading.

How Language Is Acquired: A Summary

Language acquisition is a complex process. While clearly children do imitate adult speech in some ways, it is also clear that imitation, repetition, and habit formation are nowhere near adequate to account for the acquisition of one's native language, including its grammatical patterns or rules. Neither is direct teaching. Even though parents and other caretakers may tell children the names of things, they do not directly teach babies and toddlers the grammatical system of the language.

Particularly relevant for our purposes here are the following conclusions from studies of first language acquisition:

1. At first, the underlying propositions—what we have called the deeper structure—are only minimally represented in the surface structure of a child's language. Gradually, however, more and more of the semantic and syntactic elements are represented in the surface structure of children's sentences.

2. If propositions are considered the whole of what children are trying to express, then we can logically say that language acquisition proceeds from whole to part: from a minimal representation of propositions to increasingly greater representation of the parts.

3. Adults do not—indeed, they could not—directly teach children the grammatical rules of their language. Children abstract these rules from the comprehensible input in their environment.

4. Children unconsciously form hypotheses about language structure. As the structure of the language input to which they are exposed becomes increasingly understood, children abandon less sophisticated hypotheses and formulate more sophisticated ones—all unconsciously, of course.

5. Children's competence in grammar is acquired only gradually, with successive approximations coming closer and closer to adult norms. What seem like "errors" from the viewpoint of adult language performance are absolutely necessary for language development.

6. One important factor in children's ready acquisition of language is their naturally low affective filter. Unless an adult intervenes punitively, young children will just naturally take risks in using language; they are uninhibited by fear of failure, punishment, or embarrassment.

7. There are many ways that adults facilitate children's acquisition of language: for instance, by exposing them to rich and only slightly simplified language; by considering language acquisition to be as natural a process as learning to walk, and acting accordingly; by responding to what children are trying to say rather than to the correctness of their utterances; and, in many homes, by reading to children. In fact, there is clear evidence that reading even to secondary school students generates growth not only in vocabulary and an understanding of story, but also in understanding and use of syntactic constructions (Perera, 1984, 1986).

Although a second or other language is often taught through audiolingual or grammar/translation methods (e.g., as explained in Freeman and Freeman, 1994), there is significant evidence that an additional language may also be best acquired through essentially the same processes as one's first language. Of course, formal study may facilitate and refine that process (Terrell, 1991), but it can also impede it, by encouraging language learners to overly monitor their language use and refrain from taking the risks that genuine language acquisition requires.

4

Toward a Perspective on Error

Traditionally we have viewed departures from adult standards in writing as "errors," pure and simple. This kind of thinking is revealed by the preservice teacher who worked with a first grader twenty years ago. The child had written about Puff the magic dragon, and he put periods at the end of every line rather than at the end of the sentences. The preservice teacher had explained to the child that we put periods at the end of sentences, but he had grasped only that periods go at the end of *something* and put them at the ends of lines instead. Perhaps he had been reading primers in which sentences always ended at the ends of lines (not uncommon in the basal reading programs of the 1970s). In any case, the preservice teacher was bewildered at the child's lack of compliance with her explanation. Apparently it had not occurred to her that in putting periods at the ends of lines, the child was operating upon his own developmental hypothesis about the use of periods. She viewed the child simply as failing to respond to her adult instruction.

Fortunately Grace Vento-Zogby, the teacher who recently observed a first grader apply a similar development hypothesis (see Figure 4.1), was more knowledgeable. She realized that putting periods at the ends of lines rather than sentences is not uncommon at a certain stage among children who are reinventing punctuation by developing hypotheses about its use (Cordeiro, 1988). Realizing that the child is neither stupid nor stubborn, this experienced and knowledgeable teacher will keep assisting Rachel with using periods until she abandons her original hypothesis for the convention followed by adult writers.

We saw in Chapter 3 that children do not learn the basic structures of their native language through direct instruction, but through their own discovery and by formulating increasingly sophisticated hypotheses. So it

FIGURE 4.1 Placement of periods by a first grader.

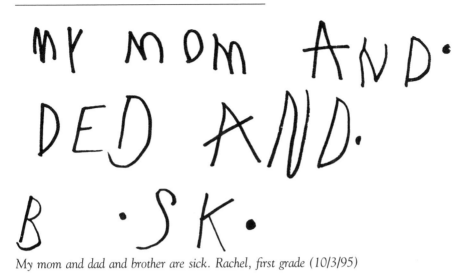

My mom and dad and brother are sick. Rachel, first grade (10/3/95)

often is with the conventions of written language. That is, children may learn many conventions through observation (both incidental and deliberate) and then generalization, more than through direct instruction—though the latter can help, when the learner is ready. Something we teachers need to learn, then, is how to recognize and deal effectively with "errors" that are actually evidence of the writer's thinking and, in some cases, clear indicators of the writer's growth in mastering the structures and conventions of written English. Thus this chapter deals with developing an informed and reasonable perspective on error and with strategies for helping writers learn to edit their writing in order to eliminate errors from their final drafts.

Errors as a Necessary Concomitant of Growth

We saw in Chapter 3 that children naturally make various kinds of "errors" as they learn the rules of their language. For the pronoun *we*, five-year-old John says "weez," because plurals take an *-s* or *-z* sound. In learning the rule, John has overgeneralized it to a word that is already plural. Jane Kiel reports this and other overgeneralizations from two children in her day care center: Tristan, just turned four, and John, age four.

TRISTAN	JOHN
Maybe the rabbit *losed* his fur. [lost]	We *goed* to Wendy's. [went]
He runs *fastly*. [fast]	I *dooed* it. [did]
	He *loseded* it. [lost]
	Dinosaurs are *extincted*. [extinct]

Notice that while Tristan applies the regular past tense ending to *lose* and produces *losed* (pronounced "loozd"), John goes him one better by making *losed* itself past tense. A regular verb that ends in a -*t* or -*d* sound takes a vowel sound plus -*d* for the past tense, and this is what John adds to *losed*, producing the double past tense, *loseded*.

As adults, we are typically amused by such overgeneralizations, knowing that they will almost certainly disappear as the child gains more experience with the language. We are similarly amused, perhaps even delighted, by the errors in children's drawings. However, we can learn from examining children's drawings some developmental characteristics that hold for writing as well.

Six of John's drawings (a different John) are included in Figure 4.2. These were collected in the sequence in which they are presented, left to right, top to bottom. In the first drawing we notice, for example, that the figure has arms, legs, and hair, but no body. The second figure shows progress, with fingers added to the hands, and feet added to the legs. The third figure has "lost" its arms, while gaining another body feature. The fourth figure has arms, hands, feet, shoelaces, and a body, with legs attached. However, it has "lost" the hair. The fifth figure includes two-dimensional legs and bodies that seem to be differentiated for male (dad and son) and female (mother, in the middle); however, it too shows no hair on the people. The sixth figure is much more sophisticated, with a neck, two-dimensional arms and legs, a beard, a crown, and, yes, hair.

What can we learn from considering this sequence of pictures? At least the following developmental characteristics:

- Learners do not typically master something correctly all at once. (For example, arms are included in the first two pictures, but they are not yet two-dimensional.) Indeed, learners may develop several hypotheses about how something is done before achieving adult or expert competence.
- Something learned may be temporarily not applied as the person is trying something else new. (The arms are missing from picture three, which includes an additional body feature.)

FIGURE 4.2 Developmental sequence in John's drawings.

These generalizations hold for emergent writers as well as for emergent artists, and for adults as well as children (e.g., Scardamalia, Bereiter, and Goelman, 1982; Cordeiro, Giacobbe, and Cazden, 1983).

In their article on error analysis and the teaching of composition, Kroll and Schafer (1978) include a chart (see Figure 4.3) that nicely compares the traditional, behavioral approach to teaching writing with a constructivist approach stemming from more recent findings in cognitive psychology (see Chapter 6 of the present book). The preceding discussion in this section illustrates particularly Kroll and Schafer's fourth paragraph in the Process column: "Errors are a natural part of learning a language; they arise from learners' active strategies: overgeneralization, ignorance of rule restrictions, incomplete rule application, hypothesizing false concepts." This observation refers to errors made in learning a language, but much the same can be said about errors made in becoming an accomplished writer (e.g., Falk, 1979), even though some of the errors we make as writers are careless ones, or conscious errors that we intend to correct by the final draft.

Spelling Errors as a Part of Learning

Since "invented" spelling has become such an issue in some communities, it seems important to demonstrate some of the natural patterns of learning in children's spelling. These will serve as exemplars of how natural growth in writing necessarily involves error.

The term *invented spelling* was intended to convey the notion that children who are first allowed to spell as best they can will naturally go through increasingly sophisticated stages in their spelling (Read, 1975; Bissex, 1980; Ferreiro and Teberosky, 1982). Just as children develop hypotheses or rules for putting words together to speak their native language, so they will develop hypotheses or rules for spelling words in order to convey meaning. Because children's invented spellings reflect their minds at work, some people prefer to use the term *constructed spellings* (Laminack, 1991). Of course, children's hypotheses about spelling are not necessarily conscious, and in fact they may know perfectly well that their spellings are not the same as adults' spellings. Nevertheless, we adults can often induce rules that seem to be guiding the children in spelling (Weaver, 1994, pp. 71–73, provides a fuller discussion). When children first start writing letters, the letters may bear no relationship to sounds (Figure 4.4a). Their "rule" seems to be something like "write some letters and hope someone else can read what you've written." Children who are just beginning to use letters to represent sounds may often seem to be operating on a rule such as this:

FIGURE 4.3 Contrast between behavioral and constructivist approaches to learners' errors (Kroll and Schafer, 1978). The fourth paragraph in the process column is credited to Richards (1971).

ISSUE	PRODUCT [BEHAVIORAL] APPROACH	PROCESS [CONSTRUCTIVIST] APPROACH
Why should one study errors?	To produce a linguistic taxonomy of *what* errors learners make.	To produce a psycholinguistic explanation of *why* a learner makes an error.
What is the attitude toward error?	Errors are "bad." (Interesting only to the linguistic theorist.)	Errors are "good." (Interesting to the theorist and teacher, and useful to the learner as active tests of his hypotheses.)
What can we hope to discover from learners' errors?	Those items on which the learner or the program failed.	The strategies which led the learner into the error.
How can we account for the fact that a learner makes an error?	It is primarily a failure to learn the correct form (perhaps a case of language inference).	Errors are a natural part of learning a language; they arise from learners' active strategies: overgeneralization, ignorance of rule restrictions, incomplete rule application, hypothesizing false concepts.
What are the emphases and goals of instruction?	A *teaching* perspective: eliminate all errors by establishing correct, automatic habits; mastery of the target language is the goal.	A *learning* perspective: assist the learner in approximating the target language; support active learning strategies and recognize that not all errors will disappear.

FIGURE 4.4a Pre-phonemic writing. The letters do not represent sounds.

I am pushing my tractor. Cory (Spring of Kindergarten, 1994, age 5)

FIGURE 4.4b Early phonemic writing. One sound per word is represented.

I am playing soccer. Cory (Fall of First Grade, 10/17/94)

> Write mainly the first sounds of the words (or of the syllables). (Figure 4.4b)

Before long, this rule gives way to a rule like

> Write mainly two or three sounds per word or syllable (usually, the first and last consonant sounds, plus perhaps other consonant and vowel sounds). (Figure 4.4c)

Of course, children then begin to add more and more letters to represent sounds within the word—not only more of the consonant sounds, but vowels too (Figure 4.4d). As children gain more exposure to written language, they begin to draw upon their visual memory to spell words and perhaps to draw upon instruction they have received about rules like "add -ed to show that something already happened" (Figure 4.4e). Gradually the proportion of invented spellings diminishes and the proportion of conven-

FIGURE 4.4c Later phonemic writing. As here, usually more of the consonant sounds are represented as the writer is just beginning to represent vowel sounds within words.

I WNT TIK r t w mi frn.

I went trick or treating with my friends. Cory (11/1/94)

FIGURE 4.4d Transitional writing. Most words include vowels; more of the sounds are represented, and some "basic" words are spelled conventionally.

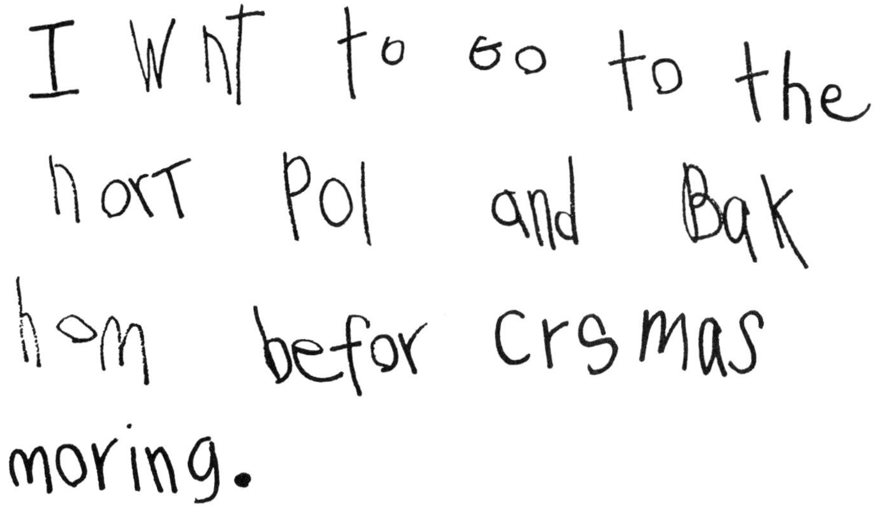

I WNT to go to the hort Pol and Bak hom befor Crgmas moring.

I want to go to the North Pole and back home before Christmas morning.
Cory (12/15/94)

Last hit   I

et my hamburg

er and tSWaloed

my tooth

Last night I ate my hamburger and I swallowed my tooth. Cory (1/11/95)

tional spellings increases (compare Figure 4.4d with Figure 4.4e). For children who are reading and writing daily, such development occurs even without direct instruction in spelling. (Compare Cory's spelling in Figure 4.4b in October with his spelling in Figure 4.4d in December and his spelling in Figure 4.4e in January. He had received spelling instruction only on a few words, during Reading Recovery tutoring.)

Figure 4.5a–c demonstrates how significant the change can be during just part of a school year. In Figure 4.5a, Sandra wrote her first rendition of "Humpty Dumpty" in late September. In late February, she was asked to write the same piece as it was dictated to her. Notice that her spacing is much better, and so is her spelling. Furthermore, it is not merely that she spells more words conventionally: the invented spellings are much more sophisticated, too. In the second example (Figure 4.5b) there is likewise a considerable difference between the first writing sample in September and the second, which was dictated to the child in June. Figure 4.5c shows something Cory wrote on November 1 and then again in June when the piece was dictated to him.

The point has already been made that such development occurs even without direct instruction. However, this is not to say that teachers should

HB⊕DDS⋀M⋀⊕W/L LH⊕D⊗FⱯGⱤF

In late September, Sandra produced this rendition of "Humpty Dumpty."

Jandy humpy Dumpy sat on a wol
humpy Dumpy had a grayt foi
ol the cings horsig and the
cings min cydint put humpy Dumpy
Back To Gesr a Gen

In late February, she produced this rendition.

not help children learn conventional spellings, or teach common spelling patterns, or help children develop strategies for changing temporary spellings to conventional spellings in final drafts. All of these are important (see Wilde, 1992, a particularly valuable resource for elementary teachers). But even if children did not receive such help, their spelling would gradually improve if they were continually exposed to books and other written texts and frequently given opportunities to write, while spelling as best they can. Furthermore, research shows that by the end of first grade, children encouraged to spell as best they can score as well or better on standardized tests of spelling than children who are asked to write using only the words they can spell correctly (Clarke, 1988). In addition, they seem to develop a better grasp of phonics, to use a much wider range of vocabulary, and of course to write more as well (Clarke, 1988; Dahl and Freppon, 1992; and several other sources cited in Weaver, 1994, ch. 7).

For teachers, the important message is to encourage students to spell as best they can when they first write down what they have to say. With children who are just beginning to write (many kindergartners and first

FIGURE 4.5b   One first grader's writing in September and in June. (Cochrane et al., 1984).

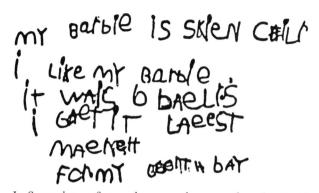

In September, a first grader wrote this story about her Barbie doll.

My BarBie is Skin colaër
I Like My BarBie
It was 6 Dolers
I Got it Last Month
for my BorThDay.

When the same story was dictated to her in June, she wrote this.

graders), it is critical to model writing for and with them—to help them hear sounds, make the letter/sound connections, and notice the conventional spellings as you compose together. Making lists of words that have the same sound/spelling patterns (lists like *night, fight, light, right, might, sight*) promotes both spelling and phonics development. When children begin using a fairly high proportion of conventional or nearly conventional spellings in their own writing, they should be ready to benefit from strategies for checking and correcting their spelling. For example, a simple strategy, one used even by adults, is simply to write a word two or three times and see which one "looks right."

Of course, this discussion is only suggestive of how to begin encouraging growth in writing and spelling (see Wilde, 1992). But it emphasizes the point that we teachers need to promote the natural growth of spelling and

FIGURE 4.5c   One first grader's writing in November and June.

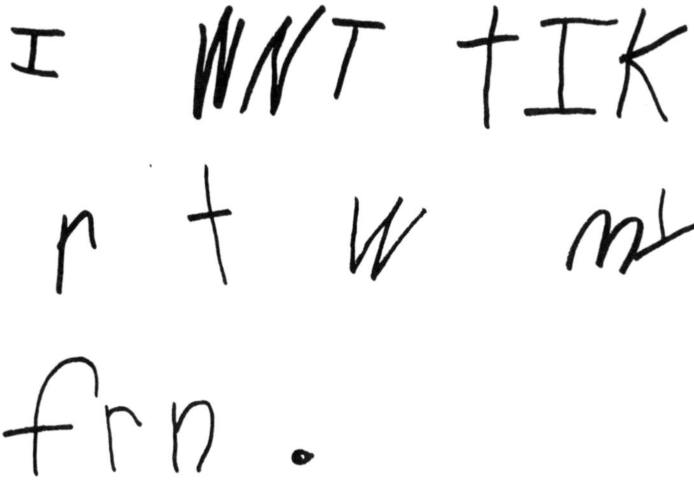

I WNT tIK
r t W mt
frn .

I went trick or treating with my friends.

I went trik or tring
with my frende's.

This is how he wrote the same thing on June, when it was dictated to him.

not expect our instruction to produce perfectly spelled drafts, especially from younger emergent writers. We don't expect toddlers to produce sentences that are grammatically correct by adult standards, and we shouldn't expect young schoolchildren to produce writing that is conventionally spelled. It takes years to spell conventionally without sacrificing meaning or rejecting the interesting words in our oral vocabulary. It takes years of experience as a writer, and the opportunity to revise and edit successive drafts of our writing. For some accessible resources dealing with the development of spelling and writing, see Figure 4.6.

Errors as a Necessary Result of Instruction

It had not occurred to me that writing growth and error go hand in hand until I read an article by Roger McCaig (1977):

FIGURE 4.6   References on the early development of spelling and writing.

Clay, M. M. (1987). *Writing begins at home*. Portsmouth, NH: Heinemann.
Laminack, L. (1991). *Learning with Zachary*. Richmond Hill, Ontario: Scholastic. Distributed in the United States by Heinemann.
McGee, L. M., & Richgels, D. J. (1990). *Literacy's beginnings: Supporting young readers and writers*. Boston: Allyn & Bacon.
Newman, J. M. (1984). *The craft of children's writings*. Richmond Hill, Ontario: Scholastic. Distributed in the United States by Heinemann.
Temple, C., Nathan, R., Temple, F., & Burris, N. (1993). *The beginnings of writing* (3rd ed.). Boston: Allyn & Bacon.
Villiers, U. (1989). *Luk mume dade I kan rite*. New York: Scholastic. (Spanish version also available)

> By literal count, good sixth grade writing may have more errors per word than good third grade writing. In a Piagetian sense, children do not master things for once and for all. A child who may appear to have mastered sentence sense in the fourth grade may suddenly begin making what adults call sentence errors all over again as he attempts to accommodate his knowledge of sentences to more complicated constructions. (pp. 50–51)

And Mina Shaughnessy noted in her landmark book *Errors and Expectations* (1977) that "it is not unusual for people acquiring a skill to get 'worse' before they get better and for writers to err more as they venture more" (p. 119).

From this point, it was only a small step to realizing that instruction in how to do something new will often result in writers making new kinds of errors. Take, for instance, a paper by a first grader (Figure 4.7). Having been introduced to the use of apostrophes in possessives, this child used the apostrophe correctly in *cow's* but unnecessarily and incorrectly in *had's* [*head's*]. She overgeneralized the apostrophe, just as preschoolers commonly overgeneralize things like past tense and plural endings. So did Cory, in the word *frende's*, which in context was an ordinary plural. (Figure 4.5c). Similarly, an earnest and eager student in one of my classes for preservice teachers wrote about *mathematic's class* after I had taught a mini-lesson on using apostrophes in possessives. I regularly find, in fact, that after such a mini-lesson, some of my students will use apostrophes in ordinary plurals and sometimes even in verbs, where the apostrophe is not called for. Such overgeneralization is typical of new learning, with both oral and written language.

Another interesting example comes from a preservice teacher who taught a group of first graders the use of commas to separate items in a

FIGURE 4.7   Use of apostrophes by a first grader.

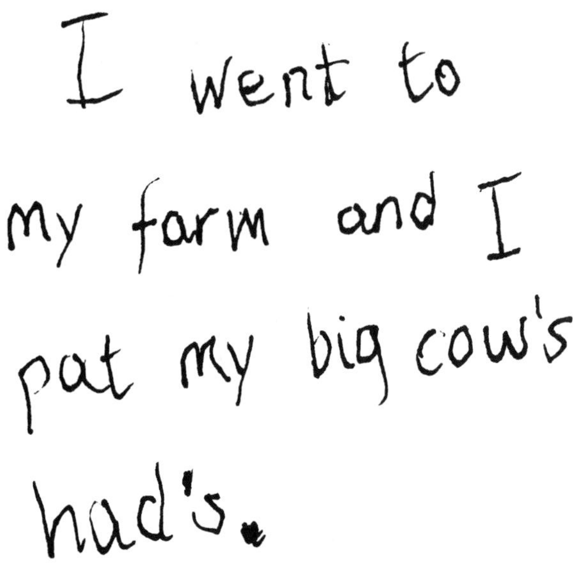

I went to
my farm and I
pat my big cow's
had's.

FIGURE 4.8   Use of commas by a first grader.

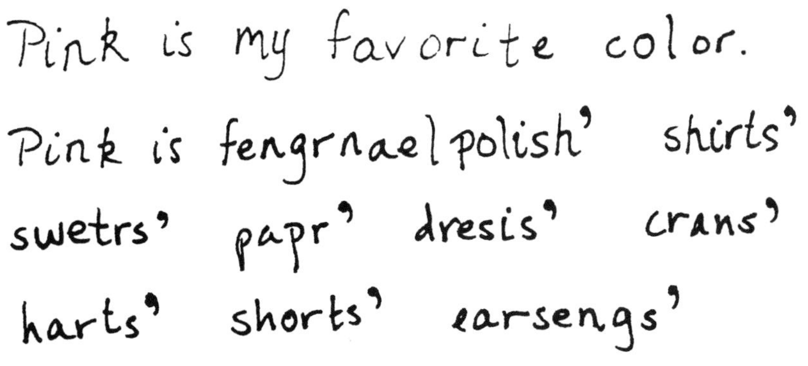

Pink is my favorite color.
Pink is fengrnael polish' shirts'
swetrs' papr' dresis' crans'
harts' shorts' earsengs'

series. They applied this lesson with varying success. One child, for example, used marks that look a lot like commas, but she put them above the
print, where apostrophes would go (see Figure 4.8).

Some of the most interesting examples I have accumulated over the
years are from students in writing classes, where I have taught the use of
the participial phrase and the absolute construction to convey narrative
and descriptive details. In retelling the Pied Piper story, one freshman wrote
a paper that included the following dangling participles:

Playing a special tune on his flute, the rats came out from everywhere, following the Piper out of town, down the road, over the hill, and right into the river, *drowning the rats*.

Taking the kids far away from town, a nearing mountain split wide open.

These sentences are not easy to reconstruct according to rule, but the first one might read something like "Playing a special tune on his flute, the Piper lured rats from everywhere out of town, down the road, over the hill, and right into the river, drowning the rats." In other words, the person playing the flute should be named right after the comma, in order to avoid having the introductory modifier dangle. This change also clarifies who is responsible for drowning the rats.

Another student wrote a marvelous description of a sea captain, with two of her seventeen "sentences" actually being participial phrases and five being absolute constructions, not grammatically complete sentence units. For example, following are five punctuated sentences from her description, with italics used for the participial fragment and the absolute fragment: "Greying eyes search the horizon for unknown hazards lurking below. *Looking for the unpredictable answers of the sea.* He reads the waters as if they were a map. An old stocking cap covers the sparse sprigs of hair. *His salt and pepper beard tattered like the sail of an abandoned ship.*"

What is a teacher to make of such results of her instruction? Fortunately by the time I encountered these examples, I had come to expect errors to accompany growth in writing. Therefore, my solution was, and is, simply to applaud the experimentation and then to help the writer punctuate more conventionally. As I wrote more than a decade ago, "The key, I believe, is to think of writing as involving more than one draft. In the first draft(s) we can then afford to encourage writers to take risks, the risks that will result in both growth and error. By allowing for error, we can encourage growth" (Weaver, 1982).

More Sophisticated Errors Replacing Less Sophisticated Errors

Another important lesson I have learned is that while old kinds of errors are disappearing, new kinds of errors are taking their place. The result is that the overall rate of errors may not lessen very much over the years.

This fact was brought home to me by John Mellon's analysis of data from the National Assessment of Educational Progress more than twenty years ago (1975). From the data on the writing of children ages nine, thirteen, and seventeen, Mellon analyzed occurrences of eight kinds of errors: spelling, punctuation, capitalization, fragments, run-ons, agreement, incorrect word choice, and "awkward constructions." Although spelling errors decreased considerably with age and writing proficiency, the other kinds of errors did not. For example, low-proficiency nine-year-olds wrote an average of 0.6 sentence fragments per hundred words while high-proficiency seventeen-year-olds wrote an average of 0.5, a slight difference indeed (p. 31).

As a teacher accustomed to observing and reflecting upon the effects of my teaching, I was intrigued. Could it be that the rate of errors in a given category remained relatively constant because "old" errors within a category were simply being replaced by more sophisticated kinds of errors? I had casually observed this with my college freshmen, so I set out to investigate with students in the elementary grades. Focusing just on sentence fragments found in two writing samples (one narrative and one persuasive), I found that the proportion of fragments leveled off at grade 4, at 0.15 fragments per hundred words. Sure enough, though, the nature of the fragments changed over the grades. Here are some examples that indicate the kind of fragment that was new at each grade (Weaver, 1982):

Grade 1   I want mom and dad to buy a pool. *because she could teach in the pool.* [An explanatory *because* clause, found in the persuasive writings.]

Grade 2   I get started on being layzy. *And not doing my work.* [The *because* clause still predominated, but the second part of a compound element was punctuated as a sentence nearly as often.]

Grade 3   I would like to do things in our science book. *Like icksrmeting on finding out.* [The new kind of fragment that appeared prominently was an explanatory phrase that elaborated on an idea.]

Grade 4   "A superduper awesome machine," said Bob. *Sam for short.* [New at this grade level was the stylistic fragment, a fragment that has the ring of artistry rather than accident.]

Grade 5   The most exciting thing that ever happened to me is. *When I first took a ride in are new Cadillac.* [New kinds of subordinate clauses were punctuated as sentences.]

Of course, changes in the nature of fragments would not necessarily be found to be the same today, when more and more children in the primary grades are being encouraged to write as best they can rather than just to complete sentences or copy writing from the chalkboard. However, the general point remains, namely, that the nature of errors seems to change *within* major categories like "fragment" (Weaver, 1982). Cordeiro found the same to be true within the general category of period placement (Cordeiro, 1988; see also Edelsky, 1983). Therefore, a nearly constant error rate over the grades is misleading. It masks more subtle changes, thus obscuring learning and growth.

It should be noted that in a more recent study, Nelson (1988) found that over the grades there *was* a decrease in certain kinds of errors, particularly in fragments and run-on sentences. One cannot help wondering whether the increase in "correctness" was purchased at the expense of syntactic growth and experimentation.

Reconsidering What Counts as Error

In a fascinating article, Joseph Williams (1981) discusses what he calls "the phenomenology of error." He wonders why certain usages are attacked with such ferocity by the writers of composition handbooks and by self-appointed language mavens such as William Safire (1993). The denunciation of certain usages is all the more strange when we notice, as Williams did, that the writers of composition handbooks often commit the same language "sins" that they rail against.

One of Williams's examples comes from Jacques Barzun. In *Simple and Direct* (1975), Barzun asserts the following rule in the middle of one page:

> In conclusion, I recommend using *that* with defining clauses, except when stylistic reasons interpose. (p. 68)

Near the top of the next page, Barzun violates the rule he has just stated:

> Next is a typical situation which a practiced writer corrects "for style" virtually by reflex action. . . . (p. 69)

Williams (1981) comments:

> Now again, it is not the error as such that I am concerned with here, but rather the fact that after Barzun stated the rule, and almost immediately violated it, no one noticed—not Barzun himself who must certainly have read the manuscript several times, not a colleague to whom he probably gave the manuscript before he sent it to the publisher, not the copy editor

who worked over the manuscript, not the proof reader who read the galleys, not Barzun who probably read the galleys after them, apparently not even anyone in the reading public, since that *which* hasn't been corrected in any of the subsequent printings. To characterize this failure to respond as mere carelessness seems to miss something important. (p. 57)

One conclusion we can draw from this and other examples Williams cites from the handbooks is that published writers do not necessarily follow the rules in those handbooks. But as the preceding quote suggests, Williams is even more interested in the fact that when published writers violate the rules we have been teaching schoolchildren and college students, usually no one notices! To make this point, Williams deliberately included about one hundred errors in his own article, including some in the passage I have quoted. As the errors became more frequent and more "serious," I began noticing more of them. However, I'm sure I did not notice anywhere near a hundred errors.

If we rarely notice (much less challenge) the "errors" in published writing, perhaps we should reconsider how we read and respond to students' papers. English teachers have traditionally been encouraged and even trained *to look for errors* in students' papers (and in my experience of teaching preservice teachers, many of them are inclined to "correct" language features that are not even considered errors in the handbooks). Traditionally, the reading of students' papers has been an "error hunt," not an attempt to appreciate what the writer has said and how he or she has said it. No wonder many students have come to hate writing!

Williams implies, of course, that we should not be more judgmental about student writing than we are about published, professional writing. Surely this is a reasonable attitude.

Handbook Prohibitions and Stylistic Effectiveness

When we move from handbook prohibitions to examining the usage of published writers, we are moving from grammar to rhetoric. As Francis Christensen has written, "Grammar maps out the possible; rhetoric narrows the possible down to the desirable or effective" (Christensen and Christensen, 1978, p. 61).

In *Notes Toward a New Rhetoric* (1967; expanded as Christensen and Christensen, 1978), Christensen has examined professional writing to determine what kinds of constructions professional writers have used in making their writing effective. Most of us have heard or read the handbook rule of not starting a sentence with *and* or *but*. What Christensen found, though, was that in the expository writing of professionals, sentences began with a coordinating conjunction (most commonly *and* or *but*) 8.75 percent of the time, while in narrative writing sentences were so linked 4.55 percent of the time (1967, pp. 50–51). In other words, nearly one out of nine sentences in informative writing began with *and* or *but*, or with a word that functions in the same way. Why, then, should we try to eradicate such usage from student writing? In so doing, we are actually teaching students not to write like published authors.

Something else published writers do is make judicious use of comma splices. That is, they occasionally use just a comma to join two or more clauses that are both grammatically complete. Irene Brosnahan (1976) has characterized the conditions that seem to govern the use of comma splices in effective writing: (1) The style of discourse is general or informal; (2) the sentences are short, and usually parallel in structure; (3) rhetorically, the sentences convey rapid movement or emphasis; and (4) semantically, the punctuated sentence cannot be ambiguous, and the relationship between the grammatically complete sentences is one of paraphrase, repetition, amplification, opposition, addition, or summary (see Figure 4.9). By trying to eradicate these kinds of comma splices from our students' writing, we may have prevented them from using some constructions used effectively by professional writers.

Another way in which we may have prevented or retarded students' development into rhetorically effective writers is by telling students never to punctuate a grammatically incomplete group of words as a sentence. In other words, we have prohibited what the grammar handbooks call fragments. What some handbooks don't mention, though, is that effective writers often use fragments judiciously. It may be true that certain kinds of fragments rarely find their way into professional writing, but other kinds do. In fact, some fragments are so accepted in formal professional writing that Kline and Memering (1977) call them minor sentences rather than fragments. They divided the fragments they found in formal writing into two major categories, independent and dependent. In Figure 4.10 (see pages 78–79), I have added examples for most of the fragments in the independent category, since Kline and Memering did not provide many. However, the examples of dependent fragments come from the professional writings that Kline and Memering examined as a basis for their categorization. For greater clarity, I have used categories that are more semantic than syntactic, though Kline and Memering provide both. Careful examination of these categories

FIGURE 4.9 Effective comma splices in published writing (Brosnahan, 1976). All but the first example were found in Brosnahan's article.

SEMANTIC OCCASIONS FOR EFFECTIVE COMMA SPLICES	EXAMPLES
1. Paraphrase	Their meeting was clandestine, it was completely secretive.—Connie Weaver
2. Repetition	This was bad, admittedly this was bad.—Helen Bevington
3. Amplification	In the morning it was sunny, the lake was blue.—D. H. Lawrence
4. Opposition	The Director was permanent, the General was temporary.—Navasky
5. Addition	School bores them, preaching bores them, even television bores them.—Arthur Miller
6. Summary	Handbook writers should admit it, teachers should teach it, students should learn it.—Irene Brosnahan
	They clambered up the grass, they clutched at each other, little ones rode on big ones.—John Steinbeck

and examples will show that the kinds of fragments found in my study of fragments in the writing of elementary school children are used for effect in the writings of professionals. Why shouldn't they be used to good effect by our students as well? Consider, for instance, the following passage from college student Lisa Lehman's narrative about kissing her boyfriend in the sixth grade:

> We had a music class, which was our favorite class because we got to choose our seats and we always sat next to each other. Perhaps I was feeling extra saucy that day, perhaps my nerve had finally healed, perhaps it was my destiny. I don't know. The only thing I do know is that when the office aide knocked on the door distracting the teacher and half the class, I closed my eyes, puckered my lips and laid my first kiss smack dab in the middle of his cheek.
>
> Sparks. I saw them before I opened my eyes. Not the Fourth of July fireworks display, but a subtle, slow haze of sparks crowning the darkness of my closed eyes, trickling down until the entire lid was aglow. Yet the spark didn't stop with my eyes. It was like someone had squashed a lightning bug in between his cheeks and my lips and all the electricity flowed between us. I opened my eyes to see my chapstick imprint on his flaming cheek. The deed was done.
>
> "Did you have to do that *now?*" was all he said. Not quite the response I was looking for.

FIGURE 4.10 Effective minor sentences (Kline and Memering, 1977). Of the examples in the independent category, only the two marked with asterisks were found in their article. In each quotation within the dependent category, Kline and Memering added italics to highlight the minor sentences.

MINOR SENTENCES (FRAGMENTS)	EXAMPLES
Independent	
1. Imperatives, exclamations, one-word interrogatives, and one-word answers	Run! Excellent! Why? Absolutely.
2. Ellipsis-based units (missing article, possessives)	That is Meyer's computer. His alone.
3. Literary	Oh, for summer.*
4. Phatic (in speech)	Oh, great. Uh-huh. Yeah, yeah.
5. Nominal, adjectival, or adverbial phrases not in the dependent category	Spring. Rain falling, grass greening, flowers blooming. A young man's fancy. A young woman's, too.
6. *How* and *what* constructions	How convenient! What a shame.
7. Subjectless, nonimperative, nonelliptical units	Just to get away.* Only five, so far.
Dependent	
8. Negation (*not* or *no*)	Emily Dickinson's poems, because they have such tension, are much more authentically in the metaphysical tradition than Emerson's are. *Not, however, that many of the values were not hers also. . . .*—F. O. Matthiesen, *American Renaissance*
9. Comparison	They then determined the number of these unrelated words recalled when the subject attempted to repeat the sentence and the sequences of words. *The more words recalled, the less memory used to store the sentence. The fewer words recalled, the more memory used to store the sentence.*—Noam Chomsky, "Language and the Mind"

10.	Afterthought and addition	It is possible, to be sure, that a thing precisely observed can be poorly rendered. *Or that it may be poorly received by the reader.*—John Ciardi, "The Art of Maxine Kumin," *Saturday Review*
11.	Clarification (dependent clauses, appositives, other adjectivals or adverbials)	I am sure no other civilisation, not even the Roman, has showed [sic] such a vast proportion of ignominious and degraded nudity, and ugly, squalid, dirty sex. *Because no other civilization has driven sex into the underworld, and nudity to the w.c.*—D. H. Lawrence, *Pornography and Obscenity*
12.	Elimination of redundancy through elliptical clauses and phrases	So what was missing from little Saalbach on that bright February morning? *Snow. Schnee. The same thing missing from so many other Alpine ski resorts this winter.*—David Butwin, "Booked for Travel: The Pleasant Slush of Saalbach," *Saturday Review*
		The spirit of the long-vanished Roman Empire, revived by the Catholic Church, returned once more to our Island, bringing with it three dominant ideas. *First, a Europe in which naturalism or even the conception of nationality had no place . . .*—Winston Churchill, *The Birth of Britain*

It seems to me that the fragments (and the comma splice sentence) make this passage more effective, not less. The writer's grammatical versatility approaches that of published writers.

Younger writers, too, can make effective use of fragments, as exemplified by the fourth grader who wrote "A *superduper awesome machine,*" said Bob. *Sam for short.* Following is another example, this time from a high school sophomore, Brooke. In revising her first draft, she has added two fragments to her introduction:

Julie watched Omar stroll lazily down the hall and laughed. He was a funny looking guy; tall and skinny with funny ears and a big nose. He was the type of guy who would flirt with any girl who would listen. Sex was his number one priority, but still Julie couldn't help but feel attracted to him. *She and almost every girl he met.* Although it seemed almost impossible, Omar seemed he was ready to settle down. *And even more impossible, settle down with Julie.*

FIGURE 4.11   References for teaching grammar as style.

GRAMMAR AND STYLE

Christensen, F., & Christensen, B. (1978). *Notes toward a new rhetoric: Nine essays for teachers* (2nd ed.). New York: Harper & Row. Relevant research and some teaching suggestions.

Gibson, W. (1968). *Persona: A style study for readers and writers.* New York: Random House. For secondary school as well as college writers and teachers.

Green, J. L. (1969). Acrobats, plowmen, and the healthy sentence. *English Journal, 58,* 892–899.

Kolln, M. (1991). *Rhetorical grammar: Grammatical choices, rhetorical effects.* New York: Macmillan. More on grammar than on rhetoric.

Love, G. A., & Payne, M. (Eds.) (1969). *Contemporary essays on style: Rhetoric, linguistics, and criticism.* Glenview, IL: Scott, Foresman. Analysis of styles.

Rice, S. (1993). *Right words, right places.* Belmont, CA: Wadsworth. Emphasizes rhetorical effects of grammatical choices.

Romano, T. (1988). Breaking the rules in style. *English Journal, 77,* 58–62. Shows some of Weathers's options as used by high school students.

Weathers, W. (1980). *An alternate style: Options in composition.* Portsmouth, NH: Boynton/Cook. The basis for Romano's experiments in teaching style.

Williams, J. M. (1990). *Style: Toward Clarity and Grace.* Chicago: University of Chicago Press.

FROM GRAMMAR TO STYLE THROUGH SENTENCE COMBINING

Daiker, D. A., Kerek, A., & Morenberg, M. (1990). *The writer's options: Combining to composing* (4th ed.). New York: Harper & Row. Textbook for college writers.

Killgallon, D. (1987). *Sentence composing: The complete course.* Portsmouth, NH: Boynton/Cook. Textbook for high school writers.

Strong, W. (1986). *Creative approaches to sentence combining.* Urbana, IL: ERIC/RCS and the National Council of Teachers of English. Professional reference for teachers.

While I might still suggest a couple of changes to this writer, I would not suggest eliminating the fragments—nor did her teacher, who considered the fragments effective.

Why, then, should we fervently try to eradicate all fragments from our students' writing? Wouldn't it be better to become more aware ourselves of what makes a fragment effective, and to help students eliminate only those fragments that are genuinely unclear or ineffective? The minor sentences characterized by Kline and Memering (1977) either stand alone or relate to an adjacent sentence, usually the sentence that comes before. In context, they are clear. Kline and Memering proffer sound advice to teachers: "We suggest as a general rule that 'fragments' will largely disappear if teachers will read student papers rapidly, attending to the substance of the sentences" (p. 109). In other words, we should read students' work the way we read the published writing of professionals. If we do, our students should have a better chance of becoming published authors beyond the classroom or school.

Figure 4.11 lists some articles and books that can help us teach for rhetorical effectiveness and style, rather than for a narrowly defined concept of correctness. Some books on sentence combining are included too, since sentence-combining activities are the one kind of grammar exercise that, more often than not, seems to have a positive effect on students' sentences (Hillocks and Smith, 1991). However, it is by no means clear that sentence-combining activities are any more helpful than direct guidance in expanding, combining, and reorganizing sentence elements (Hughes, 1975; Hartwell and LoPresti, 1985). In fact, as far as we know, directly helping our students revise and manipulate sentences in their own writing may be considerably more valuable than any sentence-combining activities we could have them do and discuss.

Responding to Errors in More Constructive Ways

One of the problems with overreacting to error is that it stunts our students' growth as writers. This was particularly true when teachers commonly assigned one and only one draft of a piece of writing—in other words, when the first draft was also the last. Under pressure not to make mistakes, students have often written less interesting pieces of writing. For example, McQuade (1980) reported that after he had taught a class in editing skills, the students wrote essays that were much worse than the essays they wrote at the beginning of the semester:

> The essays in the first set are not spectacular. . . . The essays in the second set, on the other hand, are miserable. Their principal method of organization is a series of afterthoughts, and their sentences are awkwardly and I believe self-consciously constructed to honor correctness above all other virtues, including sense. (p. 29)

No wonder, then, that McQuade concludes: "No reduction of the number of errors could be significant, I reasoned, when the post-course essays are inferior in every other way to the pre-course essays" (p. 29).

If this were not enough to convince us to restrain the traditional red pen, we might consider the following report from a teacher of English (quoted in Farrell, 1971, p. 141):

> My own research has convinced me that red-inking errors in students' papers does no good and causes a great many students to hate and fear writing more than anything else they do in school. I gave a long series of tests covering 580 of the most common and persistent errors in usage, diction, and punctuation and 1,000 spelling errors to students in grades 9–12 in many schools, and the average rate of improvement in ability to detect these errors turned out to be 2 percent per year. The dropout rate is more than enough to account for this much improvement if the teachers had not even been there. When I consider how many hours of my life I have wasted in trying to root out these errors by a method that clearly did not work, I want to kick myself. Any rat that persisted in pressing the wrong lever 10,000 times would be regarded as stupid. I must have gone on pressing it at least 20,000 times without visible effect.

As I noted in *Grammar for Teachers* (Weaver, 1979), "There seems to be little value in marking students' papers with 'corrections,' little value in teaching the conventions of mechanics apart from actual writing, and even less value in teaching grammar in order to instill these conventions" (p. 63).

Reconceptualizing the Writing Process

Over the last twenty or so years, there has been growing recognition that we need to guide student writers through the processes used by successful, published writers (Murray, 1985; Graves, 1975; Sommers, 1980; Flower and Hayes, 1981; Calkins, 1983). Before they begin writing, those writing for publication frequently know for whom they want to write and, at least in general terms, what they want to write or to write about. Even if they are writing primarily for themselves, they are not usually writing just to be writing. A period of incubation often precedes the actual writing: a period lasting days, weeks, months, or perhaps just hours or minutes. During this incubation period, writers may jot down notes, doodle, make semantic webs or outlines, or mull things over in their heads while doing the dishes or driving down the highway. Once they begin to write in earnest, the writing process does not necessarily proceed smoothly, and it

FIGURE 4.12   Model of the writing process (Michigan State Board of Education, 1994).

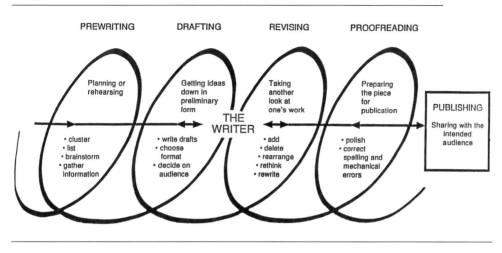

certainly does not proceed linearly in any simple way. That is, in the process of producing a first draft, a writer often rereads and revises, does more research, edits, jots down ideas for later paragraphs or sections, and so forth. After thus producing a first draft, the writer may then reread, reorder, add more information, cut out irrelevant parts. Some writers will revise sentences and edit for appropriate language and grammar while writing a first draft and again when making these larger revisions, but other writers will reserve most of this activity for still another pass through the evolving manuscript. Final proofreading usually combines with editing, or follows it—but then again, it may begin when the writer is producing the first draft.

The diagram in Figure 4.12 is an attempt to capture the complexity of the writing process. The loops and the two-directional arrows are meant to suggest that the phases of the writing process intertwine and overlap.

A first step toward dealing with errors more effectively, then, is to guide students through the intermingled phases of the writing process. This does not mean having students do prewriting on Monday, drafting on Tuesday, revising on Wednesday, proofreading (or editing and proofreading) on Thursday, and then "publishing" their writing by sharing it on Friday. It means establishing a writers' workshop in which writers can work on pieces of writing in their own idiosyncratic way, at their own pace. It means helping students with sentence structure and editing concerns when they are satisfied with the content and organization of their

FIGURE 4.13a Sophomore's first draft.

One day when I was riding in my moms car coming home ~~from~~ kalamazoo° we looked behing us and we saw ~~smoke~~ smoke coming out of the back of the car. We didn't know what it was from so we kept on driving wondering what it was from. We saw people on the other side of the road suerving away from us and the guy in front of us was trying to stop us. So we stopped on the side of the road and smoke rolled over the hood we jumped out of the car and saw our car go up in flames. We called the fire department and they put the fire out. My moms car was ~~totaled~~ totaled ~~and~~ it but the insurence company payd for another one.   [end of 1st draft]

writing and ready to turn to more superficial matters. And it means serving as an advocate, rather than an adversary: as editor, rather than as critic or judge.

As an example of how teachers can guide students in revising their sentences and editing their writing, see Figure 4.13, which includes the first and sixth drafts of the introduction of a high school sophomore's piece of writing. Notice the much greater effectiveness of the later draft, which has benefited from teacher Renée Callies's help in putting the reader "there," using participial phrases to convey narrative detail, and using punctuation conventionally. In a subsequent conference, she and the writer may still consider whether one or both of the comma splices should be left as is or eliminated. These are examples of the kinds of assistance teachers and peers can offer, particularly when the writing is ready for revising at the sentence level and for editing.

Figure 4.14 includes some books that can help teachers establish writers' workshops in their own classrooms.

FIGURE 4.13b   First paragraph of sophomore's sixth draft.

The Flaming Engine

We ran out of the car looking for someone to help, yelling at them to call 9-1-1. "We already did," they told us. Then they asked, "What happened, what happened?"

We were coming home from the mall, driving on Shaver Road, when the stoplight ahead of us turned red. We stopped, waiting for it to turn green. The light turned green, and then we slowly pulled away, going faster, we accelerated to fifty-five miles an hour. My mom looked in the rearview mirror and asked my brother to look behind us and see if the smoke was coming from us. "I think so," he said. Then we looked ahead and the guy in front of us was waving his hands and pointing to the side of the road. "I think we should get out," my mom said. My mom stopped the car and we all jumped out of the car. My brother and I ran to the back of the car, and my mom ran to the front. [end of 1st paragraph]

Then we heard the firetrucks coming. They stopped, then two guys, already dressed in their fire equiptment, jumped off the truck, got the water hose and started to put out the fire. While they were doing that one of the

FIGURE 4.14   References for instituting writers' and readers' workshops.

___

ELEMENTARY AND MIDDLE SCHOOL

Avery, C. (1993). . . . *And with a light touch: Learning about reading, writing, and teaching with first graders.* Portsmouth, NH: Heinemann.

Calkins, L. M. (1994). *The art of teaching writing.* Portsmouth, NH: Heinemann. Earlier edition published 1986.

Calkins, L. M., & Harwayne, S. (1987). *The writing workshop: A world of difference.* Portsmouth, NH: Heinemann. Ideas and activities for staff development.

Calkins, L. M., with Harwayne, S. (1993). *Living between the lines.* Portsmouth, NH: Heinemann.

Graves, D. H. (1994). *A fresh look at writing.* Portsmouth, NH: Heinemann.

Harwayne, S. (1992). *Lasting impressions: Weaving literature into the writing workshop.* Portsmouth, NH: Heinemann.

MacKenzie, T. (Ed.). (1992). *Readers' workshops: Bridging literature and literacy.* Toronto: Irwin.

JUNIOR HIGH AND SECONDARY SCHOOL

Atwell, N. (1987). *In the middle: Writing, reading, and learning with adolescents.* Portsmouth, NH: Heinemann.

Foster, H. M. (1994). *Crossing over: Whole language for secondary English teachers.* Orlando, FL: Harcourt Brace.

Rief, L. (1992). *Seeking diversity: Language arts with adolescents.* Portsmouth, NH: Heinemann.

Romano, T. (1987). *Clearing the way: Working with teenage writers.* Portsmouth, NH: Heinemann.

Romano, T. (1995). *Writing with passion: Life stories, multiple genres.* Portsmouth, NH: Heinemann.

Strickland, K., & Strickland, J. (1993). *UN-covering the curriculum: Whole language in secondary and postsecondary classrooms.* Portsmouth, NH: Boynton/Cook.

Zemelman, S., & Daniels, H. (1988). *A community of writers: Teaching writing in the junior and senior high school.* Portsmouth, NH: Boynton/Cook.

___

Alternatives to the Error Hunt

The major way of avoiding the error hunt is to help students revise and edit their writing *while it is still in process*. But what to do with errors in drafts that have been submitted as final? Both these situations are discussed here.

Teaching Final Revision and Editing/Proofreading

In helping students write, revise, and edit more effectively, teachers have found a few techniques that are especially helpful. These include brief mini-lessons explaining how to do something; individual conferences, from one or two minutes in length to more extensive; and peer group editing (provided the teacher has guided the students in learning how to do what is expected). These techniques are basic to several of the suggestions here. In her article "Developing Correctness in Student Writing: Alternatives to the Error-Hunt," Lois Rosen (1987) has culled suggestions from master teachers and her own experience. In developing the following list I have done the same, but the list draws heavily upon Rosen's because the latter is already such an excellent summary.

MAKE SURE THAT STUDENTS HAVE PLENTY OF TIME TO READ DURING SCHOOL. Students who read widely absorb a great deal about the writer's craft from their reading: a sense of the structure of different genres, vocabulary, grammar, spelling, and other aspects of mechanics. Having literature available in the classroom also provides a handy resource for studying how writers use and invent sentence structures and punctuation. Teachers may, in fact, set aside time for readers' workshop, as well as writers' workshop.

MAKE SURE THAT STUDENTS HAVE PLENTY OF TIME FOR ALL PHASES OF THE WRITING PROCESS. It may be helpful to develop not merely a readers' workshop and a writers' workshop, but a combined time for both. Reading other published authors is, in fact, one of the best kinds of preparation for writing. (See, for example, Calkins, with Harwayne, *Living Between the Lines*, 1993.) When students are asked to carry a draft through to revision and editing, it is important that they themselves have a purpose and an audience for their writing (other than their teacher), and that they themselves choose to "go public" with the writing, to "publish" it in some form, even if publication only means displaying the writing in the classroom.

DEVELOP AND COLLECT RESOURCES THAT ARE USEFUL FOR EDITING. Just having literature available is a help. Other resources would include dictionaries and thesauruses appropriate for the students, grammar handbooks (see Figure 4.15), and editing checklists. Such checklists can be developed by the teacher, but they are typically most helpful if developed by teacher and students together. Even better is an individualized editing checklist, developed with each student. For example, Figure 4.16 shows a checklist from one of Mary Ellen Giacobbe's first graders (1984). In their writing folders, Giacobbe's first graders kept a cumulative list of editing skills for which they could take responsibility in editing their own writing. Giacobbe would teach a child a new skill as the child's writing revealed the need. When the child could demonstrate the ability to apply this editing skill to his or her own writing, the child and the teacher would agree it was time to add the skill to the list. Then, if necessary, Giacobbe would remind the child to edit for the things on the list, as a piece of writing neared completion. Such individualized checklists can help writers of all ages.

MODEL HOW TO DO SOMETHING. For example, a teacher can model with the entire class how to edit a paper. One way to do this is to share a piece of your own writing that you have edited, or that a copy editor has edited for publication. The example in Figure 4.17 illustrates what I would consider sentence revision, a step that often precedes editing for correctness; however, both tasks are accomplished at the same time when a manuscript is copyedited for publication. Sharing and working through changes like this will help writers learn to revise and edit for clarity and not just for conventions or correctness.

Another way to model sentence revision or editing is to ask a student's permission to put his or her paper on a transparency, then discuss it as a class. It is important to always begin with what you and the class especially like about the paper before turning to editing concerns and conventions. Rosen's (1987) suggestions are particularly helpful:

> Once the class has had a chance to read the paper projected on the screen, the teacher opens discussion by focusing on the content of the paper. "What do you like about this paper?" or "What has the writer done well?" are good questions to ask at this point. Then the teacher directs the discussion to proofreading by asking, "Can anyone find something that needs to be changed?"—a neutral question, suggesting error-correction is a natural part of this stage in the writing process. As students identify and correct individual errors, the teacher corrects each on the transparency,

FIGURE 4.15   References for recommended grammar texts and reference books.

HIGH SCHOOL AND COLLEGE

Belanoff, P., Rorschach, B., & Oberlink, M. (1993). *The right handbook: Grammar and usage in context* (2nd ed.). Portsmouth, NH: Boynton/Cook. This book is refreshingly honest about how the language is actually used by educated people, as opposed (sometimes) to what the usual handbooks prescribe. Designed as an aid for writers, the book can also spark appreciation for the richness and diversity of language and an understanding of how language and language standards change. Valuable and interesting for teachers and for students, especially at the college level.

Ebbitt, W. R., & Ebbitt, D. R. (1990). *Index to English* (8th ed.). New York: Oxford University Press. This alphabetically organized index comes close to providing everything you ever wanted to know about grammar—provided you can figure out what headings to use. The book is particularly valuable for its honesty regarding the degree to which certain words and constructions are and are not accepted—in what kinds of writing, and by whom. The guide is not as unrealistically conservative as some of the grammar handbooks on the market, nor yet so liberal that it provides an inadequate guide to usage in the broadest sense. A valuable classroom or library reference to have available for teachers and serious students of the language.

Glazier, T. F. (1994). *The least you should know about English writing skills* (Form B, 5th ed.). Fort Worth: Harcourt. Deals with just a few of the most persistent editing problems. It has exercises and answers so students can check their own understanding. Therefore, it is useful for those motivated to teach themselves certain conventions of edited American English. Suitable for junior high through college.

Gordon, K. E. (1993). *The deluxe transitive vampire: The ultimate handbook of grammar for the innocent, the eager, and the doomed* (2nd ed.). New York: Pantheon Books. The example sentences make the book highly entertaining to many students, even though this book is not necessarily the best teaching tool. See also Gordon, *The new well-tempered sentence: A punctuation handbook for the innocent, the eager, and the doomed* (expanded and revised ed.), 1993, New York: Ticknor & Fields.

Hacker, D. (1991). *The Bedford handbook for writers* (3rd ed.). Boston: Bedford Books of St. Martin's Press. This book runs a close second to Troyka et al. in completeness and clarity of its explanations. The instructor's annotated edition provides valuable references for further exploration. This high-quality text is especially popular at the college level, perhaps in part because there are so many ancillary materials available. These include a bibliography of professional resources for teachers of writing, a collection of background readings for teachers, a guide for writing tutors, and various materials more directly linked to teaching with and from the *Handbook* itself.

Hacker, D. (1995). *A writer's reference* (3rd ed.). New York: St. Martin's Press. For simplicity, clarity, and ease of use, this handbook ranks number one. Its spiral binding is a particular blessing for those who want a book to lie flat while they are consulting it. However, the book is relatively conservative in its prescriptions. Suitable for junior high through college.

Harris, M. (1994). *Prentice Hall reference guide to grammar and usage* (2nd ed.). Englewood Cliffs, NJ: Prentice Hall. Harris's explanations are unusually clear, thanks to years of one-on-one tutoring in a university writing center.

Kolln, M. (1991). *Rhetorical grammar: Grammatical choices, rhetorical effects.* New York: Macmillan. Straightforward presentation of grammatical concepts and their stylistic effects. Especially suitable for college level, or for precollege high school students.

Lunsford, A., & Connors, R. (1995). *The St. Martin's handbook* (3rd ed.). New York: St. Martin's Press. About four-fifths of this handbook focuses on grammar, mechanics, and punctuation, but it does so in the context of writing.

Rice, S. (1993). *Right words, right places.* Belmont, CA: Wadsworth. Includes wonderfully rich examples from literature and emphasizes the rhetorical effects of language choices, not grammar for the sake of grammar. Particularly interesting to students of literature and creative writers, this book seems most appropriate for college students who are not easily intimidated by Rice's thorough explanations.

Sebranek, P., Meyer, V., & Kemper, D. (1990). *Writers Inc.* (2nd ed.). Burlington, WI: Write Source. This compendium of information has an encyclopedic quality; it includes information on various topics, grammar being only one of them. Suitable for students from junior high through college, if they can make use of a text that defines grammatical terms and concepts more than it explains them.

Troyka, L. Q., with Dobie, A. B., & Gordon, E. R. (1992). *Simon & Schuster handbook for writers* (3rd ed.). Englewood Cliffs, NJ: Prentice Hall. Of the various books listed here, this one is by far the most complete in its treatment of grammar, with a lot of insights rarely found in other books. The format is inviting and easy to read; the annotated instructor's edition is a wonderful resource of ideas for explaining grammatical concepts clearly. Most suitable for teachers and others seriously interested in understanding the structure of English and ways of explaining that structure effectively.

FIGURE 4.15, continued.

ELEMENTARY AND MIDDLE SCHOOL/JUNIOR HIGH

Kemper, D., Nathan, R., & Sebranek, P. (1995). *Writers express: A handbook for young writers, thinkers, and learners.* Burlington, WI: Write Source. Suggested for grades 4 and 5, this book—like *Writers Inc.*—has a useful reference section (maps, historical time line). However, the major focus is writing and the writing process. A chapter titled "The Proofreader's Guide" deals with punctuation, spelling, and mechanics.

Sebranek, P., Meyer, V., & Kemper, D. (1995). *Write source 2000: A guide to writing, thinking, and learning* (3rd. ed.). Burlington, WI: Write Source. Suggested for grades 6–8 but also for "students of all ages," this book is similar to the one just listed, but it has more—more of everything, including a rather complete "Yellow Pages Guide to Marking Punctuation."

Of course I make no claim to having examined *all* the grammar handbooks and chosen the best, but, on the other hand, I have selected these from among quite a few that were examined. Some readers may note that *Warriner's English Grammar and Composition* series (1986) is not included in this list, nor is the single handbook *Warriner's High School Handbook* (1992). A far better reference tool for high school and even junior high students is Diana Hacker's *A Writer's Reference*.

FIGURE 4.16   Editing checklist from a first grader (Giacobbe, 1984).

Things I Can Do

1. RAET. MY NAM.
2. RAET. THE DAET.
3. RAET THE. TAL.
4. UOS iNG.
5. UOWS 's.
6. Uollš. (Pereds)
7. Uows eo.
8. Uows " "
9. uows ' in STao of and

FIGURE 4.17 Excerpts from copyedited manuscript (Little, 1994). Typically the copy editor has tried to revise the sentences so they are less wordy or they read more smoothly.

Each student had an individualized folder ~~where he/she would~~ for record*ing* each day's goals and accomplishments and ~~where I would write~~ for my comments, encouraging remarks and suggestions for further exploration or inquiry by the student. ADHD students have difficulty monitoring and scheduling, so accounting for daily, even hourly progress was one way to help them accomplish their goals. ~~Homework was~~ Students often begun and completed within the classroom framework where they could receive immediate feedback ~~could be received~~. When ~~students~~ they did take work home, this ~~was~~ generally ~~based on~~ reflected their own interest or desire to continue or extend a project or assignment ~~which had~~ begun in the classroom.

ADHD students seem to do better with consistent routines, an offer of choice in participation of activities, and careful monitoring of their work with immediate positive feedback. Organiz~~ation of~~ing the classroom with predictable frameworks, ~~and an~~ along with overall school structuring ~~which~~ helps to compensate for impulsivity and hyperactivity demands. This organizat can greatly improve the ADHD students' chances of academic and personal success.

giving a brief explanation of the reason for the correction, and also starts a list on the chalkboard of kinds of errors identified: spelling, capital letters, run-on sentences, etc. The teacher can point out errors the students don't identify and use this as an opportunity to discuss the error, or can stop when the class has corrected all the errors it can identify. The final step is for the students to apply this process to their own papers, using the list on the board as a guide for kinds of errors to look for. (p. 65)

USE EDITING WORKSHOPS. Within the time block used for writers' (or readers' and writers') workshop, it may be helpful to set aside time at least once or twice a week for an editing workshop for those students who are ready to edit and have help with editing. The teacher can skim a student's paper briefly and call attention to whatever editing skills need attention, making sure to suggest only one or two at a time. Students can be clustered in groups to use the editing resources and to help each other.

TEACH MINI-LESSONS TO THE ENTIRE CLASS, PERHAPS DURING EDITING WORK-SHOPS. As explained in detail in Nancie Atwell's *In the Middle* (1987), mini-lessons are brief explanations of how to do something: how to write effective leads to begin a piece; how to "show" rather than "tell"; how to use quotation marks; and so forth. Because they are indeed brief (five or a maximum of ten minutes), they can be offered to the whole class. However, the teacher can also teach a mini-lesson to a group of students who all seem to need the same kind of help, or, of course, to individual students. (See Chapter 6 in the present book for a fuller characterization of mini-lessons.)

HOLD MINI-CONFERENCES WITH INDIVIDUAL STUDENTS. During writers' workshop or during a special editing workshop time, the teacher can help individual students by pointing out what kinds of matters need attention, by perhaps referring the writer to his or her editing checklist, by demonstrating how to use a grammar handbook or other resource, by demonstrating how to revise or edit for something the writer does not yet understand or cannot do independently, by suggesting that a writer confer with a peer who has already mastered something the writer does not know how to do, and so forth. For example, Figures 4.18a and 4.18b include excerpts from two students' papers, along with teacher Amy Berryhill's explanations of how she interacted with the writers during writers' workshop. Notice how she varied her responses to meet the different needs of the writers and their writings.

FIGURE 4.18a   First draft of Sherry's introduction, her teacher's comments on their conference, and Sherry's final draft.

PROPAGANDA

In the world today media controls most ~~things people do~~. ~~People are affected by what others say and do.~~ ~~Most people are influenced by the way people act, dress and speak~~. If the world did not have the media to persuade it most big business would not exist today. ~~There are so many types of advertising.~~ The companies go after many different audiences depending on what type of product they are selling. Telephone companies generally tend ~~to head for the female audience since~~ females stereotypically are the ones who talk on the phone. The three main advertisers in the telephone industry are MCI, AT&T, and Sprint. ~~These~~ three have a tendency to use any tactic possible to get people to change to their company. The American population has a habit of going after anything that is free or that promises to save that person money.

TEACHER'S COMMENTS:

In our first conference with this "Propaganda" draft, Sherry pointed to the first paragraph and asked, "Do you think I should reword this part?" My standard response is this: "Yes, I think you could word it a little more gracefully. Play around with the wording and see if you like the changes." For Sherry, this was enough! She herself initiated these sentence-level changes. This is a wonderful example of general revision for clarity. Sherry eliminated the vague phrase "things people do" and replaced it with "people's actions and emotions." She also recognized that "people" was used too frequently in the first few sentences, and her instinct to vary her word choice by substituting "society" and "others" shows me that she's got a good ear for the music of the language. Next, Sherry decided to eliminate these sentences because, although they were more specific than they had been originally, they still didn't improve the clarity of her introductory idea.

Sherry also did a wonderful job combining the following two sentences: "The three advertisers in the telephone industry are MCI, AT&T, and Sprint. These three have a tendency to use any tactic possible to get people to change to their company." The resulting combined sentence is much more effective: "MCI, AT&T, and Sprint, the three main telephone companies have a tendency to use any tactic possible to get people to change to their company." If we had conferred one more time about this piece of writing, I would have praised her combining of the sentences and demonstrated the need for a comma after *companies,* to finish setting off the free modifier. *Amy Berryhill*

FIGURE 4.18a, continued.

PROPAGANDA

In the world today media controls most people's actions and
emotions. If the world did not have the media to persuade it
most big business would not exist today. The companies go after
many different audiences depending on what type of product they
are selling. Telephone companies, for example, generally tend to
direct their advertisments towards the female audience because
stereotypically they are the ones who talk on the phone. MCI,
AT&T, and Sprint, the three main telephone companies have a
tendency to use any tactic possible to get people to change to
their company. The problem occurs because the American
population has a habit of going after anything that is free or
that promises to save that person money. *Sherry Soenen*

HELP STUDENTS LEARN TO EDIT. Many of us simply reread our writing from
beginning to end as we edit. However, writers who do not easily catch their
mechanical errors may be helped by a specific strategy. One widely used
strategy is to read one's writing aloud, looking and listening for errors—or
to read the writing into a tape recorder, then play it back while following
along in the written text. Another method is to read one sentence at a
time from the bottom of the paper up, to focus attention on sentence-level
errors rather than on the meaning of the piece. Rosen lists still other
strategies for eliminating errors from a near-final draft (p. 67).

HAVE STUDENTS HELP EACH OTHER EDIT AND PROOFREAD. This should be
done only when the habit of proofreading and procedures for proofreading
are well established—through the teacher's modeling this with the whole
class and with individuals, in one-on-one conferences. Rosen's (1987)
explanation of her own procedures is again helpful:

> When I do this with my own students, both basic writers and average
> freshmen, I usually put students in pairs after each has had a chance to
> proofread his or her own paper. The only rule I impose is that no correc-

FIGURE 4.18b First draft of Grant's introduction, his teacher's comments on their conference, and Grant's final draft.

BODY

When your watching T.V. hundreds of commercials come on everyday. The next time you see a movie commercial pay close attention to it. I'm sure when you see the commercial you probably see your favorite actor, and automotically.

Your interested. It is an avertisers job to make the viewer convinced about their product. They go out of their way to get money. Commercials always have a slogan, or something catchy to make you remember what was said. Celebrities are what make the sales. Statistics show that when cecebrities promote
Celebrities

TEACHER'S COMMENTS:

Grant used "convinced" in the rough draft of his paper, but in the second draft, when he was concentrating on creating a smooth and clear introduction, he didn't catch the newer but simpler error: "conviiced." In response, I urged him to give this paper one final edit before adding it to his portfolio. I reminded him both to use a spell checker and to check carefully himself for homonyms such as _break/brake, vain/vein,_ or _there/their/they're._ Amy Berryhill

Weekly Previews

When your watching T.V., hundreds of commercials come on everyday. The next time you see a movie commercial pay close attention to it. I'm sure when you see the commercial you probably see your favorite actor, and automotically Your interested. It is an advertisers job to make the viewer conviiced about their product. They go out of their way to get money. Commercials always have a slogan, or something catchy to make you remember what was said. Celebrities are what make the sales. Statistics show that when celebrities promote products, sales tend to rise. Movies are a waste of money and time. Grant Brooks

tions are to be made on the writer's paper without the knowledge and consent of the author. This means both writers must confer over any error on either paper and both must agree on the correction. [Grammar handbooks can be especially useful at this point.] I also ask that the editor initial all corrections he or she finds, which gives me some sense of the mechanical skills both the writer and the proofreader bring to the paper. (p. 66)

When the two writers cannot agree, Rosen helps by teaching them a mini-lesson on the topic in question. Students can also be grouped in threes or fours, with the stipulation that each group member will read all the papers and work with the author to correct any errors found. Of course, it helps if each group includes someone who is especially good at spelling and mechanics.

Although the body of research supporting such alternatives to the error hunt is still slim, the available research does suggest that editing skills are best taught as students are revising and editing a piece to be, in some sense or another, "published" (see Chapter 6).

Responding to a "Final" Draft

For teachers, one persistent question is always what to do with, to, or for a "final" draft that still has errors. Here are some possibilities.

DON'T DO ANYTHING ABOUT THE REMAINING ERRORS. Rosen (1987) calls this "benign neglect" (p. 67). She points out that this is an appropriate way to respond to journal writing and early drafts, in particular. For students whose previous writing instruction has focused heavily on "correctness," such a hands-off policy may be especially important, even in final drafts. But many teachers follow a hands-off policy for at least some final drafts, especially if the writing is not being sent to an unknown audience.

RESPOND ONLY TO SELECTED KINDS OF ERRORS. Some teachers announce in advance that only certain kinds of errors will be marked (usually no more than two or three kinds). Of course, such selective marking focuses on the particular kinds of errors that the teacher has tried to help students learn to eliminate from final drafts.

PUT A CHECK MARK IN THE MARGIN OF LINES WHERE THERE IS AN ERROR, AND INVITE THE WRITER TO FIND AND CORRECT THE ERROR(S). This works only if the writer already understands the kind of error in question, or can get help from someone who does. In other words, it works best with kinds of errors that the writer already understands, but has just missed in proof-

FIGURE 4.19 Published story by three first graders.

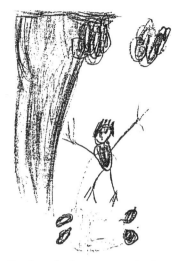

Mrs. Strawn Mows The Lawn

by Andrew Strawn
Brian Homer-Gunther
Michael Bowee

On Sunday, the lawn mower broke. Mrs. Strawn said, "What will I do?"

On Monday, she used scissors but the lawn was too big.

On Tuesday, she used a knife but it was a plastic knife and it broke.

On Wednesday, she bought a goat but it
died.

On Thursday, she used a tractor but it
got stuck on a boulder.

On Friday, she used a boomerang but it
got stuck in the trees.

On Saturday, she fixed her lawn mower.

FIGURE 4.20 "Errorwocky." After Lewis Carroll's "Jabberwocky."

ERRORWOCKY

'Twas class time, and the eager youths
    Did squirm and wriggle in their seats:
All ready were their fresh ideas,
    And their paper was clean and neat.

"Beware the Error beast, my friends!
    The jaws that bite, the claws that rend!
Beware the Run-on bird, and shun
    The frumious frag(a)ment."

They took their eraser tips in hand;
    Long time the maxome foe they sought—
Then rested they from the Error hunt,
    And wrote awhile in thought.

And, as in uffish thought they wrote,
    The Error beast, with eyes of flame,
Came whiffling through their ballpoint pens,
    And burbled as it came!

One, two! One, two! And back and forth
    The eraser tips went snicker-snack!
They left it dead, and to their teach,
    They went galumphing back.

"And have you slain the Error beast?
    You'll pass this year, victorious youths!
O frabjous day! Callooh! Callay!"
    She chortled then, in truth.

'Twas class time, and the stunted youths
    Did slouch and huddle in their seats:
All shortened were their sentences,
    And their words had met defeat.

Connie Weaver

reading. It also helps if the writing has been done on a computer and the writer can easily make one more final draft.

COMMENT ON THE ONE OR TWO MOST NOTICEABLE KINDS OR PATTERNS OF ERROR, AND INVITE FURTHER SCRUTINY. For example, a teacher might write, "You have several errors in subject-verb agreement in this paper, including this one. Why don't you see if you can find the other instances and correct them?" Again, this is especially helpful if the writing has been done on a computer and it is easy for the author to correct the errors and to print out a new "final" draft. Such response is especially meaningful if the writing is going to be published beyond the classroom.

SERVE AS A COPY EDITOR: CORRECT THE ERRORS FOR THE WRITER.   This can be especially helpful when the writing is being prepared for publication beyond the classroom. For example, a teacher may mark all the remaining errors for correction when the piece can easily be edited on a computer. Or, an elementary grade teacher or aide or parent may type a story that children have written in invented spelling, correcting the spelling, punctuation, and other mechanical features as they type. Figure 4.19 (pages 98–99) shows a story written by three first graders and then "published" in a form that classmates and future first graders would be able to read— namely, with (mostly) conventional spelling and punctuation.

Taming the Error Beast

In conclusion I would like to share with readers my poem "Errorwocky" (see Figure 4.20), a variation on Lewis Carroll's famed "Jabberwocky."

To avoid stunting students' growth as writers, we need to guide our students in the writing process, including the phases of revising and editing their sentences and words. It would also be helpful to avoid correcting the kinds of constructions that published writers use with impunity and indeed with good effect. And we need to respond positively to the new kinds of errors that reflect syntactic risk and growth. Time enough to help students correct these errors when they have gotten their ideas down on paper, experimenting with language in the process. In short, the Error Beast is to be welcomed and tamed, not slain.

5

Reconceptualizing the Teaching of Grammar

We saw in Chapter 2 that empirical research does not support the widespread belief or hope that teaching formal grammar systematically and in isolation improves students' writing, or even their ability to edit their writing for conventions of grammar, punctuation, and usage. Some students may indeed put to use the relevant aspects of what they are formally taught about grammar, but if so, the research has not been finely tuned enough to reveal this effect. Indeed, even in the research on the effectiveness of his editing skills course, Finlay McQuade was not able to demonstrate that the course had a positive effect on students' standardized test scores, or that students were significantly better editors of their own writing after taking the course. In fact, some of the students who succeeded in his course were later required to take a remedial course in the mechanics of writing, based upon samples of their writing. Furthermore, his students' post-test essays were significantly worse overall than their pre-test essays, apparently because they were trying so hard to avoid errors.

There may be several reasons why the formal study of grammar does not transfer very well to students' writing. For example:

1. Much of what is traditionally taught—identifying parts of speech and their functions in sentences, kinds of verbs and sentence types, and so forth—has little relevance to writing itself. And to the extent that the grammatical concepts taught are actually relevant to writing, they can often be taught through examples, with incidental use of terminology. An ability to analyze sentences systematically is not necessary.

2. The grammatical system is so complex that it is not easily learned or well learned. Just one of the problems is that almost everything must be defined and explained in terms of something else. Another problem is that grammatical analysis is sometimes required of children before they are capable of what Jean Piaget called "formal operational thought," although this objection (Sanborn, 1986) may have little relevance if children can attach labels to grammatical patterns and rules they induce from examples, much as they did in initially learning their native language. A related problem, however, is that many children and adults are simply not very analytic in their approach to learning. Such individuals have particular difficulty learning to analyze words, sentences, and parts of sentences.

3. Many students find the formal study of grammar boring; therefore, they do not really learn it. They may go through the motions of completing grammar exercises and tests in such a way that they *appear* to have learned the concepts, but appearance is different from the reality. Many exercises in grammar texts can be completed with only minimal understanding of the concepts. Indeed, many teachers themselves do not have a solid under-standing of the grammatical concepts they try to teach, nor is this always considered necessary by those who prepare the textbooks. I was once told that it did not matter whether an exercise was too difficult even for most of the preservice teachers in my grammar class, much less for the ninth graders for whom it was intended. "The teachers will have the answers in the teacher's manual," the editor said—as if having the answers were all that mattered.

4. The grammar, even when learned, is not applied in writing situations where it would be appropriate. There can be many reasons for this: perhaps students have forgotten the relevant aspects of grammar, perhaps they do not even think of their grammatical knowledge as something they should draw upon in revising or editing, or perhaps they do not take time to edit their work, or to edit it carefully and thoroughly. Worse yet, perhaps the students are rarely asked to write anything more than a sentence, or an occasional paragraph.

5. Perhaps the underlying learning theory is faulty. Traditional grammar texts reflect a behavioral concept of learning, according to which learning is equated with practice and habit formation. Practice exercises may be adequate if all that is required is that students pass a test that is similar,

but the application of grammatical concepts may require cognitive under-standing that is not so readily gained through practice exercises. Krashen (1993) points out, and I heartily agree, that much of what occurs in the name of teaching language—especially grammar—amounts not to teaching but to repeated testing, via the assigned exercises. Such testing-without-teaching may not be enough for meaningful learning to occur.

Whatever the reasons, it is abundantly clear that the empirical research does not support the belief that teaching grammar in isolation will typically improve writing.

On the other hand, we saw in Chapter 3 that even before they enter school, children acquire a functional command of grammar and virtually all the grammatical constructions typical of oral discourse among older speakers. Children "know" grammar, even though they don't "know about" grammar.

If our rationale for teaching grammar is primarily to improve students' writing, then it would seem that a much more limited and more focused treatment of grammar has a better chance of being effective. As we shall see in Chapter 6, there is at least a modicum of research that offers support for this hypothesis, though clearly more research would be valuable. Until research produces results that are more conclusive one way or another, we might reasonably expect our efforts to succeed best in two areas: in helping students revise for "correct" or appropriate and effective grammar, punctua-tion, and usage, and in helping them develop sentence sense, expand their repertoire of syntactic structures, and employ an increasing variety of syn-tactic structures for rhetorical effect.

In other words, our efforts at teaching grammar should probably focus on helping students revise and edit their writing, partly because whatever is first learned during revising and editing may eventually be incorporated into drafting, or into rehearsal for writing (e.g., Calkins, 1986, pp. 94–96). This suggestion assumes a multiphase model of the writing process like that in Figure 4.12.

Narrowing Our Focus and Limiting the Terminology

In *Grammar and the Teaching of Writing*, Rei Noguchi (1991) suggests that we limit our teaching of grammar and grammatical terminology to only those features that will be most valuable in helping writers eliminate errors and increase the effectiveness of their sentences. With regard to errors, he recommends focusing primarily on those that still occur relatively frequently in the writing of college students in composition classes, and those that seriously bother people who hold positions of power in the business and professional community. The errors that should receive the most attention are those that meet both criteria. Noguchi bases his argument on two research studies that I too discuss here.

After soliciting over 21,500 college composition papers from across the country, Connors and Lunsford (1988) analyzed the frequency of errors in a sample of 3,000 papers, chosen randomly from subsets of papers representing different regions, sizes of school, and types of school. After analyzing the errors in 300 of these papers, they chose the top twenty kinds of errors for further study in the sample of 3,000. These kinds of errors are rank-ordered according to frequency in Figure 5.1.

It is interesting to note that only six of the twenty kinds of errors were marked by the students' classroom teachers more than 50 percent of the time. The most frequent errors are not necessarily marked the most often; in fact, Connors and Lunsford note that the most frequently marked errors are often those that are easiest to mark and to explain. Other reasons for the incomplete marking of various errors might include the following: (1) Teachers may have felt that marking every error would be too intimidating to students, that it might convey the impression that they were more concerned about correctness than sense, and that it might discourage students from focusing on meaning or taking risks as writers; (2) they may have been unwilling to deflect their own attention from content by trying to mark all the errors; (3) they may have been ambivalent about the value of correcting errors (i.e., they may have realized or suspected that correction of one paper does not often lessen the number of similar errors in subsequent papers); or (4) they may have chosen to focus on one or two kinds of errors at a time, either the easiest to mark, the seemingly most serious, or their own pet peeves. Whatever the teachers' reasons may have been, we certainly cannot assume that the most frequently marked errors are the most frequently occurring errors or, in any sense, the most serious or stigmatizing.

A study by Hairston (1981) sought to determine what kinds of errors are regarded as most serious by business and professional people—often those in a position to make judgments about hiring and promotion of others. She sent a sixty-six-item questionnaire (see Figure 5.2) to 101 individuals, 84 of whom returned it. About three-fourths of these people were over forty, and most were between fifty and sixty years old. Three-fourths were men. The group represented sixty-three different occupations, such as state leg-

FIGURE 5.1 Frequency of errors and of teacher marking of errors in the Connors-Lunsford (1988) study. Example sentences are from Hairston's study (1981) or devised by me. Note that some of the examples in categories 6, 13, and 14 would be typical of dialects like Black English Vernacular. Connors and Lunsford did not try to differentiate between dialect features and errors.

ERROR OR ERROR PATTERN RANKED BY PERCENT OF TOTAL ERRORS	PERCENT OF TOTAL ERRORS	PERCENT MARKED BY TEACHER	RANK BY NUMBER OF ERRORS MARKED BY TEACHER
1. No comma after introductory element: *Although the candidate is new to politics she has a good chance of winning.*	11.5	30	2
2. Vague pronoun reference: *Visitors find it difficult to locate the plant, which affects business.*	9.8	32	4
3. No comma in compound sentence: *Charles drove the van and Jean drove the truck.*	8.6	29	7
4. Wrong word: *The interruption will not effect my work. Your going to love it.*	7.8	50	1
5. No comma in nonrestrictive element: *Tact not anger is the best tactic in this case.*	6.5	31	10
6. Wrong/missing inflected endings: *Jones don't think it is acceptable. Yesterday we walk home.*	5.9	51	5
7. Wrong or missing preposition: *The three men talked between themselves. Look on it this way. We went the store.*	5.5	43	8
8. Comma splice: *Never reveal your weaknesses to others, they will exploit them.*	5.5	54	6

9. Possessive apostrophe error: 5.1   62   3
   Our companys record is
   exceptional. The secretary
   claimed his' rights had been
   violated.

10. Tense shift: 5.1   33   12
    The difficult part is if the
    client refused to cooperate.

11. Unnecessary shift in person: 4.7   30   14
    People should be more
    careful. You should not start
    a fire when it's so dry.

12. Sentence fragment: 4.2   55   9
    He went through a long
    battle. A fight against
    unscrupulous opponents. The
    small towns are dying. One
    of the problems being that
    young people are leaving.

13. Wrong tense or verb form: 3.3   49   13
    When Mitchell moved, he
    brung his secretary. Then this
    kid come up to me.

14. Subject-verb agreement: 3.2   58   11
    When we was in the
    planning stages of the project,
    we underestimated costs.
    Enclosed in his personnel file
    is his discharge papers and
    job references. All but one of
    the words is spelled right.

15. Lack of comma in series: 2.7   24   19
    We direct our advertising to
    the young prosperous and
    sports-minded reader.

16. Pronoun agreement error: 2.6   48   15
    Everyone who attends will
    have to pay their own
    expenses.

17. Unnecessary comma with restrictive element: *The dog, that bit my little brother, should be quarantined.*	2.4	34	17
18. Run-on or fused sentence: *He concentrated on his job he never took vacations.*	2.4	45	16
19. Dangling or misplaced modifier: *Having argued all morning, a decision was finally reached. There were pictures of famous people who starred in movies all over the walls.*	2.0	29	20
20. It's/its error: *Its wonderful to have Graham back on the job.*	1.0	64	18

islator, computer programmer, architect, travel agency owner, bank president, newspaper columnist, realtor, oil company president, stockbroker, and federal judge. The groups best represented in the survey were business executives (six) and lawyers (seven). Only seven people were associated with the academic world; none were English teachers, and four were administrators.

The main sentences in Hairston's directions were these: "What I would like you to do is read through each sentence rather quickly and mark your response to it. That is, if you encountered the sentences in a report or business letter, would it lower your estimate of the writer, and how much?" The respondents were to choose among "Does not bother me," "Bothers me a little," and "Bothers me a lot." Each sentence was supposed to contain one error, according to contemporary and sometimes conservative conventions for grammar, punctuation, and usage.

As Hairston was aware, one of the limitations of this study was that it encouraged respondents to expect to find errors and to be bothered by them. Thus the results do not necessarily reflect how these same individuals would respond to the same errors in a business report or letter they were reading for content and clarity. (See, for instance, Williams, "The Phenomenology of Error," 1981.) Second, Hairston points out that the respondents might

FIGURE 5.2 Sentences from Hairston's (1981) study. Respondents were to indicate whether the sentence "Does not bother me," "Bothers me a little," or "Bothers me a lot." There were originally 66 items, but one had to be omitted from the results because of a typing error. Hence all the items from 8 on are numbered differently here than in Hairston's list. Contrary to what Hairston intended, sentence one is correct.

1. Extra copies will be provided for whoever needs them.
2. Tact not anger is the best tactic in this case.
3. He concentrated on his job he never took vacations.
4. Wellington said, Trains will just cause the lower classes to move about needlessly.
5. The three men talked between themselves and decided not to fire the auditor.
6. Never reveal your weaknesses to others, they will exploit them.
7. Everyone who attends will have to pay their own expenses.
8. Coventry is the most unique city in England.
9. People are always impressed by her smooth manner, elegant clothes, and being witty.
10. Almost everyone dislikes her; they say she is careless and insolent.
11. The state's hiring policies intimidate the applications of ambitious people.
12. The small towns are dying. One of the problems being that young people are leaving.
13. Having argued all morning, a decision was finally reached.
14. If the regulating agency sets down on the job, everyone will suffer.
15. The situation is quite different than that of previous years.
16. A person who knows french and german will get along well in Switzerland.
17. It is late in his term and inflation is worse and no one has a solution.
18. Our companys record is exceptional.
19. The President dismissed four cabinet members among them Joseph Califano.
20. When Mitchell moved, he brung his secretary with him.
21. Three causes of inflation are: easy credit, costly oil, and consumer demand.
22. When a person moves every year, one cannot expect them to develop civic pride.
23. We direct our advertising to the young prosperous and sports-minded reader.
24. The worst situation is when the patient ignores warning symptoms.
25. The army moved my husband and I to California last year.
26. He went through a long battle. A fight against unscrupulous opponents.
27. The lieutenant treated his men bad.
28. Sanford inquired whether the loan was overdue?
29. When the time came to pay the filing fee however the candidate withdrew.
30. The data supports her hypothesis.
31. Those are the employees that were honored.
32. Visitors find it difficult to locate the plant, which affects business.
33. Him and Richards were the last ones hired.
34. There has never been no one here like that woman.
35. These kind of errors would soon bankrupt a company.
36. My favorite quotation is, "Take what you want and pay for it.
37. The reporter paid attention to officers but ignores enlisted men.
38. If I was in charge of that campaign, I would be worried about opinion polls.
39. If Clemens had picked up that option, his family would of been rich.

FIGURE 5.2, continued.

40. Its wonderful to have Graham back on the job.
41. Calhoun has went after every prize in the university.
42. Next year we expect to send a representative to China (if Peking allows it.
43. Cheap labor and low costs. These are two benefits enjoyed by Taiwan-based firms.
44. The difficult part is if the client refused to cooperate.
45. State employees can't hardly expect a raise this year.
46. The supervisor has no objections to us leaving.
47. Although the candidate is new to politics she has a good chance of winning.
48. A convicted felon no matter how good his record may not serve on a grand jury.
49. I was last employed by texas instruments company.
50. When leaving college, clothes suddenly become a major problem.
51. Enclosed in his personnel file is his discharge papers and job references.
52. The president or the vice-president are going to be at the opening ceremonies.
53. To me, every person is an individual, and they should be treated with respect.
54. Good policemen require three qualities: courage, tolerance, and dedicated.
55. The interruption will not effect my work.
56. I have always hoped to work in that field, now I will have the opportunity.
57. Senator javits comes from new york.
58. I believe that everyone of them are guilty.
59. That is her across the street.
60. Cox cannot predict, that street crime will diminish.
61. When we was in the planning stages of the project, we underestimated costs.
62. The union claims it's rights have been violated.
63. The company is prepared to raise prices. In spite of administrative warnings.
64. Jones don't think it is acceptable.
65. Man is not the only user of tools, apes can also learn to manipulate them.

have viewed this questionnaire as a sort of test of their own grammatical knowledge. Therefore she concludes that while these professionals might be less judgmental in reading day-to-day communications, they are certainly not likely to be *more* judgmental. I agree.

Overall, on all but a few sentences, women checked a much higher percentage of "Bothers me a lot." This accords with other studies in which women have been found to be more conservative than men in their attitudes toward language use (e.g., Lakoff, 1975).

According to the frequency of the different responses, Hairston grouped these errors into five categories: *status marking, very serious, serious, moderately serious,* and *minor or unimportant*. Curiously, there are two kinds of errors (other than what we might call sheer carelessness) that Hairston omits from these groups: errors in using the apostrophe with a possessive (omission of apostrophe, or its inappropriate use in the possessive *its* or *his*, etc.), and pronoun agreement errors (which Hairston discusses but does not add to a group). In Figure 5.3, I have taken the liberty of placing both kinds of errors in groups where they seem most appropriate, given the categorizations of similar patterns of response for other items.

The status marking errors, to which there was the greatest objection, are typically the kinds of errors that would mark a person as not speaking a so-called standard dialect of English, or what is less judgmentally referred to as the Language of Wider Communication (Conference on College Composition and Communication, 1988).

It is interesting to see which of the errors that Hairston's respondents considered status marking, very serious, or serious are among the top twenty kinds of errors that Connors and Lunsford found in college students' writing (see Figure 5.4). Among their top twenty, we find only one kind of error that *may* have included examples in the status marking category: lack of subject-verb agreement. It is not clear, however, what to make of the result. Does it mean that by college age, most students have virtually eliminated status marking errors from their writing? Or that students who still use status marking features in their writing are not being admitted to college, or at least not going to college? Without more data, we really cannot tell. However, Smitherman's (1992) longitudinal study of dialect features in students' writing sheds some light on these questions. Basically, she found that such status marking dialect features seldom occur in students' writing by the time they reach age seventeen. What we still do not know, however, is the relative importance of different factors: the influence of the Language of Wider Communication as modeled on TV, for instance, or as modeled by teachers, peers, and others; the role of specific instructional attention to eliminating such features; or the role of reading as a model. Clearly, reading can be a powerful influence upon one's acquisition and use of language features (Perera, 1984; Elley, 1991; Krashen, 1993).

What else can we conclude by seeing where the errors most severely disapproved of in Hairston's study intersect with the errors most frequently made in the Connors-Lunsford study? Perhaps that we need especially to help students understand and be able to edit from their writing such errors as fragments, run-ons (fused sentences), subject-verb agreement errors, and dangling modifiers. Most teachers of writing may consider the comma splice a serious error too, but the comma splice seems not to have disturbed the

FIGURE 5.3 Categorization of errors from Hairston's (1981) study. I have added two items to Hairston's list. Based on the patterns in her raw data, I think that errors in the use of the apostrophe in possessives warrant a rating of "serious," and using the pronouns *they, them,* or *their* to refer to *everyone* or to *a person* seems to warrant a "moderately serious" rating.

STATUS MARKING	SENTENCE NUMBER (FIGURE 5.2)
Nonstandard verb forms in past or past participle: *brung* instead of *brought; had went* instead of *had gone*	20, 41
Lack of subject-verb agreement: *We was* instead of *We were; Jones don't think it's acceptable* instead of *Jones doesn't think it's acceptable.*	61, 64
Double negatives: *There has never been no one here; State employees can't hardly expect a raise.*	34, 45
Objective pronoun as subject: *Him and Richard were the last ones hired.*	33

VERY SERIOUS	
Sentence fragments: *He went through a long battle. A fight against unscrupulous opponents.* / *The small towns are dying. One of the problems being that young people are leaving.*	12, 26, 43, 63
Run-on sentences: *He concentrated on his job he never took vacations.*	3
Noncapitalization of proper nouns: *Senator javits comes from new york.*	16, 49, 57
Would of instead of *would have: His family would of been rich.*	39
Lack of subject-verb agreement (non–status marking): *Enclosed in his file is his discharge papers and job references.*	51, 52, 58
Insertion of comma between the verb and its complement: *Cox cannot predict, that street crime will diminish.*	60
Nonparallelism: *People are always impressed by her smooth manner, elegant clothes, and being witty.*	9, 54
Faulty adverb forms: *He treats his men bad.*	27
Use of transitive verb *set* for intransitive *sit: If the regulating agency sets down on the job . . .*	14

SERIOUS

Predication errors: *The policy intimidates hiring.*	11
Dangling modifiers: Having argued all morning, *a decision was finally reached.*	13, 50
I as an objective pronoun: *The army moved my husband and I to California last year.*	25
Lack of commas to set off interrupters like *however: When the time came to pay the filing fee however the candidate withdrew.*	2, 29, 48
Lack of commas in a series: *We direct our advertising to the young prosperous and sports-minded reader.*	17, 23
Tense switching: *The difficult part is if the client refused to cooperate.*	37, 44
Use of a plural modifier with a singular noun: *These kind of errors . . .*	35
Possessive apostrophe error: *Our companys record is exceptional. The union claims it's rights have been violated.*	18, 62

MODERATELY SERIOUS

Lack of possessive form before a gerund: *The supervisor has no objections to us leaving.*	46
Lack of commas to set off an appositive: *The President dismissed four cabinet members among them Joseph Califano.*	19
Inappropriate use of quotation marks: My *favorite quotation is, "Take what you want and pay for it.*	4, 36
Lack of subjunctive mood: *If I was in charge of that campaign . . .*	38
Object pronoun form as predicate nominative: *That is her across the street.*	59
Use of *whoever* instead of *whomever: Extra copies will be provided for whoever needs them.* [But this use of *whoever* is actually correct. It functions as the subject of *needs*, while the entire clause *whoever needs them* functions as the object of *for*.]	1
Use of the construction *The situation is when . . . : The worst situation is when the patient ignores warning symptoms.*	24

FIGURE 5.3, continued.

Failure to distinguish between *among* and *between:* *The three men talked between themselves.*	5
Comma splices: *Never reveal your weaknesses to others,* *they will exploit them.*	6, 56, 65
Use of *they, them,* or *their* to refer to *everyone* or to *a person: Everyone who attends will have to pay their own expenses.*	7, 10, 22, 53

MINOR OR UNIMPORTANT

Use of a qualifier before *unique: Coventry is the most unique city in England.*	8
Writing *different than* instead of *different from: The situation is quite different than that of previous years.*	15
Use of a singular verb with *data: The data supports her hypothesis.*	30
Use of a colon after a linking verb: *Three causes of inflation are: easy credit, costly oil, and consumer demand.*	21
Omission of the apostrophe in the contraction *it's: Its wonderful to have Graham back on the job.*	40

professionals in Hairston's study unduly—and indeed, comma splice sentences are used sparingly by professional writers (see Chapter 4). This discrepancy reminds us of what Connors and Lunsford repeatedly note: what is considered to be an error has differed from one decade to another, and what seems like a serious error to one person—even to one English teacher—may not bother other individuals just as well versed in prescriptive or descriptive grammar. As Connors and Lunsford express it,

> Teachers' ideas about error definition and classification have always been absolute products of their times and cultures. . . . Teachers have always marked different phenomena as errors, called them different things, given them different weights. Error-pattern study is essentially the examination of an ever-shifting pattern of skills judged by an ever-shifting pattern of prejudices. (p. 399)

We teachers need to remind ourselves that our preferences are in large measure time-bound and experience-bound as we wield the editor's blue pencil and try to get our students to adopt our standards for Edited Ameri-

FIGURE 5.4   Comparison of error ranking in the Hairston (1981) and Connors-Lunsford (1988) studies.

CATEGORY IN HAIRSTON STUDY	FREQUENCY RANK IN CONNORS-LUNSFORD STUDY
Status marking Lack of subject-verb agreement: *we was; Jones don't think*	Lack of subject-verb agreement is ranked 14, but we cannot tell what proportion of the items fit Hairston's status marking category and what proportion fit her very serious category.
Very serious Lack of subject-verb agreement: *The president or the vice-president are going to be at the opening ceremonies. I believe that everyone of them are guilty.*	
Sentence fragments	12
Run-on sentences	18
Serious Dangling modifiers	19
Lack of commas to set off interrupters like *however*	5
Lack of commas in a series	15
Tense switching	10

can English. A little humility won't hurt, nor will a certain amount of open-mindedness.

Following the line of Noguchi's argument but not the details, I would suggest that only a few of the frequently occurring errors in the Connors-Lunsford study and only a few of the status marking, very serious, or serious errors in Hairston's study require for their elimination an understanding of grammatical concepts commonly taught. And these few kinds of errors can be understood by comprehending only a few grammatical concepts (see Figure 5.5).

In short, the most critical concepts that need to be understood for eliminating some of the most frequently occurring and most "serious" kinds of errors are subject and verb (verb as predicate), independent (main) and

FIGURE 5.5   Basic grammatical concepts that need to be understood.

ERROR	RANK IN CONNORS-LUNSFORD STUDY	CATEGORY IN HAIRSTON STUDY	REQUIRES UNDERSTANDING
No comma in compound sentence	3	—	Subject and verb Independent clause
Comma splice	8	Moderately serious	Subject and verb Independent clause
Sentence fragment	12	Very serious	Subject and verb Independent clause Dependent clause Phrase
Lack of subject-verb agreement	14	Status marking or very serious	Subject and verb
Run-on or fused sentence	18	Very serious	Subject and verb Independent clause

dependent (subordinate) clauses, and phrase. Of course, this does not quite give the whole picture, as veteran grammar teachers know. For instance, in order to distinguish between independent and dependent clauses, one needs to recognize words that introduce dependent clauses and the two categories of words that can introduce and connect independent clauses. In my experience, however, the ability to recognize the category of these connectors is all that's needed: not the technical grammatical terminology, and not the ability to analyze grammatical structures in detail.

In the Connors-Lunsford study there is another group of errors that students can often learn to eliminate just by listening to their intonation as they read a paper aloud. These items are category 1—no comma after introductory element; category 5—no comma in nonrestrictive element; and category 17—unnecessary comma with restrictive element. In the Hairston study similarly recognizable errors include lack of commas to set off interrupters like *however* and lack of commas to set off an appositive. In addition or alternatively, these errors can be addressed through the concept of the modifier and the free modifier (F. Christensen, 1967). A free modifier is an optional modifying element that usually is movable within a sentence and/or is set off by commas. Introductory elements, words like *however*, appositives, and nonrestrictive elements are free modifiers that need to be set off by commas. Modifiers that are not free are not set off by commas, nor should they be.

Most of the other kinds of errors in both studies seem to be ones that we can help students learn to eliminate simply through examples. Though we ourselves may use grammatical terminology in explaining these examples, it does not seem necessary for students to learn these terms themselves in order to see how to change what they have written to the structure or form expected in Edited American English. In this category, I would put the following items from the Connors-Lunsford study: vague pronoun reference, possessive apostrophe error, tense shift, unnecessary shift in person, pronoun agreement error, and dangling or misplaced modifier.

Like Noguchi, I would suggest that teachers focus on helping students eliminate from the final drafts of their more formal writings the kinds of items that are considered status marking or serious errors. However, the errors that Hairston labeled status marking are typically ones associated with different ethnic and community dialects of English, so extreme sensitivity and caution are in order. (See in the Appendix the sample lessons on appreciating such dialects and empowering students' voices.)

It also seems sensible to help students eliminate the kinds of errors that occur most frequently even in the writing of college students. And, at whatever level we teach, we may want to do an analysis of our own students' errors to decide which need the most attention. Among the preservice and inservice teachers in my classes, the most frequent error is typically the omission of the apostrophe from possessives. Other frequent errors are ineffective fragments and comma splices, and the misspelling of common homophones like *their, there, they're; your, you're;* and sometimes *our, are.* Even *would of* and *could of* are not totally absent from their papers. Therefore, these are the items to which I typically give the most attention in mini-lessons addressed to the whole class (see the Appendix for some examples). However, only some of these matters require the understanding of key grammatical concepts.

Some basic grammatical terms are illustrated in Figure 5.6, where parts of a narrative are bracketed and otherwise marked. Here is my list and definition of those terms:

- *Clause:* A subject-verb unit. (The term *noun* is useful, but the concept of subject is more critical.)

  Its muddy waters picked up speed.

FIGURE 5.6 Narrative with T-units, clauses, and free modifiers marked.

To illustrate the concept of a grammatical sentence, or T-unit, the first three paragraphs of the narrative are divided into T-units, with square brackets marking each T-unit. Fragments that do not fit into any T-unit are left unbracketed.

To illustrate other grammatical terms, **independent (main) clauses are boldfaced**, and *dependent (subordinate) clauses are italicized*. Some dependent clauses function as nouns and therefore fill a slot in another clause. A dependent clause is boldfaced as well as italicized if it fills a noun slot in an independent clause; otherwise it is simply italicized. Other dependent clauses commonly function as free modifiers, working more or less like an adjective or adverb.

Some free modifiers—phrases rather than clauses—are boldfaced or italicized, depending on whether they go with an independent clause or with a dependent one. In addition, free modifiers are underlined.

In the last four paragraphs of the narrative, three kinds of free modifiers are underlined and labeled (appositives, participial phrases, and absolutes); the other free modifiers in these paragraphs are not underlined.

THE GRAVEYARD

"Oh, shit, NOT AGAIN!" [**The words barely had time to flit through my mind** *before the raft capsized for a second time, throwing me unceremoniously into the raging water.*] [**The raft had been swept over a modest waterfall, landing off-balance in a hole.**] [**I gulped air in the split second** *before a huge wall of water swamped me.*] [**The Indians' Graveyard had me in its grip.**]

[Early in the summer, **it had seemed a great idea to sign up for a whitewater rafting trip in Costa Rica.**] [**Rollie had been wanting to go there**]—[*there were 500 exciting miles of whitewater,* **he told me**]—[**and I was game, despite our little adventure in the Nantahala at high flood stage the previous summer.**] [True, **we had to sign up for the advanced kayak and rafter's trip,** *because I couldn't go any other time.*] [**But we cheerfully sent in our $1000 deposit to the Nantahala Outdoor Center.**]

[**I wasn't REALLY scared** *until one June day when I actually drove to the Nantahala Outdoor Center in North Carolina—conveniently arriving, after a full day's drive across the state, just too late for the last rafting trip.*] [Oh, well, **I said to myself:**] [**I can look at the rafting gear, see** *if there's anything we need for the Costa Rica trip.*] [**The friendly salesgirl was eager to help me** *when I mentioned that we'd signed up for an Adventure trip in Costa Rica.*] [**"I'd like to go there,"** **she exclaimed.**] [**She showed me a book on Costa Rican rivers** *that I bought to take home to Rollie.*] [**And she offered**

to show me a video on whitewatering in Costa Rica, *as soon as some guys were finished looking at rafting on the Colorado.*]

Well—I'm not sure I should ever have watched that video. The most frightening part was a long rapids on a river called the Général. I've repressed the rapids' exact name, but it was something like "Hell's Run." And believe me, that's what it looked like! I watched horrified as a raft tackled the rapid, only to be buried among the waves. Could the raft still be there somewhere, invisible, as wave after wave crashed over it? More to the point, could the rafters still be in the raft? All I could think of was how would they ever get you back into the raft if you got thrown out?

Then flying home from North Carolina, I read parts of the book on Costa Rican rivers. That, too, was a mistake. The authors talked about flash floods in the rainy season, describing an incident when a film crew was making a commercial—Marlboro, I think—with an actor who'd never been rafting but who looked the role of macho man, standing on a raft firmly anchored in the middle of a rapid. Unfortunately the film crew didn't count on a five foot wall of water that suddenly attacked from behind. The raft broke loose, carrying the actor downstream at incredible speed. An expert kayaker followed to rescue him, but for a while it looked as if they both were goners. This, the book said, was the kind of thing that could happen on Costa Rican rivers in the rainy season. Of course, that's when our trip was scheduled.

About that time, I remembered that a psychic friend had suggested I avoid whitewater rafting, <u>hinting at death by drowning</u> {participial phrase}. And Rollie, <u>a water lover since childhood</u> {appositive}, had been warned not to "go out too far."

So on the third day of our trip, I shouldn't have been surprised that the flooding Paçuare rose while we slept beside it for the night, <u>its muddy waters picking up speed as it swelled its banks</u> {absolute}. Nor should I have been surprised, I suppose, that we were now "going swimming" for the second time.

But this time was worse than the first. The wall of water momentarily crushed me, <u>pushing me toward the bottom of the river</u> {participial phrase}. I surfaced quickly, grateful that this time, I had not come up under the raft. Thank God! But then another wave engulfed me, <u>driving me deeper this time, much deeper, into blackness</u> {participial phrase}. I dared not open my eyes. Don't panic, I thought, don't panic, don't panic, keep holding your breath. Where, oh where is the surface, and sunshine, and AIR? Surely this way is UP? Fleetingly I remembered what Rollie kept telling himself when he was submerged in the Nantahala. I can't send HIM home alone either, I thought; gotta hang on, gotta wait 'till I surface to breathe. Then, with a thwack, I hit the surface—the surface of the raft, that is: the underneath surface. Safe, and not safe. <u>My protesting lungs ready to betray me</u> {absolute}, I worked my way to the edge of the raft and popped out from under, <u>gasping for air</u> {participial phrase}.

I'm not sure now which raft it was, the passenger raft or the oar rig that carried our gear. But no one hauled me in. Eileen paddled over with her kayak, <u>telling me to hang onto the rope on the back—not the kayak itself, the rope, the rope</u> {participial phrase}! Then I realized why no one was bothering to get me out of the river: they still hadn't located Rollie. Eileen was focusing on her watch, <u>grimly counting the seconds he'd been underwater</u> {participial phrase}. Too long. But just then he surfaced, thank God. Someone hauled him into the oar rig, <u>nearly scraping off his swim trunks in the process</u> {participial phrase}. If anyone noticed, no one cared. Eileen ferried me to the passenger raft, <u>dipping her paddle with sure skilled strokes</u> {participial phrase}, <u>keeping us from continuing downstream</u> {participial phrase}. One of the guides—Miti, I think {appositive}—reached for me, <u>urging me to hoist myself over the side</u> {participial phrase}. I couldn't. The rush of fear had left me absolutely limp, <u>my arms and legs useless</u> {absolute}. Once hauled in, for the longest time I lay in the raft like an overturned turtle, flat on my back, simply BREATHING. I knew Rollie was safe, but I didn't know until our group stopped downstream for lunch how much deeper he had been pushed by the second wave, how much closer he'd come to succumbing to the dark waters of the Indians' Graveyard. It was nearly his graveyard too.

Connie Weaver

- *Independent (or main) clause:* A clause that can stand alone as a grammatical sentence.

  The raft capsized for a second time.
- *Dependent (or subordinate) clause:* A clause that cannot stand alone as a grammatical sentence.

  before the raft capsized for a second time

  that I bought to take home to Rollie

  that the flooding Paçuare rose
- *Grammatical sentence (T-unit):* An independent clause, plus any dependent clause(s) or phrase(s) that are attached to it or embedded within it. *Each of the following sentences contains only one T-unit—that is, one independent clause plus anything that goes with it.*

I shouldn't have been surprised that the flooding Paçuare rose.

I shouldn't have been surprised that the flooding Paçuare rose while we slept beside it for the night, its muddy waters picking up speed as it swelled its banks.

I worked my way to the edge of the raft and popped out from under.

My protesting lungs ready to betray me, I worked my way to the edge of the raft and popped out from under, gasping for air.

- *Phrase:* a group of words that does not have a complete subject-verb unit.

  early in the summer

  to sign up for a whitewater rafting trip

  hinting at death by drowning

  its muddy waters picking up speed

- *Modifier:* One or more words that describe an entity or give more details about an action. (The terms *adjective* and *adverb* are useful, but not as critical as the concept of modification.)

  Another wave engulfed me.

  The huge waves *completely* obscured the raft.

  The paddle *floating downstream* was *Rollie's*.

  Early in the summer, it had seemed like a *great* idea.

  The video, *which showed people whitewater rafting in Costa Rica,* scared me to death.

  She offered to show me a video on whitewatering in Costa Rica, *as soon as some guys were finished looking at rafting on the Colorado.*

- *Free modifier:* As described by Francis Christensen (1967), the free modifier is an optional modifier that meets at least one of the following criteria, and often both: (1) it can be moved to at least one other position in the sentence; (2) it is set off by commas (or could be and possibly should be). Under "modifiers," the last three example sentences contain free modifiers that meet one or both of these criteria.

Understanding these terms will enable writers to understand such frequently prohibited constructions as the following (see the Appendix for lessons on these concepts):

- *Run-on (or fused) sentence:* Two independent clauses with no connecting word or punctuation between them.

  Rollie didn't dare breathe he was still underwater.

FIGURE 5.7   Poem with absolute constructions (1988).

A War Death

Shrapnel pounded into the dirt around me.
My buddies fell as the murderous pieces of metal embedded into their skin.
I ran. I tripped. I fell. I found myself in a ditch, *the foul smell of rotting corpses
groping at my nostrils.*
I heard the screams of others as they fell beside me, *blood oozing from their
mouths.*

I could smell the explosive powder in the air, *hand grenades whizzing overhead.*
Bombshells dropped like hailstones.
Men dropped to their knees and then to their deaths.
The death gases were now stinging my lungs.
I was dying.

A cold shiver shook my soul. I looked on as a hand grenade landed at my
feet.
It exploded. I screamed. Blood more than trickled out of my legs, for they
were only half attached. A numbness overswept my legs.
My eyelids let themselves slowly shut as a sense of peace overcame me.
I was dead.

John Weaver

- *Comma splice:* Two independent clauses joined by just a comma.
   We were happy to get signed up for the trip in Costa Rica,
   Rollie had been wanting to go there for some time.
- *Fragment:* Something punctuated as a sentence that is not
   grammatically complete (does not consist of or contain an
   independent clause). Dependent clauses and phrases are
   fragments when punctuated as sentences. (In the Glossary, see
   not only **Fragment** but **Minor sentence.**)

While focusing on only a limited number of concepts and terms is clearly
a sensible idea, other teachers may find that the needs of their students
warrant a slightly different list. For instance, in helping basic-level adult
writers eliminate errors, Mina Shaughnessy (1977) found that she needed
to focus on the use of inflectional endings (like noun plural and verb past
tense) and the tense of verbs as well as on sentence sense and agreement.
   In most circumstances, terms like *noun, verb, adjective, adverb* can be

taught incidentally, as they become relevant in discussing effective writing. Terms for connecting words can too, through lists of words that are typical of a category. Other niceties—terms like *appositive, participial phrase,* and *absolute,* for instance—can be used in the context of helping students generate and combine sentences, but the naming of these parts does not seem necessary in order for writers to be able to use them. Indeed, when I asked my teenage son where he had learned to use "those constructions" (pointing to the three absolutes that I have italicized in his poem, Figure 5.7), John simply said, "Oh, all writers know how to use those." However, absolutes had not been included in the grammar books used in his school, nor, apparently, had they been taught by his teachers; he had simply absorbed the construction through his reading. Such examples are rife among creative writers: they often demonstrate exceptional command of the syntactic resources of the language, yet they rarely can name the constructions they use. And the point is that as writers, *they don't need to.*

What Kinds of Structures Should We Emphasize for Syntactic Growth and Diversity of Style?

We saw in Chapter 3 that at least by the end of their kindergarten year, children are using in their speech all the basic sentence patterns of English. Furthermore, they are using virtually all the particular grammatical constructions found in the speech of older children and adults.

This does not mean, however, that they have ceased expanding their exploration of the syntactic resources of the language. In fact, O'Donnell, Griffin, and Norris (1967) found significant spurts of syntactic growth in children's oral language during grade 1 and grade 7. In particular, the children in their study showed significant increases in their use of nominals (constructions functioning as nouns) and their use of adverbials (constructions functioning as adverbs) (p. 89). In writing, such increases were also found between grades 3 and 5, and again between grades 5 and 7. Interestingly, it was not until grade 7 that the children's control of syntax in writing significantly outdistanced their control of syntax in speech. Other studies have found the crossover to occur even later (Loban, 1976). Apparently the nature of the oral and the written discourse situations has a lot to do with the syntactic complexity of the language used (Scott, 1988; Crowhurst and Piche, 1979).

What we cannot tell from these studies is the degree to which various factors have stimulated such growth in students' command of syntax. Has direct instruction in grammar played a significant part? Probably not for many students, given the research on the effectiveness of teaching grammar in isolation; however, we cannot tell for certain from the research on syntactic development. Has wide reading played a significant part? Probably so for at least some students, given the research on the effects of reading; but again, we cannot tell for sure from these research studies. Has extensive writing played an important part? Again probably so for some students, if they've struggled with revising their sentences for greater clarity and effectiveness.

What we *do* know, however, is some of the patterns that differentiate older students' syntax from younger students' syntax. And by comparing the syntax of proficient adult writers with the syntax of high school seniors, we can also see which kinds of constructions seem to develop naturally (perhaps aided by instruction, perhaps not) and which do not. In other words, we can glean from the research some idea of where our efforts might best be spent in trying to help students develop their command of the syntactic resources of the language.

An excellent and much more thorough discussion of the relevant research can be found in Scott's and in Nelson's articles in *Later Language Development: Ages Nine Through Nineteen* (Nippold, 1988). However, even our brief treatment here will offer some insights into patterns of development, while at the same time demonstrating the need for caution in drawing conclusions from the research on syntactic development.

Hunt's Research

Much of the pioneering research in the area of "syntactic maturity" was done by Kellogg Hunt. In his initial study (1965a), Hunt defined syntactically more mature use of syntax simply as what older students did with syntax that younger students did not do, or did not do as frequently: "the observed [grammatical] characteristics of writers in an older grade" (p. 5). Given such a yardstick, Hunt found that the best single measure of syntactic maturity in normal free writing is simply the average length of the grammatical sentence: the "minimum terminable unit," or *T-unit*, as Hunt called it (p. 21). A T-unit consists of an independent clause plus any dependent clauses or elements that may be attached to or embedded within it. The following examples and the marked paragraphs of the narrative in Figure 5.6 illustrate how sentences, T-units, and clauses are related:

I drove downtown.	[One independent clause—one T-unit]
I drove downtown and bought some art supplies.	[One independent clause, with compound predicate—one T-unit]
I drove downtown and bought some art supplies after I visited Tommy's class.	[One independent clause, followed by one dependent clause—one T-unit]
I drove downtown and I bought some art supplies.	[Two independent clauses—two T-units]

Here are Hunt's statistics demonstrating the increasingly longer T-units of students in higher grades. Included also are statistics from some superior adult writers published in *Atlantic Monthly* (Hunt, 1965a, p. 56):

	GRADE 4	GRADE 8	GRADE 12	SUPERIOR ADULTS
Average (mean) number of words per T-unit	8.60	11.50	14.40	20.30

As we can readily see, the growth in T-unit length between the fourth and eighth grades and between the eighth and twelfth grades was approximately three words per T-unit, while the difference between the twelfth graders and the highly skilled adults was approximately six words per T-unit.

But as teachers, what we want to know is not just by how many words the T-units increase, but how the internal grammar of those T-units changes or doesn't change. This will suggest some areas for trying to guide students' syntactic development.

In a controlled writing experiment, Hunt (1970) had such students and adults combine basic kernel sentences into more sophisticated sentences (see Figure 5.8). The following passages from his research indicate some of the syntactic constructions typical of children's writing at these three grade levels (pp. 64–67):

Grade 4

Aluminum is a metal and is abundant. It has many uses and it comes from bauxite. Bauxite is an ore and bauxite looks like clay. Bauxite contains aluminum and it contains several other substances. Workmen extract these other substances from the bauxite. They grind the bauxite and put it in tanks. Pressure is in the tanks . . .

Children's free writing shows more syntactic variation than this sentence-combining exercise typically did, but it is clear that in this exercise, the

FIGURE 5.8 Sentence-combining exercise (Hunt, 1970).

ALUMINUM

Directions: Read the passage all the way through. You will notice that the sentences are short and choppy. Study the passage, and then rewrite it in a better way. You may combine sentences, change the order of words, and omit words that are repeated too many times. But try not to leave out any of the information.

Aluminum is a metal. It is abundant. It has many uses. It comes from bauxite. Bauxite is an ore. Bauxite looks like clay. Bauxite contains aluminum. It contains several other substances. Workmen extract these other substances from the bauxite. They grind the bauxite. They put it in tanks. Pressure is in the tanks. The other substances form a mass. They remove the mass. They use filters. A liquid remains. They put it through several other processes. It finally yields a chemical. The chemical is powdery. It is white. The chemical is alumina. It is a mixture. It contains aluminum. It contains oxygen. Workmen separate the aluminum from the oxygen. They use electricity. They finally produce a metal. The metal is light. It has a luster. The luster is bright. The luster is silvery. This metal comes in many forms.

fourth graders' typical means of combining sentences was to conjoin two independent clauses within one sentence, using *and*.

Grade 8

Aluminum is an abundant metal, has many uses, and comes from bauxite which is an ore that looks like clay. Bauxite contains several other substances. Workmen extract these from bauxite by grinding it, then putting it in pressure tanks . . .

Several features are noteworthy here. For instance, the first four T-units in the fourth-grade example have become part of a single T-unit in the eighth-grade example: *Aluminum is an abundant metal, has many uses, and comes from bauxite.* Most noticeable in this sentence is the compound predicate, in contrast to the compound sentences in the fourth-grade sample. Second, we note the two adjectival clauses that are part of the same eighth-grade sentence: *which is an ore that looks like clay.* Third, a main clause with compound verbs in the fourth-grade sample has become a prepositional phrase with gerunds (*by grinding it, then putting it in pressure tanks)* in the eighth-grade sample. Overall, there are fewer words and fewer T-units, but more words per T-unit.

Grade 12

> Aluminum is an abundant metal with many uses. It comes from an ore called bauxite that looks like clay. It contains aluminum and several other substances which are extracted from the bauxite. They grind the bauxite and put it in pressure tanks.

One difference here is that the typical twelfth grader creates reductions of adjectival clauses: *with many uses* (rather than the full clause *which has many uses*) and *called bauxite* (rather than the full clause *which is called bauxite*). Another change is that the twelfth grader uses passives: *which are extracted from the bauxite*, and *called bauxite*.

Superior adult writers

> Aluminum, an abundant metal of many uses, is obtained from bauxite, a clay-like ore. To extract the other substances found in bauxite the ore is ground and put in pressure tanks.

Here, two more clauses have been reduced to adjectival phrases, specifically appositives: *an abundant metal of many uses* and *a clay-like ore*. Similarly, the number of full and reduced passives has increased to four. In addition, there is an adverbial of purpose: *To extract the other substances found in bauxite*.

Of course, it would be risky to assume that the kinds of growth demonstrated in this controlled sentence-combining experiment are exactly those we are most likely to find in children's free writing. Nevertheless, there seems to be some justification for hypothesizing the following trends in the syntactic development of writing:

1. First, entire sentences tend to be coordinated.
2. Then, coordination of whole sentences may gradually give way to coordination of elements within sentences, particularly to coordination of predicates.
3. At approximately the same time or soon thereafter, writers may begin to use subordinate clauses, such as adverbial and adjectival clauses (or to use more of these clauses, if they have already begun using them).
4. Then, adjectival clauses may increasingly be reduced to post-noun adjectival phrases of various kinds—particularly appositive phrases, participial phrases, and absolute constructions.

Among reduced adjectivals I have emphasized appositive phrases, participial phrases, and absolute constructions because greater use of these constructions seems often to differentiate professional writing from high school seniors' writing (see the next section). For clarification, examples of these three constructions are underlined and labeled in the last four paragraphs of the narrative in Figure 5.6.

Again, it must be emphasized that these are not hard-and-fast developmental stages but rather trends that may help us decide in what ways to nudge the syntactic development of particular students.

Walter Loban (1970) summarizes children's syntactic development as follows:

> As they [schoolchildren] mature, the low group increases its ability to use dependent clauses whereas the high group shifts to that tighter coiling of thought accomplished by infinitive clauses, participial, prepositional, and gerund phrases, appositives, nominative absolutes, and clusters of words in cumulative sentences. (p. 625)

We see such distinctions between lower, middle, and higher groups in a research study by Theone Hughes (1975). The following responses to Hunt's sentence-combining exercise are all from seventh graders (pp. 29–30):

Seventh grader no. 1

> Aluminum is an abundant metal. It has many uses. It comes from bauxite. Bauxite is an ore. Bauxite looks like clay. Bauxite contains aluminum. It contains several other substances. Workmen extract these other substances. They grind the bauxite. They put it in tanks. Pressure is in the tanks.

This writer combined only twelve of the underlying propositions (the original kernel sentences) into his eleven T-units, a ratio of about 1 to 1, or 1.09 propositions per T-unit. In Hunt's related study (1977), the closest comparison is the ratio for grade 4 students: 1.1.

Seventh grader no. 2

> Aluminum is abundant metal. It has many uses. It comes from an ore. The ore is called bauxite. It looks like clay. It contains aluminum. There are seven other substances that workmen extract from the bauxite. They grind the bauxite and put into pressured tanks. The other substances in the mass are removed by filters. A liquid remains and then they put it through seven other processes. [The errors were in the student's original.]

The writer's first eleven T-units contain the essence of seventeen of the original sentences, a ratio of about $1\frac{1}{2}$ to 1, or 1.55 propositions per T-unit. This is slightly under the average of 1.6 for the grade 6 students in Hunt's study.

Seventh grader no. 3

> Aluminum is an abundant metal that comes from bauxite. Bauxite is an ore that looks like clay. Bauxite contains aluminum and several other substances. Workmen extract these other substances from the bauxite. Then the bauxite is ground and put in tanks that have pressure in them. They remove the mass other substances have formed with filters. The liquid that remains is put through several other processes. It finally yields a white powdery chemical that is alumina. It is a mixture that contains aluminum and oxygen. Workmen use electricity to separate the aluminum from the oxygen. They finally produce a light metal that has bright silvery luster.

This writer has combined thirty-one of the original thirty-two sentences into eleven T-units. (The original sentence *It has many uses* was omitted by the student.) Thus the student has condensed nearly three underlying propositions into each grammatical sentence, a ratio of nearly 3 to 1, or 2.82 propositions per T-unit. This is very close to the average of 3.2 produced by the twelfth graders in Hunt's 1977 study. (The average number of propositions per T-unit for the five levels and the skilled adult writers is as follows: grade four, 1.1; grade six, 1.6; grade eight, 2.4; grade ten, 2.8; grade twelve, 3.2; skilled adults, 5.1.)

With sets of examples such as these, we are in a better position to understand what researchers mean when they suggest that longer T-units are only superficial evidence of what is happening to writers' syntax as they mature: they are reducing more and more independent clauses to coordinated structures, to dependent clauses, and then to increasingly sophisticated kinds of phrases. To put it more simply, they say more, in fewer words. Or to put it more technically, they are incorporating more and more propositions into each T-unit. Thus some researchers have argued that syntactic maturity might be expressed as a relationship between deep(er) structure and surface structure (e.g., DiStefano and Howie, 1979). More concretely, the syntactic maturity of a writer's sentences might be expressed as a ratio between the number of underlying propositions and the number of actual T-units in a language sample: ratios like those given for the three preceding student samples. (See Weaver, 1979, for a somewhat more thorough but still succinct introduction to additional measures of syntactic maturity and additional results from some of the research. A summary of Hunt's original research study is found in Hunt, 1965b.)

One observation we need to keep in mind is that the range and maturity of students' syntactic structures in their free writing may differ from that in a relatively artificial sentence-combining exercise such as the one devised by Hunt. I find myself wondering, for instance, whether the fourth graders in Hunt's study and the first seventh grader in Hughes's study *really* understood what they were supposed to do with the sentences, or whether they were unable to combine sentences in this contrived exercise even if they used more sophisticated sentences in their free writing. Thus it does not surprise me that the sentences in Hunt's study of students' free writing were, on the average, two or three words longer than the sentences of students in the same grade in the sentence-combining experiment. This is as great a difference as that typically found between two grade levels in the sentence-combining experiment.

To put the results from Hunt's studies in perspective, there are several other observations we should keep in mind:

- The findings from studies of syntactic maturity are limited to the kinds of discourse explicitly examined. For example, exposition and argumentation elicit certain grammatical constructions that are found much less often in narration and description, and vice versa. (See, for example, Crowhurst, 1979; Crowhurst and Piche, 1979; Scott, 1988.) Furthermore, fiction writers may suit the sentence structure to different characters and personas (Gibson, 1966, 1969; Malmstrom and Weaver, 1973, ch. 7). Thus we must be extremely cautious in drawing conclusions from the sentence-combining research.
- More syntactically mature, in Hunt's terms, is not necessarily better (e.g., Malmstrom and Weaver, 1973; Crowhurst, 1979). Relatively mature sentences can be awkward, convoluted, even unintelligible; they can also be inappropriate to the subject, the audience, and the writer's or persona's voice. Conversely, relatively simple sentences can make their point succinctly and emphatically. Often, of course, sentence variety is best.
- For these reasons, the term *syntactic complexity* seems more appropriate for what Hunt described. A syntactically mature writer, then, might be defined as one having a substantial reservoir of syntactic resources to call upon and the ability to suit

syntax to his or her purpose, audience, form of discourse, and so forth (e.g., Crowhurst, 1979).

- Hastening syntactic growth is not necessarily a desirable goal, especially for those whose syntax is already quite mature compared to that of their peers (e.g., Kerek, Daiker, and Morenberg, 1980). The research suggests that at least up to a point, such growth will probably take care of itself—particularly when students read frequently, and read at least some materials with syntax that is more complex than their own.

Christensen's Contributions

Before Loban alluded to the "tighter coiling of thought" typical of older and more proficient writers in school, Francis Christensen had discovered that this linguistic compactness was the main difference between twelfth-grade writers and professional adult writers. He has also contributed substantially to teachers' understanding of how such writers use grammar to achieve rhetorical effects and effectiveness.

In explaining the basis of his *generative rhetoric*, Christensen (1967, pp. 24–25) draws upon a statement from John Erskine (1946):

> When you write, you make a point, not by subtracting as though you sharpened a pencil, but by adding. When you put one word after another, your statement should be more precise the more you add. . . . What you wish to say is found not in the noun but in what you add to qualify the noun. The noun is only a grappling iron to hitch your mind to the reader's. . . . The noun, the verb, and the main clause serve merely as a base on which the meaning will rise.
>   The modifier is the essential part of any sentence.

Of course, it is easy for teachers to misunderstand this advice and encourage children to write sentences overburdened with adjectives, such as the following exaggeration from Christensen (1967): "The small boy on the red bicycle who lives with his happy parents on our shady street often coasts down the steep street until he comes to the city park" (p. 5). As teachers, we have also overemphasized the subordinate clause, often without realizing that to further extend students' syntactic growth we need to help them reduce some of their modifying clauses to phrases—the kinds of phrases used by professional writers.

Free modifiers seem to need the most instructional coaxing, yet they often convey the detail that makes a sentence effective. Figure 5.9 shows some examples from Christensen (1967, pp. 9–10). The main clause is numbered 1, and each "deeper" layer of modification is numbered succes-

FIGURE 5.9   Examples of writing using free modifiers (Christensen, 1967).

1 He dipped his hands in the bichloride solution and shook them,
  2 a quick shake,
    3 fingers down, [absolute]
      4 like the fingers of a pianist above the keys.

Sinclair Lewis

  2 Calico-coated, [past participle]
  2 small-bodied,   [past participle]
    3 with delicate legs and pink faces in which their mismatched eyes
    rolled wild and subdued,
1 they huddled,
  2 gaudy motionless and alert,
  2 wild as deer,
  2 deadly as rattlesnakes,
  2 quiet as doves.

William Faulkner

1 The Texan turned to the nearest gatepost and climbed to the top of it,
  2 his alternate thighs thick and bulging in the tight trousers,   [absolute]
  2 the butt of the pistol catching and losing the sun in pearly gleams. [absolute]

William Faulkner

1 He could sail for hours,
  2 searching the blanched grasses below him with his telescopic
  eyes,   [present participle]
  2 gaining height against the wind,   [present participle]
  2 descending in mile-long, gently declining swoops when he curved and
  rode back,   [present participle]
  2 never beating a wing.   [present participle]

Walter Van Tilburg Clark

---

sively. Clear examples of the adjectival constructions that are said to need most instructional coaxing—that is, the appositive, the participial phrase, and the absolute—are labeled in parentheses.

These writers have used a variety of free modifiers, typically to convey narrative or descriptive detail. While such phrases may seem particularly important in fiction and poetry, they can be useful in informative and argumentative prose as well (e.g., the Eisley quotation in Figure 5.9). Notice that most of these free modifiers occur *after* the main clause, producing a cumulative sentence, the kind of sentence that has particularly characterized twentieth-century prose (this sentence itself is an example). In

1 Joad's lips stretched tight over his long teeth for a moment, and
1 he licked his lips,
  2 like a dog,
    3 two licks,
      4 one in each direction from the middle.

John Steinbeck

1 It is with the coming of man that a vast hole seems to open in nature,
  2 a vast black whirlpool spinning faster and faster, [appositive]
    3 consuming flesh, stones, soil, minerals,   [present participle]
    3 sucking down the lightning,   [present participle]
    3 wrenching power from the atom,   [present participle]
      4 until the ancient sounds of nature are drowned out in the
      cacophony of something which is no longer nature,
        5 something instead which is loose and knocking at the world's
        heart,
        5 something demonic and no longer planned—
          6 escaped, it may be— [past participle]
          6 spewed out of nature, [past participle]
          6 contending in a final giant's game against its master.
            [present participle]

Loren Eisley

analyzing over a thousand sentences of fiction and several essays from *Harper's* magazine, Christensen found that over half of the free modifiers occurred in final position after the main or base clause, while most of the rest occurred in initial position before the main clause (this sentence illustrates both). Free modifiers occurred infrequently in medial position, between the subject and the verb, apparently because this location makes a sentence harder to read and comprehend. (See Christensen, 1968b, which is included in Christensen and Christensen, 1978.)

    With such examples as these, we can more readily see how various grammatical constructions can be used for stylistic effect and effectiveness. And without necessarily knowing the names of such constructions, we and our students can expand basic sentences into sentences that carry narrative, descriptive, and explanatory detail in rhetorically effective constructions. As Christensen (1967) noted, "Grammar maps out the possible; rhetoric narrows the possible down to the desirable or effective" (p. 39). As teachers of literature and writing, we need to help our students make this link.

Promoting Growth in Syntactic Complexity

Francis Christensen himself devised a rhetoric program to teach students to expand bare-bones sentences with modifiers such as those in the preceding section (Christensen, 1968a), but the program is now out of print. The references listed in Figure 5.10, however, are excellent introductions to sentence combining and (in some cases) to generating sentences in the tradition of Francis Christensen. I have listed my top two choices first. (See lessons in the Appendix that further clarify and suggest ways of teaching two kinds of free modifiers, the participial phrase and the absolute.)

For teachers, an important question is whether to have their students use a book such as those in Figure 5.10 with extensive work in sentence combining and possibly sentence generating. That question is not easily answered.

On the one hand, no kind of grammar teaching has produced such positive results as sentence combining, with or without sentence-generating activities. Beginning with John Mellon's study in 1969 and Frank O'Hare's study in 1973, numerous sentence-combining studies were conducted in the 1980s, mostly with positive results. In their review of the literature, Hillocks and Mavrogenes (1986) indicate that "the overwhelming majority of these studies have been positive, with about 60 percent of them reporting that work in sentence combining, from as low as grade 2 through the adult level, results in significant advances (at least $p < .05$) on measures of syntactic maturity" (pp. 142–143). Approximately an additional 30 percent of the studies found some improvement, though it was not great enough to be statistically significant. Only 10 percent of the studies reviewed were negative, showing no difference or mixed results. Furthermore, sentence combining seems to work with all levels of students, but particularly for remedial or "at risk" students. As to whether sentence combining improves the overall quality of students' writing, the evidence is mixed (Hillocks and Smith, 1991, pp. 598–599).

On the other hand, here are some questions that remain:

- Are the gains from sentence-combining activities maintained by the writers? There is some positive evidence (e.g., Morenberg, Daiker, and Kerek, 1978), but not enough research to justify reasonable confidence in the results.
- Would the writers sooner or later come to write more

FIGURE 5.10 References on sentence combining and sentence generating.

Killgallon, D. (1987). *Sentence composing: The complete course*. Portsmouth, NH: Boynton/Cook. This book includes sentence scrambling, sentence imitating, sentence combining, and sentence expanding (generating). It is described as suitable for high school or upper schools, college writing courses, or creative writing courses on any level. Separate texts for grades 10 and 11 can be purchased, but the *Complete Course* includes a synthesis of these two.

Daiker, D. A., Kerek, A., & Morenberg, M. (1990). *The writer's options: Combining to composing* (4th ed.). New York: Harper & Row. Intended for college writing classes, this excellent text will help teachers better understand free modifiers and their effectiveness. It can also be used with high school students, particularly those in more advanced writing courses. While the book emphasizes sentence combining, many of the base clauses could be used as the starting point for sentence generating.

Stull, W. L. (1983). *Combining and creating: Sentence combining and generative rhetoric*. New York: Holt, Rinehart. Like Killgallon's, this book is notable for including both sentence combining and sentence generating. Can be used for either college or high school.

Strong, W. (1981). *Sentence combining and paragraph building*. New York: McGraw-Hill.

Strong, W. (1984). *Crafting cumulative sentences*. New York: McGraw-Hill.

Strong, W. (1984). *Practicing sentence options*. New York: McGraw-Hill. Of the four McGraw-Hill books by Strong, I particularly like the last two. Intended for high school or junior high.

Strong, W. (1986). *Creative approaches to sentence combining*. Urbana, IL: ERIC/RCS and the National Council of Teachers of English. This informative resource focuses mostly on the combining of teacher-supplied sentences, but it briefly discusses sentence generating as well.

Strong, W. (1993). *Sentence combining: A composing book* (3rd ed.). New York: McGraw-Hill.

syntactically complex sentences without direct instruction? Hunt's research suggests many students would, and there is some supporting evidence at the college level also (Kerek, Daiker, and Morenberg, 1980). Such growth is most likely when students are reading a lot, and reading syntactically challenging material on a regular basis.

- Would reading and discussion of stylistically effective sentences in literature have nearly the same effect? Perhaps (see Krashen, 1993).

- Would helping students combine, expand, and revise the sentences in their own writing have approximately the same effect? It seems likely. There is at least one research study, Smith and Hull (1985), which found that a week's worth of sentence combining plus advice to use long, complex sentences produced gains in words per clause that were comparable to gains produced by an entire semester of sentence-combining practice in other studies.

While the references on sentence manipulation in Figure 5.10 are valuable, then, it may be best to use them as a teacher resource and as a source of *occasional* sentence-combining and sentence-generating activities or frequent but brief mini-lessons, not as an entire course of study. Practically speaking, perhaps the teachers in a school could agree to use different parts of the same book at different grade levels. But in any case, the teacher who has learned what these books have to offer is well prepared to help students develop syntactic resources through occasional lessons and through writing conferences with small groups and with individual students.

However, the correlations among various language measures in Loban's study (1976) should lead us to the conclusion that the least syntactically mature writers need more than mere practice in sentence combining and generating. In that study, the students in the high group were the most effective users of language as viewed by all their teachers, from kindergarten through grade 12. Those in the low group were the students similarly viewed as the least effective users of language over the years. In considering various measures of language performance, Loban discovered that the high group was high and the low group was low in *all* of the following attributes (pp. 24–25):

- Reading ability
- Writing ability
- Scores on listening tests
- Height and range of vocabulary
- Use of tentativeness: supposition, hypotheses, conditional statements (the low group was more inflexible, dogmatic, unwilling or unable to entertain nuances or ambiguity)
- Seven different measures of syntactic development and maturity

Though an examination of Loban's data clearly shows that the low group used the various kinds of syntactic structures analyzed in this study, it also shows that at every grade level, the low group used these structures less frequently than the high group (pp. 63–64). In fact, to rephrase Loban's data into the terminology used here, it turned out that in their last three years of high school, the subjects low in language proficiency were not combining as many underlying propositions into one T-unit as the high and randomly assigned groups did in grades 1, 2, and 3 (p. 65).

Considering the schools' tendency in recent decades to shunt less proficient readers and writers off to resource rooms for more skills work, one suspects that the lower group had few opportunities to read or write whole texts. This is extremely unfortunate, because studies of the effectiveness of free reading show that it has far more impact upon students' reading ability than skills work (Krashen, 1993), and furthermore, that the gains are perhaps most striking for at-risk, underachieving, allegedly dyslexic, and ESL readers (Tunnell and Jacobs, 1989). Furthermore, some of these studies, particularly of second language acquisition, suggest that reading may promote the acquisition of grammatical structures more effectively than explicit study of such structures (as summarized in Elley, 1991).

The same is true with writing. That is, it is not skills work that makes students better writers, but the opportunity to write and to receive teacher and peer help with their writing. Various teachers have clearly demonstrated that special needs and other low-achieving children and adolescents can learn to read whole books and write whole, meaningful pieces, with appropriate instructional help (e.g., Five, 1991; Stires, 1991; Routman, 1991; Atwell, 1987). It takes lots of time and patience and the conviction that the students will *eventually* make a breakthrough to literacy. But given that conviction and the determination to teach accordingly, teachers are almost never disappointed.

Instead of a crash course in writing more sophisticated sentences, then, what the less proficient and even the *least* proficient writers may need most is to spend a great deal of time in reading and writing workshops. Time spent freely discussing their reading with peers and the teacher is also likely to have an effect upon such students' use of supposition, hypothesis, and conditional statements—all of which will necessarily be reflected in greater grammatical sophistication. And syntactic complexity in their writing can be directly fostered through a limited number of lessons (see the Appendix) and by helping students revise and expand the sentences in their own writing. Even students with the least command of syntax do not necessarily need an entire program in sentence combining or sentence generating, nor will such a program necessarily benefit them as much as extensive reading and writing, with support and guidance as needed.

Scope and Sequence in the Teaching of Grammar

It would be handy, of course, to have a scope and sequence chart that would tell us what aspects of grammar should be taught at which grade levels, a chart such as we find in published language arts or grammar and composition series (also Vaura, 1994). But is using a scope and sequence chart a realistic or appropriate way to determine what to teach in helping students edit their work and revise their sentences for correctness and greater effectiveness?

Let us consider for a moment the excerpts from two papers (Figures 5.11 and 5.12), the second pages of two stories. The first paper is from a

FIGURE 5.11.   Writing sample from Nicholas, a kindergartner.

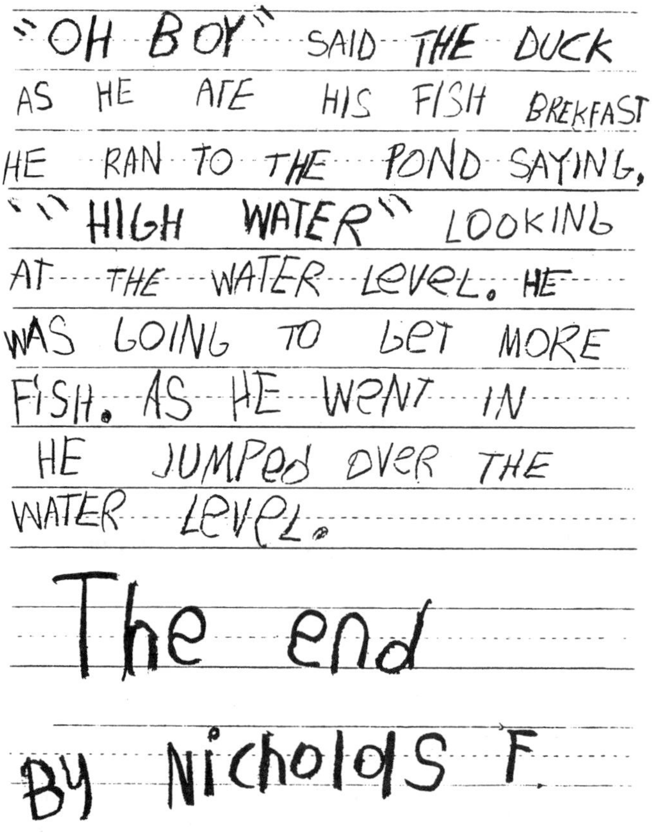

"OH BOY" SAID THE DUCK
AS HE ATE HIS FISH BREKFAST
HE RAN TO THE POND SAYING,
"HIGH WATER" LOOKING
AT THE WATER level. HE
WAS GOING TO GET MORE
FISH. AS HE WENT IN
HE JUMPED OVER THE
WATER level.

The end

BY Nicholas F.

FIGURE 5.12   Writing sample from John, a fourth grader.

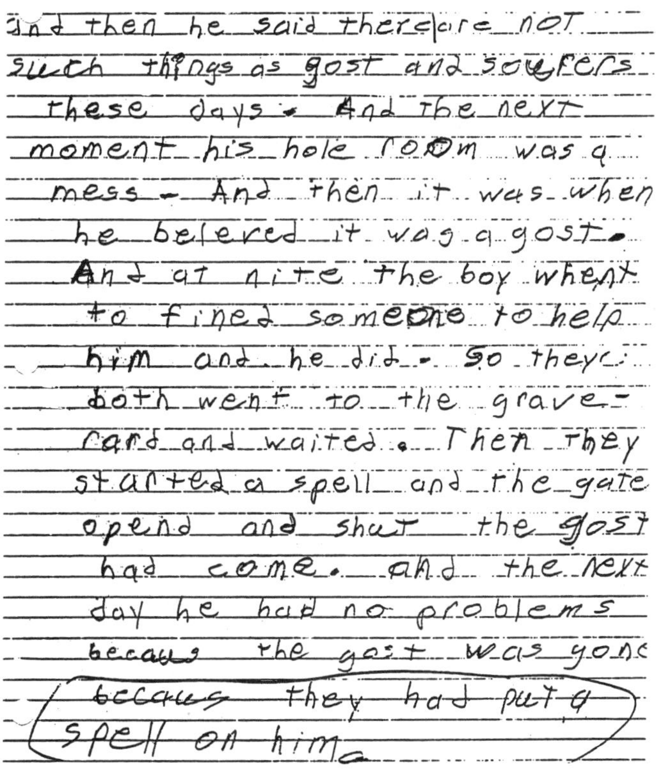

And then he said there are not such things as gost and soupers these days. And the next moment his hole room was a mess. And then it was when he beleved it was a gost. And at nite the boy whent to fined someone to help him and he did. So they both went to the grave-card and waited. Then they started a spell and the gate opend and shut the gost had come. and the next day he had no problems becaus the gost was gone becaus they had put a spell on him.

kindergartner, Nicholas, who recently completed the first grade. Because Nicholas was using dialogue in his writing, his kindergarten teacher showed him how to use quotation marks. We notice other correct punctuation, too: periods, and a comma before the duck's words "high water." Nicholas uses two participial phrases, *saying, "high water"* and *looking at the water level*, constructions that typically develop later, for most writers. Most of the words are spelled correctly too. This child was unusual in being so sophisticated a writer as a kindergartner, but he was also fortunate in having a teacher who would help him learn writing conventions as she helped him edit his writing. Equally important, he was eager to have the teacher's help in revising.

The second writer, John, a fourth grader, was not so fortunate as a student in the 1970s, before teachers understood the importance of guiding students throughout the writing process. In kindergarten, his teacher did not want students to write until they could write correctly, so all he was allowed to write was his name, in signing valentines. In first grade, his assigned writing consisted of dittos: one where he was to complete the sentence "I am happy when . . . ," and another where he was to complete the sentence "I am sad when . . ." In second grade, he copied poems from the board. In third grade, his teacher used the Workshop Way management program, in which children individually completed one task after another, in the sequence specified for the day. Most days John got to the point of doing the writing assignment, but the teacher never helped the students revise or edit their writing; she merely red-inked the errors. As a result, John was discouraged and threw the red-inked papers in the wastebasket or in a corner at home, without paying any attention to what he was supposed to learn from the error correction. Examination of his fourth-grade paper in Figure 5.12 suggests that he needed some of the same kinds of help with mechanics and grammar that the kindergartner has received. However, the red-inking of his papers in the third grade discouraged him so much that he was not able to deal with anyone's attempt to help. Until near the end of his fourth-grade year, he was emotionally unable to treat a first draft as something that need not be permanent. Thus while this piece of fourth-grade writing (and other pieces) showed a need for help with spelling the past tense of regular verbs, with strategies for noticing and correcting temporary spellings in general, and with consistent use of punctuation, he was not yet able to benefit from such help.

During his kindergarten year, then, one writer learned aspects of grammar that another, fourth-grade writer had seemingly not yet mastered and was not emotionally able to deal with. Furthermore, an examination of some of the writings in Myna Shaughnessy's *Errors and Expectations* (1977) demonstrates that many adult writers do not have as good a command of the conventions of English as these two elementary students seem to have.

Such examples demonstrate that we teachers cannot realistically hope to sequence what aspects of grammar should be taught when, to teach them systematically, and to expect students to apply what has been taught. It simply won't work, and indeed the research demonstrates that it *doesn't* work, for most students. Students vary considerably in their understanding and use of editing conventions as well as grammatical constructions. What one writer appears to need will vary considerably from what other writers in the same class will need. Furthermore, a writer's ability to accept editing help will depend upon a variety of factors, including personality, prior responses to his or her writing, and the desire to share the writing with others. We can most effectively teach sentence revision and editing through a writing process approach, with emphasis on learning to revise and to edit choice pieces for some kind of public sharing or publication, but we need to respond to each writer as an individual with different writing needs.

Thus—it bears repeating—there cannot be any sensible scope and sequence to tell us what to teach when, with regard to revising and editing. As teachers, we simply have to be knowledgeable enough about developmental trends to have some idea of when and how to intervene with particular students—and this means being sensitive to their feelings about their writing and themselves as writers too.

What I've offered in Figure 5.13, then, is an idealized scope of what aspects of grammar might be taught across the years from kindergarten through college, depending upon individual students' writing needs, abilities, and interests. This description uses a number of grammatical terms with which teachers should ideally be familiar, but again I want to emphasize that students do not need to know many of them in order to learn to edit their writing appropriately and to write increasingly varied and rhetorically effective sentences. Within some categories in Figure 5.13, it was possible to list some items in a reasonable sequence for teaching certain concepts (e.g., part 1) or in an order that more or less reflects developmental trends or increasing sophistication (e.g., part 2). However, it should not be assumed that the order of the items *necessarily* reflects an appropriate instructional sequence. Neither should it be assumed that the items in any one part should be taught before or after the items in other parts; rather, at every grade level teachers may draw items from each part, depending upon the needs of the class and especially of individual students. The Appendix includes sample lessons reflecting each part, for illustration (most derive from my teaching at the college level, but many could be adapted for other levels). Most of these lessons would be taught in the context of sentence revision and editing.

Guidelines for the Teaching of Grammar

This tentative scope-not-sequence chart needs to be accompanied by sensible guidelines for teaching grammar. Given the research discussed so far, the following guidelines seem sensible.

1. *Engage students in writing, writing, and more writing.* Give them plenty of time to write daily, in writing workshops—and see that they write not just during English and language arts, but across the curriculum. Help

FIGURE 5.13 A minimum of grammar for maximum benefits. As discussed in the text, teaching the application of these grammatical concepts does not require teaching or conscious mastery of English as a complete grammatical system; indeed, it probably requires no more than about a dozen terms.

1. TEACHING CONCEPTS OF SUBJECT, VERB, SENTENCE, CLAUSE, PHRASE, AND RELATED CONCEPTS FOR EDITING

Objectives
- To help students develop sentence sense through wide reading.
- To help students learn to punctuate sentences correctly (according to accepted conventions) and effectively (judiciously violating the rules on occasion, for rhetorical effect).
  By identifying subjects and verbs (predicates).
  By identifying fragments, run-ons, and comma splices, which includes understanding the concept of a grammatical sentence (T-unit); distinguishing between independent and dependent clauses, and between clauses and phrases (including near-clauses); recognizing when a verb is not a properly formed main verb.
- To help students learn to make verbs agree with their subjects.
  According to the conventions of Edited American English, as differentiated from the conventions of other dialects.
  In special cases, such as when the subject is modified by a prepositional phrase; when the subject and verb are inverted; when the subject is compound.
- To help students learn conventions for punctuating subordinate clauses.
  Introductory adverbial clauses (and long phrases).
  Restrictive and nonrestrictive adjectival clauses.

2. TEACHING STYLE THROUGH SENTENCE COMBINING AND SENTENCE GENERATING

Objectives
- To help students combine sentences.
  Coordinating clauses and phrases.
  Subordinating some elements to others.
  Reducing clauses to phrases.
- To help students expand their syntactic repertoire in order to write more syntactically sophisticated and rhetorically effective sentences.
  Using free modifiers (especially appositives, participial phrases, and absolutes).
  Using structures particularly associated with exposition and argumentation, such as qualifying clauses and phrases.

FIGURE 5.13, continued.

3. TEACHING SENTENCE SENSE AND STYLE THROUGH THE MANIPULATION OF SYNTACTIC ELEMENTS

Objectives
- To help students learn techniques to arrange and rearrange sentence elements for readability and effectiveness.
    Moving adverbial free modifiers.
    Using parallel grammatical elements when appropriate.
    Putting free modifiers after a clause or before it, rather than between the subject and verb.
    Eliminating dangling modifiers by moving or reconstructing them.
    Experimenting with *wh* word, *it*, and *there* transforms of basic sentence structures.
    Understanding the relative advantages of the active and passive voices and being able to use both.

4. TEACHING THE POWER OF DIALECTS AND DIALECTS OF POWER

Objectives
- To help students gain an appreciation for various community and ethnic dialects, through literature, film, and oral discourse.
- To help students understand grammatical differences between these dialect forms and the Language of Wider Communication.
- To help students determine which dialects are most appropriate in what kinds of situations (perhaps through inquiry and investigation of their own).
- To help students use, as desired, the forms of various dialects (e.g. for literary effect and rhetorical purposes).
- To help students edit their writing for the grammatical forms and word usages that characterize Edited American English (e.g., EAE subject-verb agreement, negation, pronoun use, and verb forms and use).
- To help students edit for basic usage distinctions (e.g., *it's* versus *its*, *their* versus *they're* and *there*, *your* versus *you're*).
- To help students edit for the grammatical forms and usages that differentiate the language of privilege and prestige (cultivated English) from the general English used in daily speech and writing by most people comfortable with the Language of Wider Communication.
    Editing for the finer points of subject-verb agreement, pronoun-antecedent agreement, and other issues of pronoun use.
    Editing for at least the more basic forms and usages that differentiate the English of prestige from general English (e.g., some of the distinctions listed in glossaries of usage).

5. TEACHING PUNCTUATION AND MECHANICS FOR CONVENTION, CLARITY, AND STYLE

Objectives
- To help students edit for appropriateness the relevant aspects of punctuation that are not associated with the grammatical elements in the other categories.
  Period, question mark, and exclamation mark.
  Quotation marks.
  Comma.
  Semicolon.
  Colon.
  Apostrophe in possessives.
  Other aspects of punctuation and mechanics, such as parentheses and dashes.
- To help students learn to use various aspects of punctuation not only for conventional correctness but for clarity and stylistic effectiveness.
- To help students to capitalize proper nouns used in their writings and to avoid capitalizing other nouns.

them reconsider their writing, revise for content and organization, revise again for sentence structure effectiveness, and finally help them edit and proofread their writing for publication or formal sharing of some sort. At levels where students have separate classes in different subjects, writing across the curriculum may require collaboration among teachers, but the results are well worth the effort.

2. *Immerse students in good literature, including literature that is particularly interesting or challenging syntactically.* Reading and even listening to well-written literature will promote the acquisition of syntactic structures, for speaking and writing, by both native and non-native speakers of English.

3. *Across the grades, reserve a thorough study of grammar for elective courses or perhaps units.* Teach to all students only those aspects of grammar that can help them write more effectively.

4. *Teach these relevant aspects of grammar within the context of students' writing.*

5. *Introduce only a minimum of terminology,* much of which can be learned sufficiently just through incidental exposure—for example, as we discuss selected words and structures in the context of literature and writing. For many grammatical terms, receptive competence is all that's needed; that is,

students need to understand what the teacher is referring to, but they do not always need enough command of the terms to use such terms themselves.

6. *Specifically, emphasize (as appropriate to writers' needs) those aspects of grammar that are particularly useful in helping students revise sentences to make them more effective.* These syntactic structures and revision techniques can be taught by example, with terminology used incidentally. Such teaching might include: (1) how to use "new" kinds of syntactic structures that the students haven't noticed before; (2) how to reorder and otherwise manipulate sentence elements; (3) how to expand and combine sentences. Teaching such concepts within the context of writing can help students develop more effective writing styles.

7. *Also emphasize (as appropriate to writers' needs) those aspects of grammar that are particularly useful in helping students edit sentences for conventional mechanics and appropriateness.* Such teaching might include: (1) concepts like subject, verb, and predicate; clause and phrase; grammatical sentences versus run-ons and fragments; (2) usage; (3) grammatical features that differ among the Language of Wider Communication and other dialects.

8. *Teach needed terms, structures, and skills when writers need them, ideally when they are ready to revise at the sentence level or to edit.* Structures and skills that are first practiced during revision and editing may later become sufficiently internalized that they are incorporated into drafting, but at first it is easiest and most effective to deal with them only after a draft has been written and revised for content and organization.

9. *Explore the grammatical patterns of ethnic and community dialects—through literature, film, and audiotapes, for example—and contrast these with the corresponding features of the Language of Wider Communication.* Students can make such comparisons by translating a well-known or well-liked text into a particular dialect or by writing original poems, stories, and plays in one or more ethnic and community dialects as well as in the Language of Wider Communication. Such language study and writing can help students appreciate each others' dialects as well as consider which dialects are most appropriate for what kinds of writing and under what circumstances.

10. *Offer elective courses, units, or activities that allow students to discover the pleasure of investigating questions and making discoveries about language.* A discovery approach to grammar and language will not necessarily involve learning the grammatical elements and structures from A to Z, but it can

involve investigating selected aspects of grammar for the sheer joy of discovering generalizations, appreciating ambiguity, unlocking the mysteries of syntactically challenging poetry and prose, and understanding and employing syntactic alternatives for different rhetorical effects.

11. *If you teach grammar as inquiry, draw not only upon traditional grammar but upon insights from structural, transformational, and functional linguistics.* Such teaching may involve helping students choose, develop, and collaboratively investigate some questions and problems that will lead them to discover for themselves some of the insights provided by different theoretical approaches to grammar study.

12. *Become a teacher-researcher to determine the effects of your teaching of selected aspects of grammar or your students' study of grammar as an object of inquiry and discovery.* For example: Are students better able to revise their sentences for greater effectiveness? Better able to edit? More versatile in their use of syntactic alternatives or language variants, such as ethnic and community dialects and the Language of Wider Communication? Better able to explain similarities and differences in grammatical patterns? More interested in revising and editing their writing, or in studying language? Such questions can be investigated by collecting pre-teaching data and, later in the year, comparing such data with data gathered under comparable circumstances. Other questions can be investigated by comparing your data with data from comparable students in classrooms where the teacher uses a different approach. For example: Are your students more or less competent in revising sentences and in editing than are peers in other classes who have simply studied traditional grammar but not had teacher and peer help with revising and editing? Are your students more or less competent in revising and editing than are peers in other classes who have written a lot but not had teacher and peer help in revising and editing? Are any differences in revision and editing skills (or students' growth therein) also reflected in differences in the sections of standardized tests that deal with grammar, punctuation, and usage? In standardized or state-mandated assessment of reading and writing?

As discussed further in Chapter 6, learning seems to be most enduring when the learners perceive it as useful or interesting to them personally, in the here and now. Therefore, the twelve suggested guidelines reflect such principles as the following: (1) Teach selected aspects of grammar as they become useful in the context of what the students are trying to do (write, disentangle the syntax of literature); (2) encourage syntactic experimentation and risk taking in writing, even though it leads to error, because risk taking and error are necessary for growth; (3) encourage students to consider and appreciate the alternatives, ambiguities, and nuances in grammar, instead of insisting that there is always one right answer to questions regarding grammar; and (4) create a community of language researchers in your classroom, wherein inquiry and investigation become goals for you and the students as well.

6

Learning Theory and the Teaching of Grammar

It is generally agreed that writers need strategies for revising sentences and making them more effective, as well as skills for editing their sentences for grammar, punctuation, and usage.

The traditional approach has been to teach concepts and skills from a grammar handbook or language arts series, where the primary method of teaching has been to assign grammar, revision, and editing exercises and to give tests on the material. This reflects a transmission model of education, based upon principles from behavioral psychology. Figure 6.1 lists some key principles of behavioral psychology and the transmission model, contrasted with key principles of cognitive psychology and a transactional model of learning. Considering learning to be primarily a matter of correct habit formation, the behavioralists of the 1920s suggested principles of lesson and curriculum development that continue to underly most instructional materials and programs to the present day. According to such principles, learning is best fostered through practice and more practice, preferably in a situation where it is virtually impossible to make errors and thus develop bad habits.

A contrasting view of learning derives from cognitive learning theory and concept learning research. This view is often referred to as constructivist.

In their outstanding article "Explaining Grammatical Concepts," Harris and Rowan (1989) point out that practice, practice, and more practice usually does not promote adequate understanding (see also Kagan, 1980). For example, being able to identify sentence fragments in an exercise written specifically for that purpose does not guarantee that the student knows the critical features of fragments in contrast to grammatically complete sentences, much less that the student can reliably distinguish between

FIGURE 6.1   Ends of a transmission-to-transactional continuum (Weaver, 1994).

TRANSMISSION	TRANSACTIONAL
Reductionist	Constructivist
Behaviorial psychology	Cognitive psychology
Habit formation	Hypothesis formation
Avoiding mistakes prevents formation of bad habits	Errors necessary for encouraging more sophisticated hypotheses
Students passively practice skills, memorize facts	Students actively pursue learning and construct knowledge
Teacher dispenses prepackaged, predetermined curriculum	Teacher develops and negotiates curriculum with students
Direct teaching of curriculum	Responsive teaching to meet students' needs and interests
Taskmaster, with emphasis on cycle of teach, practice/apply/memorize, test	Master craftsperson, mentor: emphasis on demonstrating, inviting, discussing, affirming, facilitating, collaborating, observing, supporting
Lessons taught, practiced or applied, then tested	Mini-lessons taught as demonstration, invitation; adding an idea to the class pot
Performance on decontextualized tests is taken as measure of learning of limited information	Assessment from a variety of contextualized learning experiences captures diverse aspects of learning
Learning is expected to be uniform, same for everyone; uniform means of assessment guarantee that many will fail, in significant ways	Learning is expected to be individual, different for everyone; flexible and multiple means of assessment guarantee all will succeed, in differing ways
Adds up to a failure-oriented model, ferreting out students' weaknesses and preparing them to take their place in a stratified society	Adds up to a success-oriented model, emphasizing students' strengths and preparing them to be the best they can be in a stratified society

the two. Those of us who have tried to teach grammar scarcely need to be told this, but personally I find it comforting to read research that validates my own experiences as a teacher. To me it seems quite clear that our traditional methods of teaching grammatical concepts are totally inadequate, and that underlying the inadequate methodology is an equally inadequate, inaccurate learning theory.

Let us approach an understanding of a more adequate cognitive/constructivist learning theory through the concept of mini-lessons that reflect that theory.

Teaching Grammar via Mini-lessons

A major thesis of this book is that one of the best ways to teach the grammatical concepts needed for sentence revision and editing may be through mini-lessons based upon cognitive and constructivist principles of learning.

This concept of mini-lessons was introduced to writing teachers in 1986 by Lucy Calkins in *The Art of Teaching Writing* and further elaborated by Nancie Atwell in *In the Middle: Writing, Reading and Learning with Adolescents* (1987). Basically, a mini-lesson is a brief explanation of something that may be helpful to students. Thus Atwell found herself teaching mini-lessons not only on various aspects of the writer's craft but also on classroom routines and management.

As developed by Calkins and Atwell, mini-lessons have several noteworthy characteristics:

1. They are brief, as the term *mini* would suggest. Typically they take no more than five to ten minutes.

2. The teacher explains directly, often without much if any overt interaction with the students. The teacher is simply offering "tips" that he or she thinks will be valuable to students.

3. Mini-lessons can be presented to the whole class when the teacher has reason to believe that several students might profit from the lesson. For instance, if several students are using dialogue but not quotation marks, this may prompt the teacher to offer a mini-lesson on the basics of enclosing in quotation marks whatever the speaker has said. When these basics have

been mastered by several students, the teacher can teach them additional mini-lessons on the finer points of punctuating direct quotes.

4. When a mini-lesson is presented to the whole class, the teacher does not assume that everyone will or should learn and immediately be able to apply what has been taught; the ideas are simply added "to the class pot," as Calkins (1986) puts it. The teacher knows that he or she will still have to help individual students apply what has been taught, to encourage students to help each other apply it, and possibly to teach similar mini-lessons to the whole class or small groups again, as more students demonstrate a need for the lesson through their writing.

5. Mini-lessons may be taught to the whole class (as explained above), to small groups, or to individuals in one-on-one conferences. Usually mini-lessons are not taught to the whole class unless the teacher has reason to believe that several students might profit immediately.

6. A key feature of mini-lessons is that students are not given follow-up exercises to practice what has been taught. The teacher simply helps them use the information if their writing suggests a need for the skill and they seem ready for it.

7. Both need and readiness are important. For instance, a writer may be presenting a speaker's exact words without using quotation marks, but if the writer is far from having mastered the conventional use of periods at the ends of sentences, the teacher should realize that the student may not yet be ready to deal with quotation marks.

8. In other words, teachers must be "kidwatchers" (Y. Goodman, 1978) in order to decide when to teach mini-lessons.

Many of these principles are captured in Figure 6.1 as aspects of an active, transactional model of learning and teaching.

More on the Different Learning Theories

The learning theory that underlies the concept of mini-lessons differs greatly from the learning theory that underlies other popular and traditional ways of teaching, such as Madeline Hunter's (1982) Instructional Theory into Practice (ITIP). What underlies traditional instruction, with its linear sequence of predetermined and prepackaged lessons, is the tenets of behavioral psychology. The behaviorialism that still permeates education today can be traced to Edward Thorndike in the 1920s. Thorndike derived the following "laws of learning" from behavioral psychologists and his own laboratory experiments with animals (as explained in K. S. Goodman et al., 1988, pp. 11–13).

Behavioral Principles of Learning

- *Law of Readiness: Learning is ordered; efficient learning follows one best sequence.* This law results in readiness materials (e.g., practice in letter formation) and in the tight sequencing of writing skills that teachers teach and learners are expected to master.
- *Law of Exercise: Practice strengthens the bond between a stimulus and a response.* This law results in drills and exercises: on the chalkboard, in workbooks, and on skill sheets. Today, the popularity of cooperative learning (Johnson and Johnson, 1985) has often resulted in students doing together the same kinds of exercises they would formerly have done by themselves. (Often, the underlying learning theory has not changed much.)
- *Law of Effect: Rewards influence the stimulus-response connection.* This law provides justification for first teaching simple writing skills (e.g., letter formation, spelling, punctuation) and then "rewarding" the learner, perhaps months or years later, by allowing the learner to compose simple texts reflecting those skills.
- *Law of Identical Elements: The learning of a particular stimulus-response connection should be tested separately and under the same conditions in which it was learned.* This law results in the focus on testing isolated skills via test questions that resemble the practice materials the students have completed.

In the 1950 *Encyclopedia of Educational Research*, H. A. Greene applies key behavioral principles to grammar instruction. He emphasizes "properly motivated drill" and habit formation: "Correct language habits are developed in accordance with the general laws of learning. The effective learning situation in language is one in which the individual is able repeatedly to produce the correct response under pleasantly motivated conditions" (p. 391). Interestingly, however, he also notes that "only a relatively small proportion of English skills is developed in the classroom" and that most students fail to transfer such skills to situations where they are needed (p. 391). He also concludes from his survey of the research that there seems to be little practical value in teaching grammar in isolation. Nevertheless, so strong was the behavioral orientation in his time that Greene seems to have taken behavioral principles and teaching methods for granted and not to have considered whether these might be less than optimal in getting students to learn and apply grammatical principles.

Today, such behavioral "laws of learning" can be found embodied in instructional procedures like Madeline Hunter's Instructional Theory into Practice. They also form the backbone of the typical instructional program, which is sequenced according to the publisher's preconceptions of what should be taught and learned, and in what order.

Cognitive/Constructivist Principles of Learning

From the cognitive (and humanistic) psychology of the last several decades, many educators have come to understand learning quite differently. They may have read books like Renate and Geoffrey Caine's *Making Connections: Teaching and the Human Brain* (1994), Frank Smith's *Comprehension and Learning: A Conceptual Framework for Teachers* (1975), or his *To Think* (1990). But even if they have not read such professional literature, they know from their own experience that they have very quickly forgotten information that was merely memorized for a test. They may have found, too, that they or their fellow learners have often not applied skills that were taught, practiced, and tested in isolation. By reflecting on their own experience, they recognize the validity of what cognitive psychologists have discovered about the learning of complex concepts, strategies, and processes. Some key insights are summarized here, as cognitive and constructivist principles of learning.

1. Learning involves not the mastery of isolated facts, but the construction of concepts. If the learner cannot or does not organize facts into concepts, they are quickly forgotten (e.g., Smith, 1975, 1990).

2. The learning of concepts is a complex process. It involves clarifying all the critical features of a concept and distinguishing these from variable or nondistinguishing features, in order to differentiate apparent from real instances of a concept (Harris and Rowan, 1989). A simple example of this complexity would be children's learning what features critically differentiate dogs from cats and other animals—that is, learning to correctly differentiate dogs from not-dogs. Only when learners can differentiate X from not-X do

they really understand the concept of X, whatever it may be. Thus only when learners can accurately distinguish sentences from not-sentences do they accurately understand the concept of a grammatical sentence.

3. Learning is by no means ordered or linear, even though the teaching may have been. Rather, learning—that which endures—is idiosyncratic, nonlinear, even chaotic, in the sense of chaos theory (Taylor, 1989).

4. Learning is idiosyncratic because learners must construct concepts for themselves. In doing so, they continually formulate hypotheses, test these hypotheses against feedback and other new input, and revise their hypotheses accordingly. This process occurs with such "simple" learning as what a dog is (in contrast, say, to a cat or a cow) and such complex processes as formulating new mathematical theorems or scientific paradigms (F. Smith, 1975, 1990).

5. Learning proceeds best when learners find the learning personally meaningful in the here and now, when they have the sense that "I can do this," and when they know they can experiment, take risks, and learn without negative consequences like punitive correction or criticism, or denigrating or downgrading of their efforts because of imperfect mastery of whatever they are trying to learn or do (Cambourne, 1988).

6. Learning proceeds best when it is relatively "natural." For instance, when people *want* to learn to do something outside of school, they commonly observe others do it, try it with the guidance of those already skilled, practice independently, and then celebrate their mastery by voluntarily demonstrating their skill to others (Holdaway, 1986). Everyday examples include learning to walk, to swim, to cook, to build or make something, to play computer games, and to drive a car.

7. Learning typically proceeds best from whole to part, for young learners. As they mature, some individuals will develop the ability to learn from part to whole, in a more linear and analytical fashion. However, many learners remain more holistic or global, most readily learning the parts of something within the context of the whole (Dunn and Dunn, 1978).

8. Learning proceeds best when others provide the kinds of support that adults typically provide for young children—for example, in acquiring their native language. This includes expecting learners to succeed eventually, and treating them accordingly; recognizing that adult mastery will develop gradually as well as idiosyncratically, over several years; expecting closer

and closer approximations to adult mastery, not perfection; responding positively to whatever the learner *can* do, rather than emphasizing what the learner cannot yet do; providing scaffolding (teacher or peer collaboration) for the learner, so that the individual learner can succeed in doing things that he or she would not yet be able to do alone (Vygotsky, 1978, 1986; Ninio and Bruner, 1978; Bruner, 1983, 1986; see, for instance, Weaver, 1994, ch. 3).

9. Much learning occurs through the observation and osmosis that are facilitated by indirect instruction, such as the natural demonstrations that others provide when they simply do what the learner would like to learn to do. Learning can also be facilitated by direct instruction. However, direct instruction typically has the most permanent effect when provided in the context of the whole activity that the learner is attempting, whether that whole be using a cookbook, building a tree house, reading a book, or writing something to share with others. In other words, direct instruction is most effective when offered within the context of the learner's interest and need.

While these principles do not correspond point-for-point to the behavioral laws of learning articulated by Thorndike, many contrasts should be apparent. Perhaps the greatest difference begins with the behavioral assumption that if only the teacher teaches something well, the student will—or should—learn it. Certainly effective teaching can help (teaching based upon an understanding of how concepts are formed, for instance). However, educators grounded in cognitive psychology have concluded that teaching does not equal learning; that is, that learning is not simply a direct reflection of teaching (e.g., Emig, 1983). If or when learning occurs, it happens because the learner has constructed concepts and knowledge for him- or herself, as a result of (or perhaps despite) the teaching. This constructivist view of learning underlies recent efforts at curriculum reform in virtually every discipline, including the English language arts, mathematics, science, social studies, and even health education.

These two contrasting views or models of learning are often called contrasting *paradigms*. A paradigm is an agreed-upon set of operating assumptions that guides people's actions, but often unconsciously. For example, teachers have for decades used instructional programs that reflect a behavioral paradigm, but they are often unaware of doing so. Change becomes possible when the unconscious set of operating assumptions is articulated and examined, as we are doing here.

Mini-Lessons as a Reflection of the Cognitive/Constructivist Paradigm

To further clarify how mini-lessons in the tradition of Atwell and Calkins differ from traditional lessons inspired by behavioral psychology, let us consider the following graphic representations of Madeline Hunter's ITIP procedures (1982) compared with the concept of mini-lessons as explained by Atwell (1987) and Calkins (1986):

ITIP	MINI-LESSONS
1. Anticipatory set and statement of objectives (objectives may be determined by prepackaged curriculum)	1. Objectives phrased in terms of sharing helpful hints or ideas (typically, the teacher determines the need for the mini-lesson by observing students' work)
2. Instruction and modeling	2. Demonstrations and explanations
3. Checking understanding	3. Guided application
4. Guided practice	4. Assessment through further observation
5. Independent practice	5. Independent application
6. Assessment	6. Further assessment through observation

In an ITIP-inspired skills approach, students are required to practice and be tested on skills in isolation; it seems simply to be taken for granted that the skills will transfer, that they will be applied when relevant. A mini-lesson approach makes no such assumption. Therefore, all the time spent practicing and being tested on skills in isolation is used instead for actual writing, revising, and editing. Mini-lessons are followed not by isolated practice and testing, but by teacher and peer assistance in applying the lesson taught. With writing, for example, students are guided in applying the concept or skill when, and only when, their own writing suggests a need and readiness. They do not do practice exercises—not even exercises dealing with pieces of writing. *Neither do they write to fulfill a writing assignment that the teacher has devised in order to provide practice in what he or she has just taught.* If students' writing suggests no need for the skill at the present time, then the teacher does not expect students to learn it. Instead, the teacher expects to help students add the new strategies to their repertoire as writers when the writers themselves are ready to construct and apply this new knowledge. Of course the teacher may nudge the students toward readiness through various kinds of mini-lessons, including those that spontaneously occur during individual conferences. And of course it may take several mini-lessons, perhaps taught in different ways, for learners to construct the concepts being introduced.

In summary, skills lessons along the lines of the ITIP model differ significantly from the kind of mini-lessons advocated by Atwell (1987) and Calkins (1986), because the former reflect behavioral principles of learning and the latter reflect cognitive principles and a constructivist paradigm of learning.

Toward a Constructivist Model of Learning and Teaching

For those to whom the cognitive principles and constructivist paradigm of learning make sense, it may be useful to have a model against which to measure one's teaching efforts. The model offered here draws heavily upon language acquisition research, the research and theory of psychologists Lev Vygotsky (1978, 1986) and Jerome Bruner (Ninio and Bruner, 1978; Bruner, 1983, 1986), and the work of such researchers and theorists as Brian Cambourne (1988), Frank Smith (1981a, 1981b, 1990), Don Holdaway (1986), Stephen Krashen (1981, 1985), Carole Edelsky (Edelsky and Draper, 1989), Bess Altwerger (1991), and others. What is new here is the way various concepts are integrated into a model (see Figure 6.2).

To the left in the outer circle are key words indicating what teachers try to provide for students when the teachers are convinced that learning is basically constructive rather than a matter of habit formation. To the right in the outer circle are key words for characteristics of the psychological experiences and state of the learner that promote learning and may even be critical for genuine learning to take place. Obviously what the teacher does is related to how the learner feels, but there is no simple one-to-one correspondence between factors. Rather, these various factors interact in multiple and complex ways, providing optimal conditions for learning.

In classrooms guided by a constructivist theory of learning, here are some of the things teachers do:

1. They provide *demonstrations* from which students can learn. For example, they may model a reading strategy that has helped them unlock a particular word, a strategy for marking parts of their writing for later reconsideration,

FIGURE 6.2   A constructivist model of learning and teaching.

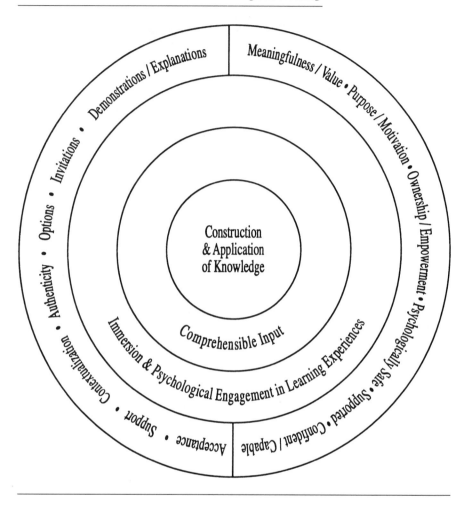

a research technique they use, a way of conducting a science experiment or figuring out a math problem. In other words, they show students some way of doing something, based upon their own experiences. Demonstrating to students how they themselves function as learners is a powerful way for teachers to affect students' learning. It helps students see the *value* of what they are being taught and *motivates* them to do likewise. Other kinds of *explanations* can likewise be important, though the constructivist teacher recognizes that teaching does not automatically equate with learning. Explanations are valuable insofar as they give learners the information they need to construct concepts for themselves, but what one student will need or be ready for is not the same as what another student will need or be ready for. Thus explanations can provide comprehensible input, but learning will not necessarily take place unless the learner is in some sense motivated to learn.

2. Teachers offer *invitations* to students: invitations to try what the teacher has demonstrated or explained or shared, for instance. Often, teachers' invitations may include the suggestion that students "try this and report back to the rest of us," or something of the sort. Teachers may also invite students to work on something together.

3. The term *invitations* obviously implies that one has a choice about the matter—and in constructivist classrooms, students do. In order to facilitate choice and decision making, teachers will offer students *options:* the option to choose what they want to read, write, or research, for example; or perhaps the option of working on one's writing, reading a book, discovering science concepts through investigation, working on or creating their own math problems, or engaging in some kind of art activity.

In classes dealing with a single content area, the choices will be narrower, of course, but even within a particular discipline, students can still be given significant options of what to read, write about, and research. Some of the decision making may be collaborative, too. For instance, in a high school literature class where the English department requires use of a certain anthology, the teacher might ask different groups of students to read a certain section of the text and decide which selections the whole class will read; alternatively, each student or group of students might decide what they will read within a given section, or which sections they will read. Such management decisions on the part of the teacher obviously require nontraditional means of accountability and assessment, but offering students the opportunity to make choices encourages them to find *meaningfulness* and *value* in what they are doing, to establish their own *purposes* and *motivation* for what they are doing, and to feel a sense of *ownership* and *empowerment.*

4. Constructivist teachers know that it is important for the options they offer to be genuine learning experiences that at least resemble the kinds of experiences from which students learn outside of school, in the natural give-and-take of growing and playing and investigating things of interest. Offering students a choice of one worksheet or another does not empower them; offering them the option of choosing what book to read does. Thus

authenticity is important for generating motivation, purpose, and the other characteristics mentioned under options. Allowing significant choices helps guarantee that the learner will perceive the self-chosen learning experience as authentic.

5. Teachers help students learn needed skills and strategies in the context of authentic learning experiences. For example, they demonstrate and explain reading strategies when students need them to deal with words and texts; they teach various kinds of writing and editing skills when students need them to strengthen their writing; and similarly, they teach research, experimentation, and problem-solving skills as students need them for investigating various topics and problems across the curriculum. In other words, authenticity and the *contextualization* of skills go hand-in-hand and have some of the same benefits in terms of students' response.

6. The teacher provides *support* for the learners, collectively and individually. One critical kind of support is a classroom community wherein students are encouraged to value each other and to work cooperatively and collaboratively. This includes not only working together on projects but simply helping each other—by showing someone how to "get" a problem word in reading, by listening to or reading a classmate's writing and offering suggestions, by helping a friend figure out how to approach a math problem or science experiment. In such a setting, both classmates and the teacher provide what Bruner (Ninio and Bruner, 1978; Bruner, 1983, 1986) calls *scaffolding* for learning: a temporary support. Working together, students can often accomplish tasks that none of them could do alone, or do as well alone. The teacher may serve as collaborator too, providing additional scaffolding for learning. Such support enables students to work in what Vygotsky (1978, 1986) calls the "zone of proximal development": to work at things that are just a little beyond what the learner could manage alone. Paradoxically, collaboration between and among teacher and students seems to be the best way to help the most students become competent and independent learners. Of course, such collaboration and scaffolding helps learners to feel *supported* in their learning.

7. Teacher *acceptance* of learners is critical. In this context, however, acceptance means more than simply accepting the learner as a unique person and treating the learner accordingly. It also means recognizing that the construction of knowledge takes a great deal of time (months and years); that

errors are a necessary concomitant of learning; that learning proceeds from the whole (an intent to mean or do) to gradual mastery of the parts (the needed skills and strategies); and that it is realistic to expect only increasingly closer approximations of adult norms, not instant perfection. As used here, *acceptance* means accepting errors as necessary to growth and even celebrating new kinds of errors that indicate progress; that is, acceptance means recognizing and rewarding successive approximations. It means responding positively to learners' best efforts, even when these efforts are less than fully successful. It means helping learners achieve goals by providing appropriate support, rather than judging them inadequate because they cannot yet achieve these goals alone. Clearly such multifaceted acceptance is critical in helping students feel that they can try new things without risking negative response and repercussions; it enables the learner to feel *psychologically safe*. Given psychological safety and the sense of being *supported* as a learner, the student is more likely to feel *confident* that he or she is *capable* of engaging successfully in the learning experiences offered. And this in turn promotes *motivation, empowerment,* and other associated characteristics that are critical for learning.

Returning to Figure 6.2, we need only point out the relationship between the outer circle and the inner circles. The implication of the outer circle is that learning proceeds best when students see meaningfulness and value in what they are doing and are sufficiently motivated to develop their own purposes and agendas for learning; when they feel safe in taking risks because they know they will not be criticized or penalized if their efforts are less than fully successful; and when they feel supported in their learning and confident that they are capable of doing and succeeding at whatever they are attempting. In addition, the outer circle implies that teachers can promote these characteristics by offering demonstrations and explanations, invitations, and options; by offering learning experiences that will likely seem authentic to the students; by helping students learn needed skills in the context of their use; by providing support of various kinds; and by accepting and applauding students' efforts at learning.

The outer circle, then, may be viewed as conditions conducive to *immersion* and *psychological engagement* in learning—an emotional commitment to what one is doing, rather than the unthinking completion of tasks one finds meaningless or boring. The act of being engaged in learning experiences will itself provide *comprehensible input* for the learner. Together, engagement in learning and the availability of comprehensible input provide conditions for the *construction and the application of knowledge*.

Constructivism Contrasted with Behavioralism

The notion that psychologically engaged learners construct knowledge themselves from comprehensible input is vastly different from the behavioralists' notion that learning consists of habit formation. Thus the cornerstones of behavioralism and constructivism differ sharply.

Superficially, though, some of the more extreme examples of behavioral instruction have some key characteristics in common with constructivist teaching, as well as some key differences. For example, teachers using Direct Instruction materials from SRA publishing company (programs such as *Reading Mastery: DISTAR* and *DISTAR Language*) may support students' learning more than teachers traditionally have done, but they do so by (1) reducing learning to bits and pieces of language and concepts; (2) engaging students in "repeat-after-me" kinds of drills; and (3) testing the students on the same kinds of activities they have been doing. With such support, in a psychologically safe environment, many students who have done poorly in traditional classrooms feel more capable of accomplishing the expected, and they do succeed—but succeed at *what*? They are not engaging in the kinds of reading, writing, and researching that best facilitate concept formation and independence in learning.

The kind of support provided in constructivist classrooms is very different. Teachers help learners do things they cannot already do, and in this process the students eventually learn how to do them independently. Examples might include how to choose a book, how to write a letter to the editor, how to locate resources and information on a topic of interest, and how to introduce and reference quotations taken from published sources. Skills are taught in the context of their use (contextualization) and mastered gradually, while students engage in authentic learning experiences that, frequently, they themselves have chosen. With processes like reading and writing, the teacher aims for fluency first, then clarity, and finally correctness, following the natural sequence in which children develop the ability to read and write (Mayher, Lester, and Pradl, 1983; Mayher, 1990). Furthermore, the teacher facilitates learning and collaborates with the learners, instead of dispensing information and testing students on it. Therefore, learners are more likely to see meaningfulness and value in what

FIGURE 6.3   References on whole language as constructivist learning and teaching.

UNDERSTANDING WHOLE LANGUAGE AS CONSTRUCTIVIST THEORY
Fulwiler, L. (1992). The constructivist culture of language-centered classrooms.
    In C. Weaver & L. Henke (Eds.), *Supporting whole language: Stories of teacher
    and institutional change*. Portsmouth, NH: Heinemann.
Goodman, K. S. (1986). *What's whole in whole language?* Richmond Hill,
    Ontario: Scholastic. Distributed in the United States by Heinemann.
Lester, L. (1991). *Learning with Zachary*. Richmond Hill, Ontario: Scholastic.
Weaver, C. (1990). *Understanding whole language*. Portsmouth, NH: Heinemann.

EXPLORING WHOLE LANGUAGE AS CONSTRUCTIVIST CURRICULUM
Foster, H. M. (1994). *Crossing over: Whole language for secondary English teachers*.
    Orlando, FL: Harcourt Brace Jovanovich.
Manning, M., Manning, G., & Long R. (1994). *Theme immersion: Inquiry-based
    curriculum in elementary and middle schools*. Portsmouth, NH: Heinemann.
Routman, R. (1991). *Invitations: Changing as teachers and learners K–12*.
    Portsmouth, NH: Heinemann.
Strickland, K., & Strickland, J. (1993). *UN-covering the curriculum: Whole
    language in secondary and postsecondary classrooms*. Portsmouth, NH:
    Boynton/Cook.

they do, to have motivation and purpose for their activities, and to experience ownership and empowerment as learners. These characteristics are vastly different from those experienced by most learners when instruction is guided by behavioral principles and methods.

In literacy education, this constructivist paradigm of learning has become a cornerstone of what is known as whole language education. Figure 6.3 provides some references for better understanding whole language theory and practice. The references on the teaching of writing (Figure 4.14) also help clarify whole language practices. As a 1992 article by Laura Fulwiler suggests (see Figure 6.3), whole language learning theory is relevant all across the curriculum because it is essentially a constructivist theory of learning.

An Invitation

Considering a particular example can be an excellent way of testing one's understanding and critiquing—even challenging—the concepts presented. You may find it worthwhile, then, to consider in what ways the sequence of mini-lessons described by Doris Master (1977) reflects the constructivist model, and in what ways it does not. Reflecting upon the model itself as well as upon this sequence of lessons, you may wish to consider whether the sequence is or is not likely to be more effective if more of this model's "conditions for learning" are met.

Master used this step-by-step procedure to teach the use of quotation marks to a group of self-selected children who had already attempted to use quotation marks in their writing, and who were already writing complete sentences fluently. She invited them to join a "Quotation Mark Seminar" wherein they carried out the following steps (paraphrased from her article "Build a Skill, Step by Step," 1977):

1. First, they discussed comic strips and how the author and artist used balloons to indicate the exact words of a character. The children agreed that this was not a feasible way to indicate a character's words in a story. This conclusion gave Master the opportunity to explain how punctuation marks are used in direct quotations.
2. The group made up "funny or exciting statements for the cartoon characters on the board" and then punctuated them together.
3. The students were assigned the task of finding a three-frame comic strip, pasting it on paper, and rewriting the conversation using quotation marks.
4. The following day, Master assigned some pages from an English textbook dealing with direct and indirect quotations. The group discussed these pages, then completed and corrected the exercises.
5. Next, the children were directed to their writing folders to find a piece of writing that contained conversation, then to rewrite it with correct punctuation of the direct quotes. They were encouraged to use dialogue from their classmates' writing if their own writing did not contain dialogue.
6. The next step involved writing a dialogue between characters in one of the pictures Master showed the children. Of course, they were to try to punctuate the dialogue correctly.
7. Later, Master made up a progress report (instead of a report card) for a fictional character, Marvin Termite; the progress report contained poor grades and comments. The children were asked to write the conversation between Marvin and his mother about the progress report and, of course, to punctuate the dialogue correctly.
8. Children who still needed more practice were asked to write a conversation that might have taken place between Marvin's mother

and his teacher, as well as a conversation between Marvin's parents about the progress report.

After describing this sequence of activities, Master comments: "I hope that after the completion of this series of structured exercises, the children's writing will contain more examples of dialogue correctly paragraphed and punctuated. Evaluation of the efficiency of the instruction will be made by the presence and use of punctuation marks in the children's free writing. Should some children still demonstrate the need for further instruction, additional exercises could be designed" (p. 92).

Mini-Lessons and Other Constructivist Teaching Strategies

Master's step-by-step sequence for teaching the use of quotation marks is anything but a mini-lesson, yet it does seem to reflect some principles of cognitive learning theory, with its emphasis on active construction of concepts.

First of all, Master worked with *self-selected* students who were already using dialogue in their writing and experimenting with quotation marks. Thus, the situation met the conditions of need and motivation.

Second, Master engineered a situation in which the children themselves would conclude that something other than dialogue balloons is needed to show, in writing, the actual words of a speaker. (Of course, this step may have been unnecessary, since the children were already experimenting with quotation marks.)

Third, she did not test the students on quotation marks in isolation from real writing (though indeed some of the activities may seem rather artificial). She went from teaching the concepts to application, however artificial the application activities may seem.

From a constructivist point of view, though, we might ask, "Wasn't there way too much practice in artificial activities apart from the children's editing of their own writing?" Obviously Master was trying, through such practice, to increase the students' understanding of the concepts she had taught, and to ensure that they could apply the concepts. Was the amount of practice too much, too little, or perhaps just right?

Teachers newly introduced to the concept of the mini-lesson often find it difficult to even understand how you could teach something and expect that at least some students will have partially learned it, unless they practice

FIGURE 6.4 Brainstorming/clustering and subsequent writing in a "Show, don't tell" lesson.

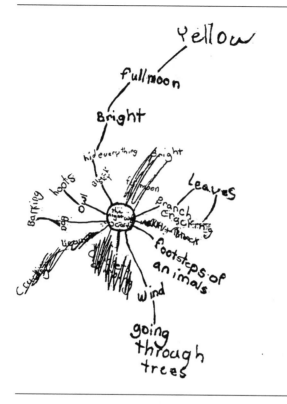

the skill under the teacher's guidance and correction. And indeed, such expanded or extended mini-lessons may be valuable, particularly for learning grammatical concepts that are relatively difficult to grasp. Thus the Appendix of this book includes four major kinds of lessons, each reflecting—in some way, and to greater or lesser degree—a constructivist view of learning. Often, these kinds of lessons are intermingled, so that I have made no attempt to identify them in the Appendix itself. But for clarification, here are what I see as the four major kinds of lessons.

Incidental Lessons

The teacher teaches something through conversation and casual mention: that is, through exposure more than through direct instruction. For example, in helping students brainstorm for words to describe something, the teacher can casually ask for words and phrases to identify "this naming word, this noun." The describers can be referred to as "adjective" words and

FIGURE 6.4, continued.

Show- Not Tell

Name Amy

Tell: The night was scary!

Show: I walked outside of the house
it was pitch black and the
only thing you could see is the
bright yellow full moon above you
I felt the wind going through the
trees like ice cream melting in the
summer. Then I stepped on a branch
and fell into a crunchy pile of le
that sounded like someone eatting
chips. I herd the dog barking
like a broken record. I looked
behind me and eyes as big as
the moon, the owl, was hotting
at me. I herd footeps, I cun'imi
and I ran through the dark
and was locked out of my
house intill morning.

---

phrases, which "modify" the noun. Figure 6.4, from one of Scott Peterson's fourth graders, shows an example of the kind of brainstorming and clustering that naturally calls for the use of terms like *noun* and *adjective*, when done first as a whole class. This sample of Amy's work shows her own brainstorming and then the piece she wrote. If her writing were later put on transparency and shared with the class, Scott might ask the class what words Amy used to describe the moon. Then he might summarize by mentioning that *moon* is a noun, a naming word, and that words that describe or modify a noun are called adjectives. Scott might lead the class to note, too, the *-ing* phrases that modify *wind* and *ice cream*. Both of these modifiers are present participial phrases, but the teacher might just note that these phrases, too, work like adjectives, to modify naming words. Repeated use of the terms for basic parts of speech helps students grasp the concept in much the same way they have learned what a sweater is, or a car, or a chair. Just as it takes repeated use of words like *sweater* and *sweatshirt* and *jacket* to differentiate them, so it will take repeated use of grammatical terms for students to grasp their most essential features. However, such incidental use can be valuable preparation for later focusing on the noun-plus-verb (subject-plus-predicate) essence of sentences, or for the concept of free modifiers that add detail and style to sentences. (See the Appendix for examples of how grammatical terms can be taught and learned incidentally, through picture books.)

Dorothy Strickland of Rutgers University offers the following description of how parts of speech—in this case, adjectives—can be explored through literature and the students' and teacher's own writing, in a series of activities that extend over several days. As the students read and employ descriptive language, the teacher can teach the use, concept, and term of adjective (and the concept of adjectival, which includes anything functioning the way an adjective does). Strickland points out that several literary pieces should be used to help students get a "feel" for the language element under study (in this case, adjectives) as demonstrated by professional writers, the teacher, and each other. Students learn *about* language as they use it. The capital letters to the left of the explanation indicate the steps of the lesson sequence that correspond to the conditions for language and literacy learning articulated by Cambourne (1988). (For discussion of some of these conditions, see Chapter 3 of the present book.)

IMMERSION	The teacher briefly introduces and reads the poem *Honey I Love*, by Eloise Greenfield (1978). This is essentially a descriptive list of things that the poet, or the persona of the poem, loves. After soliciting open-ended response, the teacher gently guides discussion toward certain matters, such as the question of whether the poet might be drawing upon personal experiences from her own childhood. Particular attention is paid to visual imagery.
Read aloud & response	
Second reading	Before reading the poem for a second time, the teacher tells children to listen for and create "mind pictures" of their favorite parts. These parts and the children's mind pictures are discussed and described (they have not yet seen the text or the pictures). Discussion follows about how poets and authors help readers create mind pictures.

DEMONSTRATION Write aloud	The teacher writes his or her own short piece (free verse or prose) about something the teacher loves. This is a brief write-aloud in which the teacher demonstrates idea generation, drafting, and editing.
EXPECTATION Brainstorming	The students brainstorm for what they might write about and discuss ways to make their readers visualize what they read. Some students share examples of how they might phrase something.
RESPONSIBILITY Drafting USE	Over the next few days, students work on their pieces. Writing conferences are held in which descriptive language is a major focus. The term *adjective* is used to describe some of the kinds of words that are used. Students are helped to see that the use of adjectives is only one part of what makes a passage descriptive.
APPROXIMATION Revising	Students share and discuss the use of language in their pieces. The teacher gives extra help to students who need assistance in revising what they have written. Other students who have already drafted and revised may be helped to collect metaphors and other interesting uses of language from the work of Eloise Greenfield and other writers; these examples are shared with the class.
Editing	Students continue to confer as they edit their writing; those who need it receive additional help from the teacher.
RESPONSE Conceptualizing, naming, publication	As students read and respond to each others' work, the teacher guides them in coming to a definition of what adjectives are and an understanding of how adjectives and adjectivally functioning groups of words assist in description and help the reader create "mind pictures." They publish their work in some way, such as through a class book of "I love" poems or prose.

Imitating syntactic constructions can teach the use of grammatical patterns incidentally too. Take, for example, *Bears in the Night* (Berenstain and Berenstain, 1971), which served as the model for Kendall's "story" in Figure 6.5; a similar book with prepositional phrases is *Rosie's Walk* (Hutchins, 1968). The first graders' story "Mrs. Strawn Mows the Lawn" (Figure 4.18) was likewise based on a book in the children's classroom. Many books for young children have syntactic patterns that invite imitation. However, students of all ages can be invited to compose something based on a literary model having syntax that might extend their own grammatical resources as writers, through imitation.

FIGURE 6.5   Part of story by Kendall, a kindergartner.

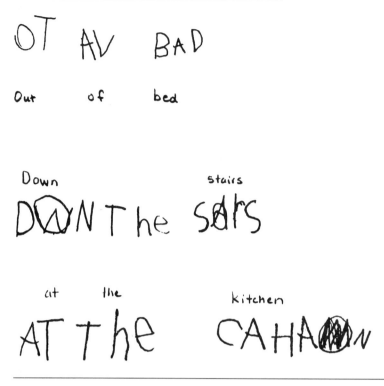

Inductive Lessons

An inductive lesson is one in which students notice patterns and derive generalizations for themselves. Teachers often structure such lessons so that certain conclusions are inevitable; an example is the lesson in the Appendix emphasizing certain patterns with auxiliary verbs. (Note, though, that the teacher may end up pointing out the patterns, in which case the lesson has become deductive, with direct teaching of rules and examples.) While such structured lessons may be most common (to save class time, if for no other reason), inductive lessons can be much less structured, with the possibility that students will discover something or see patterns that the teacher has not noticed. The kinds of grammatical exploration and investigation described in Postman and Weingartner's *Linguistics: A Revolution in Teaching* (1966) can be delightful ways to learn to draw generalizations as a scientist does, when sufficient class time can be devoted to such investigation.

Mini-Lessons

As described by Atwell (1987) and Calkins (1986), a mini-lesson is a five-or ten-minute explanation of something. It is direct and to the point. For example, the teacher can present a brief mini-lesson sharing one of his or her strategies for generating writing topics, or demonstrating what it means to "show, don't tell," or explaining how to use the semicolon to connect grammatical sentences. (See the Appendix for a mini-lesson on the last topic.) Over time, the teacher may present a set or sequence of mini-lessons on the same or related topics, such as the structure of clauses and grammatical sentences, subject-verb agreement, and the nature and uses of free modifiers. Several sets or sequences of mini-lessons are included in the Appendix. Although the mini-lesson reflects direct teaching, which is commonly associated with a behavioral paradigm, it is constructivist in other ways. Namely, students are not required to practice the concept in isolation from authentic learning activities like writing pieces of interest to them, nor are they required to take a test on the material taught. Instead, they are given help in applying the concepts to what they are doing as readers, writers, and learners.

Extended Mini-Lessons

This is my own concept, based on my teaching practices and those of others. It often seems that a mini-lesson will be most successful in conveying a concept if students actively try to demonstrate or apply it, briefly and collaboratively. For example, if I present to the whole class a mini-lesson or lessons on using the apostrophe in possessives, I may conclude with three or four examples on transparency where students are to decide whether the apostrophe is needed and, if so, where it should go. Or, if I present a mini-lesson on demonstrating the effectiveness of participial phrases or absolutes as free modifiers, I may extend the lesson by having the class do a sentence-combining activity (as a whole class or in smaller groups) to help them learn to use such constructions. Or, I may ask them to write an "I am" poem or something similar in which they try to use one or both of these constructions. (Such lessons are included in the Appendix.) Granted, the latter is an artificial kind of writing activity, but quite often a number of writers produce poems that they really like. If not—well, the activity is brief and may stimulate the use of free modifiers in other pieces of writing. Notice, however, that the "practice" is designed to clarify the concepts, not necessarily to ensure mastery, as in a behavioral paradigm of teaching. I fully expect to have to guide writers individually in combining and expanding their sentences with free modifiers. This is why I think of such lessons as extended mini-lessons, still within the constructivist paradigm because they involve learners actively and include what I hope will be just enough practice to solidify the concept.

Commercially Produced Mini-Lessons: The Daily Oral Language Program

At least some aspects of a constructivist paradigm are reflected also in McDougal, Littell's set of twelve teachers' manuals (for grades 1–12) which provide mini-lessons on punctuation, capitalization, usage, and writing skills. All the manuals except the one for first grade have thirty-six weeks of lessons, five lessons a week, with two sentences a lesson to be corrected. The manuals suggest that the teacher put the two sentences to be corrected on the chalkboard—perhaps before class begins or at lunchtime, so that the sentences will catch the students' attention as they enter the classroom. Each sentence has more than one point that needs "correcting." The authors of the Daily Oral Language program (Vail and Papenfuss, 1989/1990) suggest that the teacher invite the students to volunteer needed corrections orally, while the teacher writes them on the board. Each two-sentence lesson should require no more than five to ten minutes daily, they suggest. However, the teacher may have all the students copy the two sentences on paper and try to correct them, before the corrections are shared orally. This may generate involvement on the part of more students. Such lessons seem to reflect at least some aspects of the constructivist paradigm.

The teachers' manual includes a page for each week, with five lessons per page. In the first column for each page is a list of skills to be covered; in the second column are sentences for the board; and in the third column are the correct(ed) sentences. Figure 6.6 includes three days' lessons from level 8. When teachers first give up the security of traditional grammar books, they may find it reassuring to teach such commercially prepared mini-lessons. However, they soon realize that the kinds of errors in the sentences being corrected are often not the kinds of errors their own students are making most frequently. When this happens, many teachers abandon the teachers' manual and create mini-lessons using their own students' writing.

Lessons Within the Constructivist Paradigm

Notice that all these kinds of lessons—incidental, inductive, mini-lessons, and extended mini-lessons—can potentially be offered to the entire class, to small groups, or to individuals in one-on-one conferences. Teaching such

FIGURE 6.6 Sample lessons from level 8 of the Daily Oral Language program (Vail and Papenfuss, 1989/1990).

DAY	SKILLS COVERED	SENTENCES FOR THE BOARD	CORRECT SENTENCES
3	Subordination, Comma (introductory adverbial clause), Proper noun (beach)	1. It was overcast and drizzly we decided not to go to bradford beach	1. (Since or Because) it was overcast and drizzly, we decided not to go to Bradford Beach.
	Proper noun (river), Comma (introductory adverbial clause), Reduction (elimination of redundancy)	2. because they enjoyed rafting on the snake river this year they plan to return to the snake river next year	2. Because they enjoyed rafting on the Snake River this year, they plan to return there next year.
4	Verb (know), Capitalize I, Colon (series), Commas (series)	1. i knowed i would receive these gifts for my birthday a sweater a calculator and a basketball	1. I knew I would receive these gifts for my birthday: a sweater, a calculator, and a basketball.
	Comma (introductory participial phrase), Proper noun (relationship), Dangling modifier	2. entering the theater the smell of the popcorn made dad hungry	2. Entering the theater, Dad smelled the popcorn and became hungry.
5	Misplaced modifier, Comma (direct quotation), Quotation marks (direct quotation), Capitalize first word of direct quotation, Exclamation point	1. the guard at the gate taking tickets shouted get away from that fence	1. The guard taking tickets at the gate shouted, "Get away from that fence!"
	Proper nouns (month, short story), Determiner, Quotation marks (short story), Comma (nonrestrictive clause), Verb (write)	2. in march them students will read the short story wheldon the weed which was wrote in the twentieth century	2. In March (those or these) students will read the short story "Wheldon the Weed," which was written in the twentieth century.

lessons to small groups and individuals is particularly feasible when the teacher has created a writing workshop in the class (see Chapter 4), and of course the smaller the group, the more likely the lessons are to be understood and used. Certainly there may be other kinds of grammar lessons that reasonably fall within the constructivist paradigm: lessons that recognize and treat the learner as an active constructor of meaning, either because of the nature of the lesson itself (e.g., incidental and inductive lessons especially) or because of the nature of the follow-up and teachers' expectations (assistance in applying concepts in "real" writing, rather than isolated practice and testing). However these four kinds of lessons, and various combinations thereof, describe the grammar lessons that seem most valuable to me as a teacher of writing.

Early Studies Supporting a Constructivist Model for the Teaching of Grammar

There is a great deal of research documenting the success of a constructivist model in literacy education. Some of that research consists of naturalistic observations; some of it consists of case studies and anecdotal records; and some of it consists of experimental research comparing the effects of an experimental approach with the effects of a traditional approach as a control (for summaries, see Stephens, 1991; Weaver, 1994). However, only a few of the experimental studies deal with teaching grammatical concepts through active involvement in writing.

In critiquing summaries of the research on the teaching of grammar, Martha Kolln (1981) does mention some studies that have shown the teaching of grammar to be more effective in the context of writing than in isolation.

The oldest of these studies was conducted by Ellen Frogner, who compared the effects of a "grammar" approach and a "thought" approach (1939, as reported in Kolln, 1981). The formal grammar group learned to recognize infinitives, gerunds, and various kinds of modifying phrases (prepositional, appositive, participial) and to identify their use in sentences. In addition, they applied the grammatical concepts by effectively combining short, choppy sentences and then discussing and correcting errors such as misplaced prepositional phrases and dangling modifiers. The "thought" group focused on discussing and combining sentences, without being drilled in the recognition of grammatical constructions. "They thought about and discussed coordination and subordination of ideas, parallel structure, and the relationship of punctuation to meaning" (Kolln, p. 146). What they wrote, however, were still decontextualized sentences; apparently they did not deal with sentences in their own writing.

Unfortunately, Frogner used only objective tests and not actual writing to compare the effectiveness of the two approaches. Even so, the results from the "thought" approach were more positive, suggesting that teaching sentence combining was more productive than teaching grammatical concepts, even when both approaches involved discussion of stylistic effectiveness. Interestingly, this approach sounds very much like the sentence combining that has typically shown positive results in more recent studies (see the summary in Hillocks and Smith, 1991).

Another study, somewhat similar in nature but more impressive in scope, is that done by Roland Harris (1962), reported at length by Braddock, Lloyd-Jones, and Schoer (1963). Working with junior high classes in five London schools in 1960, Harris investigated the effects of "formal grammar" compared with "direct methods of instruction" in grammatical concepts relevant to the students' writing and editing. All the classes had the same instruction for four of their five class periods each week; only the fifth class was different. During the fifth class period, the students in the "direct method" engaged in various writing projects and in "drawing illustrative sentences, points of usage, and paragraphs from the stories to teach the improvement of writing" (Braddock et al., p. 78). Apparently these lessons dealt with aspects of "'sentence building and structure' which came to the teachers' attention as they read the children's writing, treating common errors in the classroom and in compositions 'by means of example and imitation, instead of by the abstraction and generalization of the approach through formal grammar'" (p. 71). The "formal grammar" group studied traditional grammar in a program that integrated grammar and composition lessons; they never had time to engage in the longer writing projects that occupied students who were taught grammar directly, but in the context of their own writing.

The differences in the treatment of usage can be illustrated by the different ways that the teachers handled subject-verb agreement. In the "formal grammar" class, the students tackled errors like *Me and Jim was going into the cave* by using traditional grammatical terminology—for instance, by explaining that *me* is the object form and should be replaced by the nominative form *I,* and by pointing out that the subject is compound and hence grammatically plural; therefore the verb should be *were,* the plural form. In contrast, the "direct instruction" approach involved leading students to the same conclusions by helping them think things through for themselves. For instance, the teacher might ask, "Would you say 'Me was going into the cave?'" When a student would respond no, that he would use "I," the teacher could then point out that *I* is the appropriate form even if there is another person too. Or the teacher might ask, "Would you say 'We was going into the cave'?" When a student admits that no, she would say "We were going into the cave," the teacher could point out that two singular subjects together also require the plural form *were* (based on the quote from Harris, as cited by Braddock et al., p. 71).

At the end of two years, Harris analyzed compositions that were written at the beginning and end of the experiment, using eleven different measures. These included sentence length, frequency of subordinate clauses and compound sentences, sentence variety, and the number of essays containing each of several kinds of common errors. Of the 55 differences computed at the end of the two-year study, only 11 were statistically significant, but all 11 favored the "direct instruction" group. Of the 25 differences represented by the 5 most reliable measures, only 6 favored the "formal grammar" group, and none of these were statistically significant (Braddock et al., p. 80). In addition, Harris noted that the procedures used with the "direct instruction" group elicited "'not only enthusiasm but also a certain self-criticism and purposive modification of habits of writing'" (Braddock et al., p. 72). Today, we might call this "direct instruction" method an inquiry method, since it involves the students actively.

Though we don't know enough about these studies to know which or how many of the conditions favoring learning were operational in them, one important factor is clear: students seemed to benefit most from the approaches in which the learning of grammatical concepts was contextualized and in which they took a more active role. Also clear from both studies is the fact that studying grammatical terminology was less helpful than simply discussing and revising or manipulating sentences.

More Recent Research on Grammar in the Writing Process

In 1980, Calkins reported the learning of punctuation in two third-grade classrooms. In one classroom, the teacher taught simple sentences, periods, and other aspects of mechanics directly, through dittos and with pre-tests and post-tests; her teaching reflected the behaviorally based concept of direct instruction that is common today. Though practicing punctuation extensively, her students rarely wrote. In the other classroom, students never studied punctuation formally, but instead wrote for an hour a day, three days a week, learning punctuation as needed to make their meaning clear, and learning it from the teacher and their peers and the books they were reading.

At the end of the year, Calkins interviewed all the children in each class to determine what they knew about punctuation. The children who had studied punctuation day after day could explain, on the average, only 3.85 marks of punctuation, typically by reciting the rules they had learned for the period, question mark, and exclamation mark. In contrast, the students who wrote instead of studying isolated aspects of mechanics could explain, on the average, 8.66 marks of punctuation. More than half of these students explained the period, question mark, exclamation mark, apostrophe, paragraph sign and caret used in editing, dash, quotation marks, and commas. Nearly half could explain the colon, parentheses, and asterisk. These children tended to explain such marks of punctuation not by reciting memorized rules, but by explaining or demonstrating how the marks were used in their own writing.

For example, Calkins quotes a third grader, Alan: "If you want your story to make sense, you can't write without punctuation. . . . Punctuation tells people things—like if the sentence is asking, or if someone is talking, or if you should yell it out." Another third grader, Chip, said that punctuation "lets you know where the sentence is heading, so otherwise one minute you'd be sledding down the hill and the next minute you're inside the house, without even stopping" (Calkins, 1980, p. 569). The children used punctuation for special effects, as well as clarity. Eight-year-old Andrea, for instance, remarked, "I keep putting in new kinds of punctuation because I need them. Like sound effects—it takes weird punctuation to put *thud-thud* or *splat!* onto my paper" (p. 571). Calkins summarizes: "When children need punctuation in order to be seen and heard, they become vacuum cleaners, sucking up odd bits from books, their classmates' papers, billboards, and magazines. They find punctuation everywhere, and make it their own" (pp. 572–573).

Calkins did not begin her study at the first of the school year, matching children on the basis of I.Q. tests or in some other way. Nor did she have any kind of pre-test that would have facilitated rigorous before-and-after comparisons. However, this lack of scientific rigor does not seriously compromise the obvious conclusion: that children learn punctuation better not by studying it in isolation but by trying to use it effectively in writing for purposes of their own.

Another, more extensive and more formal study is reported by DiStefano and Killion (1984). Faced with district writing skills objectives and "objective" tests of those skills, a group of Colorado teachers proposed to the district that they compare the effectiveness of direct but decontextualized teaching of skills with a writing process approach to teaching those same skills. Also, they proposed that a writing sample be the measure of effectiveness, rather than an objective test. The district agreed, provided that all the district writing skills would be assessed. These included capitalization, punctuation, spelling, sentence structure, format, and usage. The teachers added a seventh criterion, organization.

Five levels of proficiency were established for each criterion at each grade level. Since the proficiency levels changed for each grade level, scores could be compared only within a given grade level, fourth through sixth. Six elementary schools participated in the study, with three randomly chosen to be in the process group (the experimental group) and the other three assigned to the skills group (the control group); teachers in the experimental schools received thirteen hours of in-service instruction from colleagues experienced in the writing process approach. Students in all three grades wrote on an assigned topic in September and again in May.

Results from analyzing the students' papers and assigning proficiency ratings showed that growth in punctuation, capitalization, and format did not differ significantly between the groups. At all three grade levels, the experimental group did significantly better on organization. Differences in sentence structure also favored the experimental group at the two higher grade levels; this criterion involved using a variety of sentence types, with no fragments or run-ons. Usage and spelling also favored the experimental group at all three grade levels. DiStefano and Killion (1984) conclude:

> The control group did not do better than the experimental group on any criterion at any of the three grade levels. Overall, the process model was a huge success when the results of those schools participating in the program are compared with the results of the control group. This study also demonstrates that traditional skills can be measured by looking closely at actual writing. (p. 207)

Of course, such results are not surprising to anyone convinced of the validity of a constructivist model of learning and teaching.

Summary of the Research

As we have seen in earlier chapters, research does not support the teaching of formal grammar systematically and through isolated lessons and drill, on the grounds that a knowledge of grammar is useful to writers, readers, speakers, and listeners, or to students learning another language. From this and other bodies of research, the following conclusions seem warranted:

1. Studying grammar as a system, in isolation from its use, is not in fact the best use of instructional time if better writing (or reading) is the intended goal of grammar study.

2. In learning their native language, young children acquire the major grammatical constructions of their language naturally, without direct instruction. They develop an intuitive grasp of syntax that they use in writing and reading as well as in speaking. Therefore, they do not need to be taught grammar in order to write or read.

3. Wide reading may, in fact, be one of the best routes to the further acquisition of grammar; indeed, even listening to literature read aloud has been shown to stimulate the acquisition of syntax, as well as vocabulary.

4. Writing, of course, is equally critical. But students will not necessarily learn new grammatical constructions from writing alone, unless teachers help them learn to combine sentences and manipulate syntax.

5. Focusing on certain aspects of grammar may have some place in the acquisition of an additional language, particularly for adults and adolescents, and particularly after they have acquired the basics of the language. However, studying the grammatical system of a new language does not facilitate the acquisition of that language as readily as being immersed in and attempting to use the language in all its modes (listening, speaking, reading, and writing).

6. In general, analyzing language—the focus of traditional grammar instruction—is much less helpful to writers than a focus on sentence generating, combining, and manipulating.

7. Similarly, attending to usage, punctuation, and other aspects of mechan-

ics and sentence structure in the context of writing is considerably more effective than teaching usage and mechanics in isolation. Students revise their sentences and edit their writing more effectively when sentence revision and editing skills have been taught in the context of their own writing.

The Need for Informal as Well as Formal Research

The traditional, systematic teaching of grammar in isolation reflects a behavioral theory of teaching and learning. In contrast, a constructivist theory of learning and teaching underlies the teaching of selected aspects of grammar, mostly when issues arise and needs are observed within students' writing. Some teaching practices, of course, fit somewhere in between. For example, the Daily Oral Language program seems to reflect the notion that practice (week after week, year after year) makes perfect, a behavioral concept. Also, the lessons are taught according to a timetable, not according to what the teacher perceives students' needs to be (and it would be difficult to choose lessons based on need, because each lesson covers more than one point and the lessons are not categorized to facilitate selective use or reordering). On the other hand, the lessons are intended as relatively brief; they focus on the *use* of grammatical concepts, rather than the isolated study of grammar; and they involve students actively, at least in theory. In these respects the daily lessons reflect a constructivist paradigm.

Clearly, more formal research is needed. For example, we might want to know whether teaching grammatical skills only in the context of their use works best, or whether it is more effective to teach daily oral language lessons in "correcting" sentences and, in addition, to focus on skills as they are needed.

Before or instead of doing experimental research, though, most of us will surely want to experiment informally with different ways of teaching grammar from a constructive paradigm, mostly in the context of students' writing. Thus the purpose of the Appendix is to share some of my own experiments, so that others can draw from and improve upon the lessons that seem most appropriate for their own teaching—and keep observing what does and does not work, and keep refining their own lessons and teaching too. Such informal teacher research is critical in improving our instruction, whether or not it later forms the basis for experimental research.

AFTERWORD
Conclusion and a New Beginning

June 17, 1995. Yesterday I conducted a half-day workshop on teaching grammar in context with some teachers from the Spring Arbor, Michigan, area. I shared with them some of the research, arguments, and recommendations from this book:

- The general conclusion from ninety years of research: that teaching grammar in isolation, as a school subject, does not seem to have much effect on the writing of more than a few students.
- The research suggesting that teaching selected aspects of grammar in the context of writing is more productive.
- The observation that teaching all the parts of speech and structures commonly taught in traditional grammar books seems to be an inefficient way of accomplishing our aims as teachers of writing. We can accomplish more with less.
- The recommendation that we not try to teach grammar as a complete description of the structure of English (except, perhaps, in an elective course or unit), but instead that we focus our teaching on those concepts and terms that are most helpful in discussing sentence expansion, revision, and editing.
- The suggestion that we focus instructional attention on those aspects of grammar that are particularly helpful in creating, rearranging, and revising sentences for greater stylistic effectiveness.
- The suggestion that we also attend particularly to those aspects of grammar that are most critical in helping students punctuate sentences conventionally.
- The suggestion that while a few basic grammatical concepts may be taught in separate language lessons, such concepts should generally be taught and reinforced as students are revising and editing their writing.
- The suggestion that we use methods that are highly motivating, in order to encourage students to develop and apply relevant

concepts (a constructivist concept of learning, in contrast to the behavioral concept that has dominated the traditional teaching of grammar throughout the twentieth century).

- The suggestion that we not bother testing students on their command of grammar but rather that we help them apply and learn to apply the most useful concepts—again, a reflection of the constructivist rather than the behavioral concept of learning.

In addition, I shared some of my experiments in teaching grammar in context, most of which are included in the Appendix.

Here are some of the conclusions that emerged from the teachers' responses, our discussion, and my further reflection upon it:

- "Research" can be used to prove almost anything. Therefore, we must read the research thoughtfully, looking for what it does not tell us as well as what it does.
- On the other hand, we can use this truism as an excuse to avoid examining the assumptions and teaching practices we are comfortable with.
- As teachers, we need to be open to learning from research, but also to be discerning critics of it. We need to value and validate our own experience, but also to reconsider our preconceptions and be willing to take risks that may make our teaching more effective or efficient.
- We need to keep in mind that new learning involves not only risks, but new kinds of errors and less than fully successful experiments, on the part of both teachers and students.
- It is also important to reconsider our traditional attempt to ferret out the alleged errors in students' writing—partly because published writers break the rules, and even more important, because by focusing too soon or too much upon errors, we limit students' growth as writers. Time enough for judicious editing after students have drafted and revised their writings for content, organization, sentence structure, and style.
- We also need to remember that no matter what we do in teaching grammar, not all of our students will immediately, or even eventually, become versatile stylists and expert copy editors. Learning to use a greater range of syntactic structures more effectively and to edit according to accepted conventions takes years, not days or weeks. We need to be patient with ourselves and our students, and to recognize and help others understand

that new methods do not have to accomplish miracles in order to be better than old methods.

The struggle to reconsider the old and take risks with the new was exemplified in our workshop by Pat Short, who became interested a year ago in the possibility of teaching less grammar, but teaching it more efficiently and in ways that would have more impact on students' writing. One of my extended mini-lessons during the workshop involved using present participial phrases in "I am" poems describing ourselves. Pat wrote:

> I am anxious . . .
> Worried my students will, like Anthony's Roman citizens,
> "Rise up and mutiny,"
> Changing lesson plans in mid-hour, sometimes mid-sentence,
> Searching for self-esteem builders, theirs and mine,
> Encouraging writing that rings with voice and validity,
> Swearing to honor writers but still red-marking writing,
> Praying to validate colleagues while trying to destroy the "five paragraph essay" syndrome.
>
> I am still in process . . .

Like Pat, the teachers in the grammar support group I mentioned in the Preface are in process—as I am too, of course. We are not necessarily ready to undertake, or interested in undertaking, comparative research that will help demonstrate the superiority of teaching grammar in context rather than in isolation. However, we are continuing to experiment with teaching less grammar in such ways that our teaching may have more effect on students' writing. We invite you to join us in our quest for better ways of teaching those aspects of grammar that seem most important for writers. Join with us and with Susan Spear, who writes:

> I am a question mark
> Seeking, searching
> Open to more and more ideas
> Wondering if a period is truly at the end

We think not.

Appendix
Sample Lessons on Selected Aspects of Grammar

In developing and choosing lessons to share in this Appendix, I have illustrated the different kinds of lessons described in Chapter 6: incidental lessons, inductive lessons, mini-lessons, extended mini-lessons, and various combinations and sequences thereof. Teachers who need more background in grammar to adapt and expand these lessons or develop their own might find Diana Hacker's *A Writer's Reference* (1995) particularly useful. More realistic in its assessment of how the language is really used by educated people is *The Right Handbook: Grammar and Usage in Context,* by Belanoff, Rorschach, and Oberlink (1993). Both of these would also be excellent references for students at the high school and college levels.

Usually, it works well for the teacher to make transparencies for the concepts being taught, and to use different colored transparency pens to clarify particular constructions, marks of punctuation, and so forth. I prefer to use examples from students' own writing or examples from literature, such as the many published examples in Scott Rice's *Right Words, Right Places* (1993); in practice, though, I all too often find myself concocting short examples that can easily be printed by hand on a transparency. All these lessons can be taught to the entire class or to a smaller group of students, but follow-up application commonly needs to be guided individually. *Or to put it bluntly, without further guidance, such lessons will not necessarily transfer to students' own writing any better than traditional grammar book exercises have done; they simply reflect a more efficient use of time than the traditional practice exercises and tests. Students will inevitably need guidance in applying these concepts during revision and editing.*

This Appendix also includes at least one and sometimes several lessons reflecting each category in Figure 5.13, A Minimum of Grammar for Maximum Benefits:

- Teaching concepts of subject, verb, clause, sentence
- Teaching style through sentence combining and sentence generating

- Teaching sentence sense and style through the manipulation of syntactic elements
- Teaching the power of dialects and dialects of power
- Teaching punctuation and mechanics for clarity and style

The lessons are not always in this order, though. Rather, the ordering reflects the interrelationships among concepts and skills. Generally, I have made no claim or suggestion as to the grade levels at which lessons of a particular kind might be taught. The individual teacher needs to decide, based on assessment of what will benefit his or her students. It is also important to note that several of the lessons might be better taught as two or more separate but related mini-lessons.

In examining these lessons, you will notice that I have freely used not only the grammatical terms suggested as basic in Chapter 5, but other terms as well. I include them partly because some readers will want to see the terms with which they are familiar, but also because I think such terms can be used to communicate even when the reader does not necessarily have a prior concept of the term. In other words, I use such terms incidentally, without expecting everyone to be familiar with them or to learn them. I think we can use such terms the same way with our students. However, in the Glossary I have defined and illustrated the terms that have been particularly emphasized in this book, including all the terms in listed in Chapter 5.

Most of these are lessons I have taught with students in various classes at the college level, but particularly with the preservice and inservice teachers in my Grammar and Teaching Grammar class. In working with those enrolled in this course, I have usually had a dual or triple aim: to teach something that could benefit them as writers themselves; to suggest and exemplify something that they might profitably teach to their students, at least in simplified form; and to model possible ways of teaching grammar in context. Here, these suggestions often look like rather formal lesson plans, with goals indicated and the reader addressed as "you." But to emphasize the fact that these lessons represent ongoing experimentation, some lessons or parts of them have been written in a more conversational tone—to share what I have done as a teacher at the college level and sometimes to make suggestions for how my experiments might be modified to achieve goals at other levels. This, I hope, will also emphasize the fact that adaptations will usually be necessary as well as desirable: that we must all to some extent reinvent the wheel of effective instruction in our own classrooms, even while we share our efforts with each other, collaborate with one another, and benefit from others' experiences. Without further ado, then, here are some of my experiments with teaching grammar in context—beginning with a lesson that does not fit comfortably under any of the five preceding categories.

Teaching the Meaningful Parts of Words

This topic does not fit comfortably under the heading of *grammar* unless we expand that term to include the internal grammar or structure of words. But because the meaningful parts of words seem to be so infrequently taught these days, I have chosen to include a mini-lesson to remind teachers of the importance of this topic to our students as readers and writers.

GOAL   To help readers learn to decipher words and expand their vocabularies by attending to the meaningful parts of words.

RATIONALE   This kind of lesson is valuable for students across the grades. The meanings of common prefixes are often taught in the primary grades, while the meanings of common Latin and Greek bases can be introduced as early as the intermediate grades and taught throughout high school and beyond.

POSSIBLE PROCEDURES   To decide what to teach, choose a meaningful element that occurs in words the students are likely to know. Brainstorm for words that include this element, then ask students what the element is likely to mean, considering the meanings of the words they have brainstormed. Once the class has decided the meaning through discussion, offer two or three more words that contain the element. Invite students to consider what these words might mean or to explain how the meaning of the element contributes to the meaning of the whole word.

Examples

1. Brainstorm for words that include the element *ped*: *pedal*, *pedestal*, *moped*, *pedestrian*, and so forth. Try to determine the meaning of *ped*. (It comes from a Latin word meaning "foot.") Other words for discussion might include *pedometer*, *peddler*, *pedicure*, *centipede*, *expedite*, *impede*; words with the same root spelled differently are *tripod* and *octopus*.

2. Brainstorm for words that include the element *trans: transportation, transit, transcontinental,* and so forth. (It comes from Latin and means "across.") Other words for discussion might include *transact, transfer, translate, translucent, transmission,* and *transparency.*

TEACHER RESOURCES   For lists of Latin and Greek elements, teachers can consult Gentry and Wallace, *Teaching Kids to Spell* (1993). A much more complete resource is Smith, *Dictionary of English Word-Roots* (1966).

Teaching Grammar Incidentally: Basic Parts of Speech and Structures

Both the names for parts of speech and the use of grammatical constructions can be taught and learned incidentally, in the course of reading and writing.

1. Learning the Names of Basic Parts of Speech

GOALS/RATIONALE   As explained in Chapter 6, I firmly believe that students can develop considerable familiarity with some grammatical terms simply through our using the terms repeatedly, in a context that makes their meaning reasonably clear. This, for example, is how children commonly learn most of the words in our language. We may explicitly repeat, for our babies and toddlers, some of the basic naming words of the language, while pointing to the object: words like *ball,* for instance, or *doggie.* But most words—even most nouns—are surely learned incidentally, as we and others use the words in meaningful sentences and later as our children read books and more books.

At the college level, I want to refresh my students' memory of basic terms like noun, verb, adjective, and adverb. Even though these terms are not all equally necessary for talking about style or the conventions of language, they are useful—and it is relatively easy for students of all ages to develop some understanding of the terms without formal study and analysis.

POSSIBLE PROCEDURES   One mini-lesson involves sharing the alphabet book *Animalia* (1986), by Graeme Base. I typically read the descriptions for the first four letters of the alphabet, then hand the book around the class. Beforehand, I have put these four descriptions on a transparency, which we examine. In "An armored armadillo avoiding an angry alligator," we have the opportunity to comment upon nouns, adjectives, and what appears to be a verb: *avoiding*. We note that we would need *is* or *was* for the verb and the sentence to be complete. Adverbs occur too in the phrases for C and D, as in "Diabolical dragons daintily devouring delicious delicacies." Sharing this book gives me the opportunity to share a resource that can be used with students of all ages, to reiterate the point that we can teach basic grammatical terminology just by using it, and to explain that students may learn the terms as well or better through such incidental teaching as through grammar book exercises and testing. (After all, do we test children on the meanings of words like *coat, chair, desk, pants,* and *love?* Usually not, but they learn the essential meanings of these and thousands of other words from being exposed to them in meaningful contexts.)

2. Expanding Awareness of Basic Parts of Speech

Another incidental lesson, an additional or alternative one, involves sharing four books by Ruth Heller. In groups, students examine and comment on these books, learning whatever is meaningful to them. The books are *Merry-go-round: A book about nouns* (1990), *Kites sail high: A book about verbs* (1988), *Many luscious lollipops: A book about adjectives* (1989), *A cache of jewels and other collective nouns* (1989).

3. Expanding Awareness of Parts of Speech During Writing

Another mini-lesson involves sharing how I use grammatical terms incidentally in the context of encouraging and discussing students' writing. For example, in pointing out effective use of verbs and adjectives, I simply use those terms without pre-teaching them, giving practice exercises on identifying verbs and adjectives, or testing students on their ability to identify words functioning as verbs or as adjectives. Other teachers I know do the same thing. With college students, I also use some terms to which they may never have been introduced: terms like *participial phrase* and *absolute* (see later in the Appendix for a set of lessons on those constructions). Chapter 6 includes a discussion of two writing activities wherein grammatical terminology was used incidentally.

4. Learning Grammatical Structures by Imitating Literature

Wide reading is one of the best ways to acquire the ability to comprehend and use a wide range of syntactic structures. However, imitating sentence patterns in writing is valuable too. Any good-quality literature is a good candidate. In the elementary grades, children can imitate the structure of patterned books in writing of their own; see, for instance, the examples in Chapter 4. Examples of very simple books for imitating the use of prepositional phrases are *Bears in the Night* (Berenstain and Berenstain, 1971), *Rosie's Walk* (Hutchins, 1968), and *A Dark, Dark Tale* (Brown, 1988). Bernard Most's *If the Dinosaurs Came Back* (1978) encourages imitation of the hypothetical *if* clause. Possibilities abound for imitating various kinds of structures used by published writers. By the middle school or junior high level, many students should benefit from imitating literary sentences that feature constructions like the appositive, the participial phrase, and the absolute. Some students (like the kindergartner in Figure 5.11) will have begun using such structures much earlier and can therefore probably benefit from additional guidance in their use. Examples can be drawn from good-quality picture books, for many of their authors have used sophisticated grammatical constructions.

Teaching Subject, Verb, Clause, Sentence, and Related Concepts for Editing

GOALS/RATIONALE   As explained in Chapter 5, students need to understand some basic grammatical concepts if they are to punctuate by rule rather than just by intuition. Not that intuition is bad: it goes a long way, for many writers. But in order to eliminate ineffective fragments and comma splices from their writing, most writers probably need to understand the following concepts, at a minimum,

- Subject and verb
- Clause, as distinguished from phrase
- Independent clause, as distinguished from dependent clause

The concepts of subject and verb are also important in understanding subject-verb agreement, another concept relevant in editing.

It should be noted that traditional definitions of the sentence are, in themselves, not very helpful in identifying sentences. A sentence is commonly defined as "a group of words that expresses a complete thought" or as "a group of words that contains a subject and a predicate and expresses a complete thought." But even the latter definition is not precise enough to serve as the basis for a discovery procedure, a procedure for determining what is and what isn't a sentence, grammatically speaking. For example, a subordinate clause has a subject and a predicate, but it is not grammatically complete. Students often consider a construction like *the reason being that we were late* to be a sentence, because it has a subject of sorts *(reason)* and a verb form *(being)*, not to mention a subject and verb in the subordinate clause. In context, such a construction often seems complete, at least to some students; after all, it completes the sentence that came before! However, *being* is not a complete verb and therefore the construction is not a sentence or clause. Similarly, an absolute construction is nearly an independent clause, but not quite. For example, the absolute *its muddy waters picking up speed* needs a BE verb to be grammatically complete: *its muddy waters were picking up speed*. (Alternatively, the absolute could be changed to a clause: *its muddy waters picked up speed*.) In any case, these examples of students' confusion should help teachers understand why the traditional definitions of the sentence are insufficient as the basis for discovery procedures. See, too, the discussion in Chapter 6, which mentions Harris and Rowan's research (1989) into college students' common confusions when asked to identify what is and what is not a sentence. As Hartwell (1985) puts it, most definitions of the sentence are COIK: clear only if known, if the concept of a sentence is already understood (p. 119).

To predetermine older students' grasp of the concept of a sentence, one might replicate the study by Harris and Rowan (see Figure A.1 for their sentences). Another option is to have students divide into T-units the part of "The Graveyard" narrative that hasn't already been so divided (Figure 5.6). What I myself usually use is "The Frog" essay in Gary Paulsen's *The Island* (1988). Allegedly written by the fourteen-year-old protagonist of the book, this essay is a challenge because it sometimes embeds T-units within other T-units. I type the essay without sentence end punctuation and ask my students to work in groups to set off the T-units with brackets. After checking the T-unit divisions, we move from grammatical to rhetorical considerations, discussing the ways we think this adolescent's narrative "should" be punctuated; finally, we compare it with the original and appreciate Paulsen's skill in capturing the voice of an adolescent writer.

The following lessons are designed to introduce my students to these concepts in ways that they might profitably adapt to teaching at their various grade levels (to the extent that the concepts are appropriate). These lessons are divorced from the writing process but provide a foundation that the teacher can draw upon in helping students edit their writing. Because students often learn and remember more when they are actively involved through manipulating data and even things, some of these lessons involve

My Brothers

(1) The phrase I heard only too often when I was younger was "You're too little to play." (2) Whatever my older brothers did I wanted to do, wherever they went I wanted to go. (3) Pat being two years older than myself and allowed to hang out with Randy, being four years older. (4) Since there was such a difference in age, I developed different and unique relationships with each.

(5) My brothers have clashing identities. (6) Total opposites of each other. (7) First, Pat is the kind of brother you see on television. (8) The kind that would help you with your homework and your problems. (9) Randy, on the other hand, isn't the smartest brother in the world but, he's been around and knows a lot. (10). The best summary of Randy is that he's the Mr. Hyde of Pat. (11) Not exactly bad, though a lot different. (12) He has no patience especially when he gets angry. (13) Then he goes on apologizing for days.

(14) There are traits in both of my brothers that I dislike. (15) First, Pat is too perfect. (16) Much too perfect for his own good. (17) The biggest annoyance is that he gets great grades. (18) And he's always so nice to people that bother him. (19) Because he thinks it's important to be polite. (20) Not to mention his mannerisms are good at all times. (21) Randy likes to move around a lot. (22) He gets bored with a job fast and easy. (23) He just can't stay in the office very much. (24) Which makes him a very good salesman.

(25) To sum up, we have our differences. (26) But that's just like any other family. (27) I still like them both very much. (28) Any differences that I may have because of age or size which wasn't resolved or will be through time. (29) For a final note to this assignment. (30) I would never say any of this to their faces, just on paper.

---

manipulables. However, there is always a trade-off in having students manipulate things and draw conclusions: that is, the lessons take longer and are anything but "mini."

Because there are so many lessons in this set, an overview is given here:

1. Subject and verb, and the concept of clause
2. Subjects and verbs: emphasis on auxiliary and main verbs
3. Basic subject-verb agreement
4. Subject-verb agreement when a prepositional phrase modifies the subject
5. Connecting independent clauses

6. Independent and dependent clauses, and the concept of fragment
7. Eliminating run-ons and comma splices
8. Making limited but effective use of the comma splice
9. Phrases contrasted with clauses; more on the fragment
10. Eliminating fragments; using fragments sparingly but effectively
11. Fragments, fused sentences, and comma splices (differently sequenced set of lessons)
12. Connecting clauses with conjunctive adverbs and punctuating them conventionally
13. Comparing the uses of, and punctuation associated with, coordinating conjunctions, subordinating conjunctions, and conjunctive adverbs

1. Understanding Subjects and Verbs, and the Concept of Clause

GOALS   To help writers understand that sentences consist of at least a subject plus a verb as predicate, and that the verb can actually be a phrase of several words.

RATIONALE   Editing for subject-verb agreement requires understanding and being able to identify subjects and verbs. Such an understanding will also be helpful for writers who punctuate most sentences correctly, but who cannot consistently correct comma splices, run-ons, or fragments because they don't have a firm grasp of what constitutes a subject and verb.

POSSIBLE PROCEDURES   One way to teach basic awareness of subjects and verbs is first to put on a transparency several sentences, each with a verb phrase that differs in complexity from the others (see the next lesson for more examples). Following are simple examples, with (to save space) just a proper noun as subject and a verb that has no object. The lesson can be either expanded or simplified, as needed.

1. Explain that grammatically correct sentences always have at least a subject and a verb:

SUBJECT / VERB
Brian | waited.
Brian | is waiting.
Brian | has been waiting.

SUBJECT / VERB
Barbara | laughed.
Barbara | was laughing.
Barbara | had laughed.

Brian | might be waiting.	Barbara | must have laughed.
Brian | must have been waiting.	Barbara | may have been laughing.
Brian | is going to be waiting.	Barbara | ought to be laughing.

2. Explain that when the verb consists of more than one word, it may be called a *verb phrase*.

3. Explain that an easy way to determine the verb part of the sentence is to ask, "Which words tell what is going on?" The answer will be the verb part of the sentence (also known as the simple predicate): *laughing, was laughing, must have been laughing*. The rest is the subject (unless there are adverbial elements that modify the entire subject-verb unit). This test for predicates and subjects could be a separate mini-lesson. The test is derived from DeBeauregard (1984), but he explains it a little differently. He suggests formulating a question like "Who laughed?" The answer is the subject of the original sentence, while the predicate is all the words used in the question, other than the initial *who* or *what*.

4. Explain that a subject-plus-complete-verb unit is a clause. Grammatically speaking, a sentence has at least one clause that can stand alone, that does not depend on another clause.

2. Understanding Subjects and Verbs (Emphasis on Auxiliary and Main Verbs)

To use procedures similar to what I've tried in this inductive-deductive lesson, teachers need to know the basic kinds of auxiliary verbs:

MODAL AUXILIARIES [present, past]	FORMS OF HAVE	FORMS OF BE	
can, could	has, have	am, is, are	[present]
shall, should	had	was, were	[past]
will, would	having	being	[present participle]
may, might	had	been	[past participle]
must			

The following words may show subject-verb agreement but otherwise function more like modals:

ought to
want/wants/wanted to
has/have to
am/is/are/was/were going to

Possible Procedures

Procedures can be varied, but the following illustrates one possibility.

1. Prepare different colored strips of card stock or colored paper for nouns, auxiliary verbs, and main verbs.

For simplicity, choose main verbs that do not need to have anything after them (intransitive verbs). To make it clearer that a past participle has a different function from the past tense, choose verbs that have a distinctive past participle form—ideally, verbs ending in *-en*, or *-n*. Some possible verbs and their irregular past participles are *fall (fallen); rise (risen); speak (spoken); begin (begun); fly (flown); go (gone); grow (grown); sing (sung).*

Put all the basic forms of a main verb on one side of one verb card. For example:

falls, fall
fell
falling
fallen

Put various kinds of auxiliary phrases on strips of one color. Here are some examples (where putting words on different lines is meant to indicate that only one of the words can be used at one time):

can	has	is
will	have	are
shall	had	was
		were

may ⎫
    ⎬ be
could ⎭

has ⎫
have ⎬ been
had ⎭

should ⎫
       ⎬ have
must ⎭

might ⎫
      ⎬ have been
would ⎭

ought to have   has/have to have been

Many other combinations are possible but, as we shall see, they occur in a consistent and predictable order.

Select nouns that can reasonably go with some of the main verbs you have chosen, including nouns that may create "poetic" sentences when coupled with some of the verbs. For simplicity, you might want to avoid any modifying words and instead choose nouns like *Carla, Elvis Presley, courage, science, summer, poems, stars, tigers, astronauts.*

2. Prepare for each group of students a packet of cards containing nouns, auxiliaries, and main verbs. (A plastic sandwich bag with self-gripping zipper works well.)

3. Include in each packet directions such as these:

> As a group, first assemble at least half a dozen sentences in the following order:
>
> One green card, for subject + one pink card, for helper verb(s) + one purple card, for main verb.
>
> (Yes, put your cards in this order; and yes, be sure to create sentences that reflect the normal grammar of English, even if some are a bit poetical.) Sometimes you will have to choose one form of a word or another, or even to select from among totally different words. At least one person, acting as scribe, should write down the sentences you have created.

4. When each group has constructed and written several sentences, write some of their sentences on a transparency, being sure to write all the modal verbs in a column, all the HAVE verbs in the next column, the BE verbs in the next column, and the main verbs last. With luck, your set of sentences might look something like the one in Figure A.2. (It's okay to insist that sentences to be added to this list must follow the pattern of green, then pink, then purple card.)

5. Such a list allows for the students or the teacher to draw various kinds of generalizations, depending upon the purposes of the activity, the time available, and the grammatical sophistication and needs of those involved. These generalizations include the following:

- A main verb can stand alone, or it can have one or even two or three helper verbs.
- If a verb form carries a distinctive marker for tense, that tense marker always occurs on the first verb form, whether it is an auxiliary or the main verb.
- Modals always occur before any other kind of helper verb. HAVE forms occur next, while BE forms are the last to occur before a main verb.

FIGURE A.2 Subjects and verbs, with emphasis on auxiliary and main verbs.

Noun (subject)	Modal	HAVE	BE	Main verb
Courage				sings.
Elvis				went.
Stars			are	speaking.
Carla		has	been	growing.
Astro-nauts	might	have	been	flying.
Elvis	ought to	have		gone.
Science	will		be	rising.
Poems	shall			begin.
Tigers		had		fallen.
Summer			was	beginning.

- A HAVE auxiliary is always followed by a past participle form (whether it is the auxiliary *been,* or the main verb).
- A BE auxiliary is always followed by a main verb in the present participle form, as long as the sentence is active rather than passive.

For a lesson putting more emphasis on discovery of such patterns, the teacher can put the three major kinds of auxiliary verbs on different color cards, such as blue, red, and yellow. This will make it easier for students themselves to notice the invariable order of different kinds of auxiliaries.

REMINDERS AND NOTES   This activity is not yet meant to teach subject-verb agreement, but only to make students more aware of it through the examples shared.

If students ignore the restriction of combining one green card with one pink card and then one purple card, in that order, seeming anomalies will occur. For instance, one thing to anticipate is that someone will probably use a form of HAVE or a form of BE as a main verb. This does not break the pattern. Rather, it is simply true that certain forms of HAVE (*have, has, had*) can each function either as an auxiliary verb or as a main verb. Similarly, certain forms of BE (*am, is, are, was, were*) can function both ways. To emphasize the point, it may be helpful to have the students add these forms on whatever color strips the teacher has used for main verbs.

When restrictions are ignored, another seeming anomaly that occurs is the passive sentence, such as *Stars have been sung*, a sentence with the singer not specified. The passive has a BE form that is followed by the past participle, in this case *sung*. However, the corresponding active form follows the patterns above: [*Someone*] *has sung stars*.

3. Understanding Basic Subject-Verb Agreement

GOALS/RATIONALE   To help writers understand basic subject-verb agreement, so they can edit their writing for the conventions of subject-verb agreement.

Basic subject-verb agreement can be taught in a brief mini-lesson, at least to writers who already have some understanding of subjects and verbs and for whom dialect-switching is not an issue. Ideally such a mini-lesson would be offered when some students' writing is being prepared for publication beyond the classroom, and when the writers might benefit from using the forms associated with Edited American English, or what is sometimes called the Language of Wider Communication.

Possible Procedures

1. Put on a transparency some basic examples of subject-verb agreement. For example:

He wants to leave.   The *players want* to leave.
Cinda blames you.   The *teachers think* you did it.

2. Point out the basic teeter-totter relationship:

When the subject names just one person or thing, the verb carries -s: *wants, blames.*

When the subject names more than one, the subject carries -s: *guests, teachers.*

3. Show how this relationship is marked in other, less obvious examples:

SINGULAR
Harley has ripped the box apart.
That *guitarist is* awesome.
Nobody blames you.

PLURAL
The *girls have* ripped the box apart.
Those *musicians are* awesome.
People think you did it.

4. Suggest to students that as they edit their writing, they check for subject-verb agreement. Posting on the wall some examples of conventional agreement from their own writing may help.

4. Understanding Subject-Verb Agreement When a Prepositional Phrase Modifies the Subject

GOAL   To help writers learn to edit their writing for subject-verb agreement when the subject is modified by a prepositional phrase. Students need to have a basic understanding of the concept of subject-verb agreement.

Possible Procedures

1. First, explain the concept of a prepositional phrase. Many teachers do this by relating a number of prepositions to a single noun, such as *box: on the box, in the box, under the box, over the box, around the box, toward the box,* and so forth. (See Figure A.3 for some common prepositions.) After

FIGURE A.3   Common prepositions.

about	beside	from	outside	toward
above	besides	in	over	under
across	between	inside	past	underneath
after	beyond	into	plus	unlike
against	but	like	regarding	until
along	by	near	respecting	unto
among	concerning	next	round	up
around	considering	of	since	upon
as	despite	off	than	with
at	down	on	through	without
before	during	onto	throughout	
behind	except	opposite	till	
below	for	out	to	

the teacher gives two or three examples, students should contribute others, which can be added to a list on transparency.

2. Give packets with sentence elements to students working in groups. Again, nouns for the subject can be put on green cards, and entire verb phrases and predicates can be put on a different color of cards. Be sure that the "nouns" include some grammatically singular pronouns like *she*, *something*, and *nobody*, and some grammatically plural pronouns like *we*, *both*, and *all*. (Special problems crop up with *everyone* and *everybody*, so perhaps they are best omitted at this point.) Some groups could be given only singular nouns and pronouns, while other groups could be given only plurals.

3. After the students have formed and written down sentences using their cards, give them cards of a different color, each containing a prepositional phrase that could reasonably modify two or more of the nouns they have used as subjects. To groups that have singular nouns and pronouns, give prepositions that end in plural nouns, and vice versa. For example:

The group [of boys]   We [on the team]
Nobody [among my friends]   The sandwiches [on the menu]

Ask the students to expand their sentences by adding one of the prepositional phrases after each noun phrase they have used.

4. Write some of the students' sentences on a transparency. Explain that the prepositional phrase (which is on a different color card) does not change what the subject is. Therefore, the verb form remains the same.

5. Connecting Independent Clauses

GOALS/RATIONALE   To punctuate conventionally, writers need to know common ways of joining independent clauses. In the most basic lessons, the concept of an independent clause can be equated with a complete sentence.

Possible Procedures

1. Put on a transparency some simple sentences that can logically be joined by *and*, *but*, or *or* (the most common of the coordinating conjunctions),

FIGURE A.4   Coordinating conjunctions and correlative conjunctions.

COORDINATING CONJUNCTIONS	CORRELATIVE CONJUNCTIONS
and	both . . . and
but	either . . . or
or	neither . . . nor
	not only . . . but also
nor	whether . . . or
so	
yet	(These pairs link grammatically equal elements.)

and show that the sentences can be connected with a comma plus one of these conjunctions. (See Figure A.4 for some coordinating conjunctions and correlative conjunctions.) For example, here are some sentences after they have already been connected:

> Cindy brought a pizza over, *and* we had lots of fun eating and listening to CDs.
> Cindy brought a pizza over, *but* we didn't like her vegetarian pizza.
> Cindy will bring a pizza, *or* Carmen will bring a giant submarine sandwich.

2. Depending on the sophistication and needs of the writers, you can similarly demonstrate the use of a semicolon to connect two sentences, as in

> There wasn't much else we could do; we were trapped in that cave.

In explaining this use of the semicolon, I make the point that the semicolon essentially consists of a comma plus a period. The comma part signals the close relationship between the ideas, while the period part signals that each part before and after it is grammatically complete, an independent clause, a grammatical sentence.

6. Understanding Independent and Dependent Clauses and the Concept of Fragment

GOALS/RATIONALE   For writers to consciously eliminate run-ons, comma splices, and fragments from their writing (or to use these constructions deliberately, for effect), they need to understand independent and depend-

FIGURE A.5 Common subordinating conjunctions.

CONTRAST	TIME, SEQUENCE	CAUSE	CONDITION
although	after	as	if
even though	as	because	unless
though	before	in order that	whether
	since	since	
whereas	till	so that	
while	until		
	when		
rather than	while		

ent clauses, and how these figure into grammatical sentences and are punctuated. An extended mini-lesson such as this can be used to introduce the basic concepts, but follow-up lessons may help, too: lessons drawing examples from the students' own writing.

Because dependent clauses that function like adverbs are much easier to understand than adjective and noun clauses, it can be useful to begin with adverbial clauses. Adjective clauses come with their own set of punctuation rules and therefore require separate lessons.

Possible Procedures

1. Give examples of how a grammatical sentence (an independent clause) can be made into less than a sentence, by putting a subordinating word in front of it. (See Figure A.5 for some subordinating conjunctions.) For example:

I turned out the light.   [complete sentence, an independent clause]

when I turned out the light   [all subordinate clauses, not grammatically
until I turned out the light   complete]
because I turned out the light
unless I turned out the light
before I turned out the light

2. To extend this basic lesson, invite students to collaborate in adding a main clause to each of these sentences. In the process, demonstrate con-

ventional punctuation: the fact that a comma is used after an introductory subordinate clause like this, but is optional before such a clause:

> *When I turned out the light,* at first I couldn't see anything.
> The house didn't really become pitch black *until I turned out the light.*

3. To further extend the lesson, point out that when a dependent clause is not attached to a main clause within the same punctuated sentence, it is considered a fragment. During editing, such fragments are usually attached to the sentence to which they most closely relate, which is typically the preceding sentence.

7. Eliminating Run-on Sentences and Comma Splices

GOALS/RATIONALE   To enable writers to eliminate run-on sentences and comma splices from their writing, except when they seem particularly effective (see Figure 4.9 for examples from published writers).

POSSIBLE PROCEDURES   Prepare a transparency with some examples of ineffective run-ons or comma splices. It is particularly helpful to take these examples from your students' own writing. Show two or three ways of correcting each sentence, and discuss as a group which way seems most effective.

SUGGESTIONS AND NOTES   In working with college students, I have discovered that the reason they don't identify and eliminate run-on and especially comma splice sentences is often that they don't recognize the second "sentence" as being grammatically complete, with a subject and a verb. In their research, Harris and Rowan (1989) found the same thing. Students were less likely to recognize the second independent clause as having a subject and verb when (1) the subject was a pronoun, like *he, she, it, we, you, they, this, these*; or (2) the verb was a form of BE, namely, *am, is, are, was, were.* Students were especially likely to think that the second clause did not have a verb when it was a contracted form of BE. Here are some examples from my own students' papers. In each case, the student did not recognize the second part of the sentence as having a subject and a verb:

> All people in this world are born into a certain sex, they are either male or female.

Reports are like people, they all have different results and conclusions.

There are more safer ways we can solve the energy crisis, one is solar energy.

Every race has different cultures and traditions, that's what makes each culture unique.

One of these experimental drugs was cinanserin, this drug was administered to humans after minimal animal studies.

There are many reasons transsexuals turn to prostitution, here are a few.

Of course, a teacher encountering some of these sentences in a student's paper may want to suggest some change other than merely fixing the comma splice. The point here, however, is that the writers understood the concept of the comma splice but did not recognize their sentences as instances of the comma splice.

8. Making Limited but Effective Use of the Comma Splice

GOALS/RATIONALE   Once students understand the concept of the comma splice, they are better prepared to distinguish between effective uses of it and ineffective uses that would conventionally be changed during editing.

Possible Procedures

1. Put on a transparency the examples of published comma splice sentences from Brosnahan (1976) and from Figure 4.9. (Another interesting example is the first sentence of Charles Dickens's A *Tale of Two Cities:* "It was the best of times, it was the worst of times, it was the age of wisdom, it was the age of foolishness, it was the epoch of belief, it was the epoch of incredulity, it was the season of Light, it was the season of Darkness. . . .") Invite the students to decide whether these comma splice sentences are effective and, if so, why. See if they can describe some of the conditions that Brosnahan suggests are typical of the published, effective comma splice.

2. Explain how Brosnahan characterized the examples in the chart.

3. Invite students to compare these uses of the comma splice with some from their own papers (which, perhaps, you have already put on a trans-

parency). Do their comma splice sentences meet the conditions described by Brosnahan? Are they as effective? Why, or why not?

9. Understanding Phrases Contrasted with Clauses; More on the Fragment

GOALS   To enable writers to distinguish between clauses, which may or may not be independent, and phrases, which are usually grammatically dependent.

Possible Procedures

1. Put on a transparency some complete sentences (independent clauses), and point out phrases within these clauses (or put some phrases on a transparency). For example:

> Shane lives *on the lake*. [*On the lake* is a phrase within the independent clause; it does not have a subject-plus-verb nucleus.]
>
> There we stood on the dock, *abandoned by our cruise ship*. [The phrase *abandoned by our cruise ship* contains the verb form *abandoned*, but does not itself have a subject. The entire phrase is working as a modifier of *we*.]
>
> It was late, *much too late to catch the ferry*. [Again, the italicized phrase has a verb form, *to catch*, but it's not functioning as part of a subject-verb unit.]
>
> She stared incredulously, *her eyes accusing him of betrayal*. [The italicized phrase, an absolute phrase, would need *were* to be a complete clause.]

2. Explain that when a phrase is punctuated as a complete sentence, it is commonly called a fragment.

10. Eliminating Fragments; Using Fragments Sparingly but Effectively

GOALS   To enable writers to punctuate ineffective fragments conventionally, while making judicious use of fragments for particular effects.

Possible Procedures

1. Using some examples from lesson 6 in this sequence, remind students that a dependent clause is technically a fragment when it occurs alone as a punctuated sentence.

2. Remind students that the same is true of phrases punctuated as complete sentences.

3. Have available on a transparency some examples of fragments, ideally from the students' own writing—fragments that you, at least, consider ineffective. Discuss and demonstrate how to connect these to whatever they modify or go with. The following examples illustrate some common kinds of fragments:

> There wasn't anything we could do. *Until the coach arrived.* [dependent clause]
>
> The good sportsmanship award went to Carter. *The funny kid who sat next to me in science.* [This appositive phrase has a dependent clause modifying it, not an independent clause.]
>
> Hot, molten lava rolled down Mount St. Helens. *Causing havoc everywhere.* [present participial phrase]
>
> Don knew what he had to do. *Turn the sailboat around, fast.* [verbal phrase]
>
> The dog looked at me. *Its eyes pleading.* [absolute construction]
>
> Joe borrowed my car for Saturday night. *The deal being that I can use his CD player for the party Sunday.* [absolute; the verb form *being* cannot stand alone as a main verb]
>
> I won't be in class on Friday. *The reason being that the debate team is going to a tournament.* [absolute, with incomplete verb *being*]
>
> I can't go out tonight. *Being that I have to study for a math test.* [dependent clause, introduced by the colloquial *being that*]

4. Share with students the chart in Figure 4.10, which shows *dependent* fragments. Are these effective? Why, or why not? Under what conditions do dependent fragments seem to be effective?

5. Return to the fragments used for step 3. Do some of these meet the conditions for being effective as fragments, as minor sentences? Discuss.

6. Share with students some examples of independent fragments, and discuss their effectiveness. Invite students to draw upon the literature they are reading in order to contribute examples to a wall chart of published, effective fragments.

11. Fragments, Fused Sentences, and Comma Splices: A Differently Sequenced Set of Lessons

ASSUMPTIONS   This possible sequence of mini-lessons assumes that (1) the students have some sense of a subject-verb unit, but an imperfect ability to identify subjects and verbs; (2) students are writing expository and argumentative prose that naturally demands the kinds of connecting words indicated here; (3) students are making errors of the kinds indicated; (4) teachers will draw upon examples from the students' own writings in contrasting fragments and comma splices with grammatically complete sentences; and (5) steps would be skipped or reordered, depending upon the needs seen (or not seen) in the students' writing.

1. Begin with fragments that are phrases, choosing examples of common kinds.

> He closed the door. *And waited breathlessly.* [second part of compound predicate]
>
> We'll catch up soon. *In about ten minutes.* [prepositional phrase]
>
> I bought a new computer program. *Also a book.* [phrase introduced by word like *also, just, only*]
>
> She slammed the door hard. *Then left.* [phrase introduced by word like *then, first, next*]
>
> I have a lot of work to do. *For instance, wash the car.* [phrase introduced by expression like *for example, such as*]
>
> Uncle Chuck is great. *Somebody I can really admire.* [phrase that performs an appositive function]
>
> I saw him, all right. *Running down the street.* [participial phrase]
>
> Carla was exhausted. *Absolutely wiped out.* [participial phrase]

Demonstrate that these phrases are not grammatically complete; that is, they are not clauses, much less independent clauses.

Show how these phrases can become part of the independent clauses that precede them.

Collect examples of phrases from various published sources (ads, junk mail, appeals for money, published articles, novels); together, try to decide in what syntactic and rhetorical contexts and genres a fragment may be effective.

2. For another lesson, choose absolute phrases, which are near-clauses.

I washed the car. *The deal being that I get to use it today.* [Explain that *being* is not a main verb in such sentences.]

We hurried to the basement. *The tornado less than half a mile away.* [Note the absence of a main verb; show how the absolute can be connected to the clause by a comma plus *with*.]

She stood smiling in the doorway. *Her arms laden with packages.* [Note that the verb phrase is incomplete; show that the sentence can be repaired by adding *were*, or by attaching the absolute with a comma.]

3. For another lesson, choose dependent clauses punctuated as complete sentences.

I fell asleep studying. *Because I was so tired.* [adverbial clause]

I can't buy a car. *Until I earn enough money.* [adverbial clause]

Show how independent clauses can, in effect, be made dependent by putting a subordinating conjunction in front of them.

Brainstorm for subordinating words. Expand the list (see Figure A.5) and post in the classroom. Compare these with coordinating words (such as *and, but*) as necessary.

Include noun and adjective clauses later, if need be. (They occur as fragments less frequently.)

4. Consider fused sentences, if necessary, and common kinds of comma splices.

We made snowballs Greg started a snowball fight. [no connecting word or punctuation]

Show the two independent clauses. Fused sentences are often a result of haste rather than lack of understanding.

There is no way to prove this, *it* must be taken on faith. [pronoun as subject in the second independent clause]

Kim is dating Karl, he*'s* a nice guy. [contraction as verb in the second independent clause]

We didn't know what to do, we *were* really lost. [form of *be* as a main verb in second independent clause]

Perhaps the most common reason why students write two independent clauses with only a comma to connect them is that they don't recognize the second sentence as an independent clause when its subject is a pronoun or its verb is a contraction or form of BE. Explain, showing ways of repunctuating or recasting the clauses.

There are restrictions, *for instance* you cannot return it if you were responsible for damaging it. [phrase like *for example* or *such as* introducing the second independent clause]

I can't see much sense in buying lottery tickets, *however* one might get really lucky. [conjunctive adverb like *however* or *nevertheless* introducing the second independent clause]

Students often think that they should use a comma before an exemplifying phrase or a conjunctive adverb when it introduces an independent clause. Contrast the punctuation used before coordinating conjunctions (like *and* and *but*) with the punctuation used before these other kinds of connectors (a period, a semicolon, or even a colon or dashes before exemplifying phrases). Discuss the appropriateness of alternative choices. Make lists of the different kinds of connectors and post these in the classroom, with correctly punctuated sentences as examples.

12. Connecting Clauses with Conjunctive Adverbs and Punctuating Them Conventionally

GOAL   To demonstrate how to punctuate sentences conventionally when using conjunctive adverbs to connect two independent clauses.

Possible Procedures

1. Prepare and share a transparency with some examples of conjunctive adverbs used to connect two sentences (see Figure A.6 for some common conjunctive adverbs). If possible, use some conventionally punctuated sen-

FIGURE A.6   Common conjunctive adverbs.

also	accordingly	as a result
besides	consequently	for example
hence	furthermore	for instance
indeed	however	in fact
instead	meanwhile	of course
then	moreover	on the other hand
thus	nevertheless	
	therefore	

tences from students' writing. Give examples where the conjunctive adverb begins a second, separately punctuated sentence and examples where the two independent clauses are joined by a semicolon. Emphasize the use of the semicolon as contrasted with the use of a comma.

> We didn't get packed in time to catch the 8 o'clock bus. *Therefore,* we'll have to drive.
>
> Psychologically, I wasn't ready; *however,* I had to play my solo next. [Note the comma after the conjunctive adverb, *however.*]
>
> Susan is waiting in the wings; Josh, *meanwhile,* is superb in his dramatic monologue. [Note the comma before and after *meanwhile.*]

2. Take from students' writing some unconventionally punctuated sentences that include conjunctive adverbs (typically, these are comma splice sentences). Put these on a transparency, then discuss and demonstrate the conventional punctuation needed. Some examples from college freshmen:

> There are restrictions on the press, *for instance,* in a rape case the name of the victim raped is not allowed to be released.
>
> If white and black children can play together when young, how come they can't grow up together and share the same benefits, *then* each would have an equal chance to gain status.

And from preservice teachers:

> A student's uniqueness is supported and encouraged, *thus* the students do not feel the need to imitate each other.
>
> It's difficult to explain a method of teaching in its entirety, *therefore* I will explain whole language by simply comparing it to the traditional way that previous generations were taught.

He doesn't come right out and say "I am sandpaper," *rather* he leads us to try and guess who he is.

13. Comparing the Uses of, and the Punctuation Associated with, Coordinating Conjunctions, Subordinating Conjunctions, and Conjunctive Adverbs

GOAL   To clarify how different connecting words are used, with emphasis on the punctuation associated with them.

Possible Procedures

1. One of many ways to do such an activity would be to use manipulables. For instance, prepare strips of construction paper or pieces of card stock with independent clauses on them (but omit capitals and end punctuation). Try to include clauses that could be related to one another in more than one way (that is, with more than one kind of connective or subordinator). Take, for instance, the sentences *We drove all night through the mountains* and *We needed a rest,* which could logically be combined in such ways as these:

> We needed a rest, *but* we drove all night through the mountains.
>
> *After* we drove all night through the mountains, we needed a rest.
>
> We drove all night through the mountains; *therefore,* we needed a rest.

2. Put various connecting words on construction paper too, using a different color for each of the three major kinds of connectors: coordinating conjunctions, subordinating conjunctions, and conjunctive adverbs.

3. Divide the students into groups, and give each group a set of six or eight interrelatable independent clauses and several connectors from each category. Invite the students to connect pairs of sentences, using any connector they think appropriate. Ask them to write two or three of these sentences on a transparency, using the conventional punctuation, and then explain their examples to the rest of the class.

Figure A.7 is based on a chart of punctuation DOS and DON'TS that I once developed for students in our developmental writing classes at the university. However, I now realize that such a chart is much more valuable to writers if *they* help develop it, gradually.

FIGURE A.7 Punctuation DOS and DON'TS.

TO SEPARATE SENTENCES (INDEPENDENT CLAUSES)

DO	Example	DON'T	Example
Use a period.	*Sue brought the pizza.* *Al supplied the pop.*	Don't write two independent clauses without punctuation.	*Sue brought the pizza* *Al supplied the pop.*

TO JOIN SENTENCES (INDEPENDENT CLAUSES) CLOSELY RELATED IN MEANING

DO	Example	DON'T	Example
Use a semicolon.	*Sue brought the pizza;* *Al supplied the pop.*	Don't use just a comma.	*Sue brought the pizza,* *Al supplied the pop.*
Use a semicolon or a period plus a heavyweight connector.	*Sue brought the pizza; therefore* *Al supplied the pop.* *Sue brought the pizza. Therefore,* *Al supplied the pop.*	Don't use just a comma plus a heavyweight connector.	*Sue brought the pizza, therefore* *Al supplied the pop.*
Use a comma plus a lightweight connector.	*Sue brought the pizza, and Al* *supplied the pop.*	Don't use just a comma without a lightweight connector.	*Sue brought the pizza, Al* *supplied the pop.*
On rare occasions, use a period plus a lightweight connector.	*Sue brought the pizza.* *But Al supplied the pop.*	Don't use just a comma with words like *it, this, that, we, you, he, she, they.* These words are not connectors.	Joe had a party last night, it was great. Joe had a party last night, he invited everybody.

Figure A.7, continued.

TO MAKE ONE SENTENCE SUBORDINATE TO ANOTHER, CREATING A SUBORDINATE CLAUSE

Use a subordinator. When the subordinate clause begins the sentence, it should be followed by a comma. The comma is optional when the subordinate clause ends the sentence.

Since Sue brought the pizza, Al supplied the pop.

Al supplied the pop because Sue brought the pizza.

Don't let a subordinate clause stand alone as if it were a complete sentence.

<u>Since Sue brought the pizza.</u>
Al supplied the pop.

Al supplied the pop.
<u>Because Sue brought the pizza.</u>

Heavyweight Connectors
(Conjunctive Adverbs)
(Four or More Letters)

also	accordingly
besides	consequently
hence	furthermore
indeed	however
instead	meanwhile
then	moreover
thus	nevertheless
	therefore

as a result
for example
for instance
in fact
of course
on the other hand

Lightweight Connectors
(Coordinating Conjunctions)
(Three or fewer letters)

and   or   yet
but   nor   so

Subordinators
(Subordinating Conjunctions)

Contrast	Time, Sequence	Cause	Condition
although	as	as	if
even though	after	because	unless
though	before	in order that	whether
	since	since	
while	till	so that	
whereas	until		
	when		
rather than	while		

Teaching Style Through Sentence Combining and Sentence Generating

1. Introducing Participial Phrases

GOALS   To help writers see the effectiveness of using present participle phrases, when used as free modifiers. In addition, to help writers see that they can sometimes move such phrases for greater effectiveness, as they revise. Such lessons are most appropriate for writers who provide few narrative and descriptive details in their writing, or writers who provide such details in separate sentences, instead of appropriately subordinating some details in modifying phrases.

BACKGROUND   One of the constructions that most distinguishes professional writers from student writers is the participial phrase used as a free modifier—that is, as a modifier that is not absolutely essential to the sentence and therefore is set off by punctuation—usually by commas in prose, but sometimes just by line divisions in poetry (Christensen and Christensen, 1978). The present participle phrase commonly conveys action, whether it is used in poetry, fiction, or nonfiction. Such free modifiers most commonly occur at the end of the clause, even if they modify the subject of that clause. The second most common position is before the subject-predicate unit. Least common is a participial free modifier occurring between the subject and the predicate.

Possible Procedures

1. Put some examples on transparencies and discuss them with the students. For example:

> I watched the flashing past of cotton fields and cabins, *feeling that I was moving into the unknown.*
> Ralph Ellison, *Invisible Man* (1952)

> "I wish we could get wet," said Lily, *watching a boy ride his bicycle through rain puddles.*
> Amy Tan, *The Moon Lady* (1992)

Father,
All these he has made me own,
The trees and the forests
Standing in their places.
    Teton Sioux, *The Trees Stand Shining* (H. Jones, 1993)

Still laughing, Mama bustled about the kitchen until her masterpiece was complete.
    Phil Mendez, *The Black Snowman* (1989)

Far below, a sea of purple and orange clouds churned, *dashing like waves in slow motion against the mountain's green forests and reddish-brown volcanic rock.*
    Tom Minehart, "On Top of Mount Fuji, People Hope for Change" (July 17, 1993)

The river that used to surge into the Gulf of California, *depositing ruddy-colored silt that fanned out into a broad delta of new land at its mouth,* hardly ever makes it to the sea anymore.
    Paul Gray, "A Fight over Liquid Gold" (1991)

2. Discuss the placement of the participial phrases. In most cases, the participial phrase is probably most effective as is. However, what about putting the participial phrase before the subject in the second example?

> Watching a boy ride his bicycle through rain puddles, Lily said, "I wish we could get wet."

Is this order perhaps as good as the original, even though the focus has changed? By thus discussing the effects and effectiveness of placing modifiers differently, students develop a sense of style and an ability to suit the grammar to the sense of what they are writing.

3. You might also discuss examples like the following sentences from Richard Wright's poem "Between the World and Me" (1935), wherein two past tense verbs are followed by a present participle phrase:

> The dry bones stirred, rattled, lifted, *melting themselves into my bones.* And then they had me, stripped me, *battering my teeth into my throat till I swallowed my own blood.*

FIGURE A.8a Examples of "I am" poems in which the writers were encouraged to use participial phrases. The top three poems were written by sixth graders and the bottom two by seventh graders.

I am an elegant, proud daisy
Dodging life-taking lawnmowers
Spreading out my leaves and petals
Taking in carbon dioxide
Giving out a gift of oxygen.

Rachel Nieboer

PINTO

I am a widely blotched black and
white pinto
Gliding smothly into my rocky canter
Tipping over my green grain bucket
Mouthing my metal snaffle bit.

Jennifer Richardson

I am a young speedy pup.
    Brigning aggravation to my family
    Eating all in sight
    Destroying whatever I can
    Chewing away at life.

Chris Colyn

I am a long, rectangular bumper sticker
sticking on a small red car
smelling the horrible stench of the
    exhaust pipe
telling everyone that my owner loves
    New York.

Aaron Knox

I am a strong lasting tool.
    Nailing friends together
    Pounding kindness into the world
    Sawing through problems
    Sanding rough edges in life

Helen Karsten

Why might the poet have switched from past tense verbs to present participle phrases at the ends of these sentences? How is the effect different?

ADDITIONAL MINI-LESSONS Students may benefit from follow-up lessons in which they listen to or read more literary excerpts making effective use of present participle phrases. The teacher can encourage the students to find and share examples themselves. Another kind of mini-lesson can involve taking a bare-bones sentence from a student's paper and brainstorming together about details that might be added in free modifying -ING phrases. Similarly, one can demonstrate how to combine already written sentences during revision. See also the following lessons in this category.

FIGURE A.8b Examples of "I am" poems. The top two were written by college freshmen encouraged to use participial phrases as free modifiers. The bottom two were written by teachers, under less stringent conditions.

LEAVES IN THE FALL

I am a red leaf
  Floating through the brisk air
  Changing from green to fiery red
  Crumbling after being walked on
  Disappearing after crumbling
  Growing new leaves next year.

Tracey Chambers

I am ten o'clock
  steadily ticking toward noon.
A calculator, tracking my progress,
  planning my future.
I am concrete, a foundation for the
  architecture of my life.
Yet I am also a string instrument,
  vibrating with living melodies
A prism absorbing the spectrum of life
  and tossing out multicolored glints
Hungry, determined, I am my own
    canvas
  never complete

Pat Reeves

I am a soccer ball
  rolling down the field
  bouncing off the player's head
  curving around the goalie
  flying through the air
  scoring a point to win the game.

Joel Parsons

I am "Four Strong Winds" and the
    "Moonlight Sonata,"
  melancholy yet serene.
I am a Bilbo's pizza with whole wheat
    crust,
  tomato bubbly and cheese gooey
I am 5 a.m., a nun
  greeting the morning solitude,
  grateful for the absolution of a new
    day.
I am a midnight lover,
  cherishing and tender,
  tracing a smile in the dark
  with my fingertips.
I am a whitewater raft,
  sturdy yet flexible,
  bouncing over hidden rocks
  to rest beyond the whirlpool.

Connie Weaver

2. Using Present Participle Phrases as Free Modifiers

POSSIBLE PROCEDURE   Suggest to writers the option of writing "I am" poems (see Figure A.8) in which they equate themselves metaphorically with things that reflect their interests, suit their personalities, suggest their goals. Emphasize the possibility of using present participle free modifiers by sharing examples in which the writer has used them effectively.

1. A HERD OF WILD HORSES RACES ALONG A BEACH.
   Their hoofbeats carve patterns in the sand.
   Their hoofbeats churn the surf.
      [A herd of wild horses races along a beach, their hoofbeats carving
      patterns in the sand and churning the surf.]
2. Manes are flying
   Legs are flailing
   THE HORSES SURGE FORWARD INTO A DEEPENING MIST.
      [Manes flying, legs flailing, the horses surge forward into a deepening mist.]
3. THE THUNDERING HERD ALMOST DISAPPEARS.
   The herd is veiled by a blue haze.
      [The thundering herd almost disappears, veiled by a blue haze.]
4. Two stallions emerge suddenly.
   TWO STALLIONS BEGIN TO FIGHT.
      [Suddenly emerging, two stallions begin to fight.]
5. THEY REAR ON THEIR POWERFUL HIND LEGS.
   They circle each other in a deadly dance.
      [They rear on their powerful hind legs, circling each other in a deadly
      dance.]
6. The stallions have fought to a stalemate.
   THE STALLIONS RACE TO THE FRONT OF THE HERD.
      [Having fought to a stalemate, the stallions race to the front of the herd.]
7. THE HERD STAMPEDES.
   The herd is panicked by an inferno.
      [The herd stampedes, panicked by an inferno.]
8. The herd is singed by the flames.
   The herd is choked by the smoke.
   THE HERD PLUNGES DESPERATELY INTO THE SEA.
      [Singed by the flames and choked by the smoke, the herd plunges
      desperately into the sea.]

3. Creating Participial Phrases and Absolutes Through Sentence Combining

GOAL   To encourage writers to use participial phrases (both present and past) and absolute constructions in their writing. Also, to consider the stylistically effective placement of these free modifiers.

Possible Procedures

1. Put the sets of sentences shown in Figure A.9 on transparencies, leaving plenty of room to write the changes that the students suggest. It may be

9. Their fears are forgotten.
   THE HORSES FROLIC IN THE WAVES.
   They dive into the depths.
   They surface again.
   > [Their fears forgotten, the horses frolic in the waves, diving into the depths, then surfacing again.]
10. The horses are restored.
   THE HORSES MOVE BACK TOWARD THE SHORE.
   > [Restored, the horses move back toward the shore.]
11. THE SHORE IS NOW SOFTENED BY TWILIGHT.
   The shore is tinted with muted pinks and lavenders.
   > [The shore is now softened by twilight, tinted with muted pinks and lavenders.]
12. THE HORSES GALLOP IN SLOW MOTION.
   Their manes are suspended in twilight.
   Their hooves trace deliberate patterns in the sand.
   > [The horses gallop in slow motion, their manes suspended in twilight, their hooves tracing deliberate patterns in the sand.]
13. The herd runs dreamily.
   THE HERD FADES INTO THE DISTANCE.
   The herd leaves sea and shore undisturbed.
   > [Running dreamily, the herd fades into the distance, leaving sea and shore undisturbed.]

helpful to provide a copy of the activity for each student, so that students can more easily focus on the task and keep a record of the sentences they have created. Adapted from Allyn & Bacon's *The Writing Process*, Book 9 (1982), the sentences describe a short nonverbal motion picture titled *Dream of the Wild Horses.*

2. Explain that, for now, you want the sentences in each set combined into a single sentence, with the sentence in capitals remaining untouched and the others reduced to parts of sentences (free modifiers), but kept in the same order. Do the first two or three with the students. If the students reorder the parts of the resultant sentence or choose a different original sentence to leave unchanged (which is common), you can accept these variations but, whenever possible, discuss which version works better in the flow of the narrative. Don't worry, for now, about examining the structure of the newly created parts of sentences; that can be done after the narrative is created.

3. After creating a satisfying narrative, you can call students' attention to the three kinds of free modifiers they have created:

> *Running dreamily*, the herd fades into the distance, *leaving sea and shore undisturbed*. [present participle phrase. The *-ing* in these free modifiers shows that the phrases are present participles. They are verb phrases functioning as modifiers.]
>
> The herd stampedes, *panicked by an inferno*. [past participle phrase]
> *Singed by the flames and choked by the smoke*, the herd plunges desperately into the sea. [past participle phrase. The *-ed* forms in these free modifiers show that the phrases are past participles. They, too, are verb phrases functioning as modifiers.]
>
> *Their fears forgotten*, the horses frolic in the waves. [absolute phrase. The absolute has a subject and retains the essence of the verb phrase. Often, the absolute can be restored to a complete sentence by adding *am, is, are, was,* or *were*, as in *Their fears were forgotten*.]
>
> The horses gallop in slow motion, *their manes suspended in twilight, their hooves tracing deliberate patterns in the sand.* [The first absolute consists, in effect, of a subject plus a past participle phrase. The second absolute has a subject followed by a present participle phrase. The addition of *were* would restore each absolute to a complete sentence.]

As these examples illustrate, the participial phrase is essentially a verb phrase functioning like an adjective, to modify a noun. The present participle phrase typically connotes present action, while the past participle phrase connotes completed action or description. The absolute construction is effective for conveying descriptive detail, without giving it the full weight of a grammatically complete sentence.

Teacher Resources
Christensen, F., & Christensen, B. (1978). *Notes toward a new rhetoric: Nine essays for teachers* (2nd ed.). New York: Harper & Row. These essays by Francis Christensen are valuable in helping us understand some of the characteristics of today's prose style.

Daiker, D. A., Kerek, A., & Morenberg, M. (1990). *The writer's options: Combining to composing* (4th ed.). New York: Harper & Row. Intended as a text at the college level, this book is also especially valuable to teachers interested in implementing sentence-combining activities that draw upon the research of Christensen and others.

Killgallon, D. (1987). *Sentence composing: The complete course*. Portsmouth, NH: Boynton/Cook. Excellent book for students, especially at the high school level.

Figure 5.10 includes these and other references.

4. Appreciating and Using Absolute Constructions

GOALS   To help writers appreciate the absolute construction as a means of conveying descriptive detail, and to help them become sufficiently aware of the absolute construction to use it in their writing.

NOTE   See Figure 5.6 and the Glossary for other examples of the absolute. Technically the absolute is a phrase, because it's not quite grammatically complete as a sentence. Because the absolute has a "subject" and the *essence* of a verb, it can also be described as a near-clause.

Possible Procedures

1. Locate some effective absolutes from literature. The references cited in the lesson immediately above are good resources, as is Scott Rice's *Right Words, Right Places* (1993). The absolute construction is particularly common in narrative fiction and poetry—even in many picture books for children. Here are some further examples:

> I saw the giant bend and clutch the posts at the top of the stairs with both hands, bracing himself, *his body gleaming bare in his white shorts.*
>   Ralph Ellison, *Invisible Man* (1952)

> Before me, in the panel where a mirror is usually placed, I could see a scene from a bullfight, *the bull charging close to the man and the man swinging the red cape in sculptured folds so close to his body that man and bull seemed to blend in one swirl of calm, pure motion.*
>   Ralph Ellison, *Invisible Man* (1952)

> A sudden blow: *the great wings beating still*
> *Above the staggering girl, her thighs caressed*
> *By the dark webs, her nape caught in his bill,*
> He holds her helpless breast upon his breast.
>   W. B. Yeats, "Leda and the Swan" (1924)

Notice how the three absolutes in the Yeats excerpt keep the reader suspended before the main clause, as Zeus in the form of a swan approaches and then claims the girl.

2. As a follow-up, encourage students to experiment with absolutes in their own writing. As a preparatory activity, you might encourage "boast" poems like this:

> My car is a sleek gray cat,
>> its paws leaping forward the instant I accelerate,
>> its engine purring contentedly.

3. Often in students' narrative writing, one finds simple sentences like *My car is a sleek gray cat,* sentences that could benefit from including more descriptive detail in absolute phrases. When writers are ready to revise at the sentence level, the teacher can help them consider ways of expanding some sentences through absolutes that convey descriptive detail. Past participle phrases can also add descriptive detail, while present participle phrases are often effective in conveying narrative detail.

Teaching Sentence Sense and Style Through the Manipulation of Syntactic Elements

Free modifiers can often be located in more than one place in a sentence; indeed, that is one reason they are called *free* modifiers. Theoretically, from the viewpoint of grammar alone, many free modifiers can occur at the end of a sentence (that is, after the subject-plus-verb of an independent clause), at the beginning of the sentence, or after the subject and before the verb. For example:

> The boat moved forward, *plowing through the waves.*
> *Plowing through the waves,* the boat moved forward.
> The boat, *plowing through the waves,* moved forward.

While all three positions are technically possible, probably only one or two will seem rhetorically effective or appropriate, to most readers. In this case, most of us would probably agree that the first alternative is especially effective in placing the free modifier at the end.

In addition to discussing the placement of free modifiers like participial phrases and absolutes, we can often help writers make their sentences more effective by moving some other kind of modifying phrase. With college students, I have sometimes used examples from the first draft of my own writing, as illustrated in the following lesson.

1. Moving a Medial Modifier

GOAL   To help writers understand that a sentence can be unnecessarily difficult to process if there is a long modifying phrase that comes after the subject and before the verb, and to help them gain experience in moving a modifier to the front of the sentence to get it out of the way.

POSSIBLE PROCEDURES   Put on a transparency some sentences like the following, and demonstrate how to move the medial modifier to the front of the sentence:

> Michael Gordon, *a psychologist experienced in working with schools to help ADHD kids*, suggests no more than 30–45 minutes of homework for ADHD children in the elementary grades, and no more than an hour or so for older children.

This sentence is probably clearer if the modifying phrase (an appositive) is moved to the front of the sentence:

> *A psychologist experienced in working with schools to help ADHD kids*, Michael Gordon suggests . . .

2. Putting the "Given" Information First and Ending with the "New"

GOAL   To help writers learn to put the "new" or most important information at the end of a sentence, where it is psychologically more effective.

PROCEDURES   Put on a transparency some examples from your own or your students' writing, and revise the sentence so as not to end it with the less important information:

> Children in whole language classrooms read for meaning better, corrected more of their mistakes (miscues), and retold more fully the stories they read than did children in the traditional classrooms.

In examining this sentence I'd written, I concluded that it ended weakly. Therefore, I revised it as follows:

> In comparison with children in the traditional classrooms, children in whole language classrooms read for meaning better, corrected more of their mistakes (miscues), and retold more fully the stories they read.

Now the sentence ends with the ways in which children in the whole language classrooms excelled; in other words, it ends with the point I wanted to emphasize.

3. Using a WH Word Transform or an it Transform for Emphasis

GOAL   To enable writers to see the advantages of using a WH word transform or an *it* transform for emphasis, and to experiment with such constructions.

Possible Procedures

1. Put on a transparency some examples like the following untransformed sentence (to use the terminology of transformational grammar) and then the transformed version:

> You probably realized that I was bothered by your decision. *However, you may not have realized that I was particularly bothered by your choice of directors.* [untransformed]
> You probably realized that I was bothered by your decision. *What you may not have realized, however, is that I was particularly bothered by your choice of directors.* [transformed]

The transformed version calls greater attention to what "you" may not have realized. Other examples:

> I didn't really want steak, though. *What I really wanted was Chinese food.*
> It was hard to imagine how she had finished the job so quickly. *What really amazed me, though, was the quality of the work.*

Sentences like this are sometimes called cleft sentences because the basic message is cleft, or divided, by an added word. With WH word transforms, that added word is a form of the BE verb.

The following examples are similar, but involve an *it* transform rather than a WH word transform:

> Nationalism tries to check the growth of world civilization.
> [untransformed]
>
> It is nationalism that tries to check the growth of world civilization.
> [transformed, with *that* added]
>> J. B. Priestley, "Wrong Ism"
>
> Joe Dillon introduced the Wild West to us.
>
> It was Joe Dillon who introduced the Wild West to us. [transformed, with *who* added]
>> James Joyce, "An Encounter"

Almost always, these cleft sentences build upon something that came before. For example, the sentence from Priestley was most likely preceded by a sentence indicating that something was inhibiting the growth of world civilization. Similarly, the sentence from Joyce was most likely preceded by a sentence mentioning the Wild West. The same pattern holds for the WH-word transforms, which are usually preceded by a contrasting statement to which they implicitly refer. In each of the following examples from published writing, you can see how the sentence must build upon something that came before:

> What followed was a series of countless individual and collective decisions that together added up to making a difference in how English language arts is—and will be—taught and learned in Michigan.
>> Ellen Brinkley (Michigan State Board of Education, 1994)
>
> In *The Input Hypothesis* (1985), Krashen discusses some of the evidence for his theory of second language acquisition. What I would like to do here is review some of the evidence. . . .
>> Constance Weaver, *Reading Process and Practice* (1994)
>
> What the research tells me is that if children or less literate adults start reading for pleasure, however, good things will happen.
>> Stephen Krashen, *The Power of Reading* (1993)

2. Invite students to create WH word transform sentences to follow statements like these:

> I didn't really want X. What I wanted was . . .
>
> He knew where to go. What he didn't know was . . .

4. Using it and there Transforms to Avoid Awkward Sentences

GOAL   To help writers understand that beginning a sentence with the introductory *it* or *there* is sometimes effective, despite what the grammar handbooks commonly say.

POSSIBLE PROCEDURES   Put on a transparency some sentences like the following. Demonstrate and discuss how much more awkward (or downright impossible) it would be to eliminate the introductory *it* or *there*.

> It is almost a truism among students of architectural history that the use of the arch and the vault began with the Romans.
> "Arches and Vaults in the Ancient Near East" (1989)

To avoid the introductory *it,* we would have to reword the sentence something like this:

> Among students of architectural history, the idea *that the use of the arch and the vault began with the Romans* is almost a truism.

This version has a long modifier after the subject and before the verb, making the sentence more difficult to comprehend. The *it* transform is clearer. Take another example:

> It is almost impossible to project your psychotic image life into the mind of another via telepathy and keep the hallucinations from becoming sensually weaker.

This time, the untransformed sentence was the published version:

> The task of projecting your psychotic image life into the mind of another via telepathy and keeping the hallucinations from becoming sensually weaker is almost impossible.
> Ray Bradbury, *The Martian Chronicles* (1950)

Note, though, the greater difficulty in processing the sentence when an extremely long phrase separates the subject, *task,* from the verb and the rest of the predicate, *is impossible*.

Here are some examples of the *there* transform functioning effectively:

> There are other streets in Paris as ugly as the Boulevard Raspail.
> Ernest Hemingway, *The Sun Also Rises* (1926)

There was no funeral. There was no music. There was no period of mourning. There were no flowers. There were only silence, quiet weeping, whispers, and fear.

Richard Wright, *Black Boy* (1937)

If desired, a mini-lesson could follow on the topic of subject-verb agreement in sentences beginning with an introductory *there*. Several of the published examples in this section are taken from Scott Rice's *Right Words, Right Places* (1993, pp. 37–42).

5. *Using the Passive When Naming the Agent Is Not Necessary*

GOAL   To demonstrate to writers that the passive construction has its uses, despite what the grammar handbooks commonly say.

POSSIBLE PROCEDURES   Put on a transparency a passage that makes appropriate and effective use of the passive construction: perhaps a news story about a murder, wherein the journalist must avoid saying who committed the crime. My favorite example is one from Postman and Weingartner's *Linguistics: A Revolution in Teaching* (1966). The passage they cite is the opening paragraph of "The Great Wall of China," by Franz Kafka. In the translation they have used, it begins this way:

> The Great Wall of China was finished off at its northern-most corner. From the south-east and the south-west it came up in two sections that finally converged there. This principle of piecemeal construction was also applied on a smaller scale by both of the two great armies of labor, the eastern and the western. It was done in this way.

Postman and Weingartner quote the entire paragraph and pose three "problems" that lead students to draw conclusions about what difference it makes to use the passive rather than the active in describing how the Great Wall was built.

Teaching the Power of Dialects and Dialects of Power

Many teachers have taught students to "correct their usage" without realizing that the students' language patterns reflect a viable and equally valid communication system, from a linguistic point of view. We have simply thought we were teaching students to speak and write "correctly," without realizing that their speech *is* correct, for the language community in which they have been nurtured or with which they identify. In short, we have not always taken into account that our students' different dialect is, in many circumstances, more appropriate than ours. Instead of focusing on the dialects of the powerful within the larger society, then, the following mini-lessons are designed to help preservice and inservice teachers better understand the viability and power of dialects and the importance of valuing all dialects and voices, rather than trying to eradicate our students' native dialects in favor of our own. Given this acceptance, we are then in a better position to help students learn to switch dialect patterns to suit their audience and situation.

1. Accepting Others' Language Patterns and Voices, and Examining Attitudes Toward Dialects

GOALS To encourage appreciation for others' dialects and acceptance of so-called nonstandard dialects in the classroom, in order not to stifle our students' voices. To consider and reconsider, as teachers, what stances we should take toward dialects and dialect differences.

POSSIBLE PROCEDURES Share with students the poem "Parsley," by Rita Dove (1983). Explain that according to the poet's note, on October 2, 1957, Rafael Trujillo (1891–1961), then dictator of the Dominican Republic, ordered 20,000 blacks to be killed because they couldn't pronounce the letter *r* in *perejil*, the Spanish word for parsley. To facilitate discussion, you might use the following comments from Noguchi (1991) regarding the commonly observed fact that "the social status of a language variety is intimately linked to the social status of its users" (p. 115):

> Like other primates of the animal kingdom, humans seek, in one way or another, to signal, enhance, and ultimately, protect status. (Note, for example, the often painstaking care we take in the purchase, display, and maintenance of clothes, cars, and abodes, a care sometimes far exceeding the utilitarian purposes of these artifacts.) Language partakes in these activities insofar as linguistic form conveys not just cognitive meaning but often social status as well—high, low, in between, insider, outsider. . . . (p. 114)

Noguchi goes on to suggest that professionals, including teachers, who engage excessively in looking for "errors" in others' speech or writing may

FIGURE A.10   References on dialects versus the Language of Wider Communication.

Christensen, L. (1994). Whose standard? Teaching standard English. In B. Bigelow, L. Christensen, S. Karp, B. Miner, & B. Peterson (Eds.), *Rethinking our classrooms: Teaching for equity and justice*. Milwaukee, WI: Rethinking Schools.

Conference on College Composition and Communication. (1974). *Students' right to their own language*. Urbana, IL: National Council of Teachers of English.

Conference on College Composition and Communication. (1988). *The national language policy* (position statement). Urbana, IL: National Council of Teachers of English.

Delpit, L. D. (1992). Acquisition of literate discourse: Bowing before the master? *Theory into Practice, 31*, 296–302.

Farr, M., & Daniels, H. (1986). *Language diversity and writing instruction*. Urbana, IL: ERIC Institute for Urban and Minority Education and the National Council of Teachers of English.

Seymour, D. Z. (1971). Black children, black speech. *Commonweal Magazine*, November 19. Reprinted in P. Eschholz, A. Rosa, & V. Clark (Eds.), *Language awareness* (6th ed., pp. 122–130). New York: St. Martin's Press, 1994. See also in the same book the article by R. L. Jones, pp. 131–134.

Sledd, J. H. (1969). Bi-dialectalism: The linguistics of white supremacy. *English Journal, 58*, 1307–1315.

Smitherman, G. (1972). English teacher, why you be doing the thangs you don't do? *English Journal, 61*, 59–65.

(whether they realize it or not) be trying to "signal, enhance, or protect their own status or the status of their group" (p. 114).

With teachers especially, here are some thought-provoking questions that might be raised. Does Noguchi imply that teachers and other members of the middle class have looked down upon other dialects because they have looked down upon the speakers of these dialects? If so, and if Noguchi is correct, what are some of the implications: for us as teachers, for students whose dialects have not been valued by many in the middle and upper classes, and for the students who ordinarily speak the valued Language of Wider Communication? Can we break out of the tendency, and help our students break out of the tendency, to use language as a means of preserving and enhancing status? Must we instead, or also, help students become comfortable with using the Language of Wider Communication, the language that has traditionally signaled greater status in many formal situations? For different perspectives on this matter, consult such references as the ones listed in Figure A.10.

Rayford's Song

Rayford's song was Rayford's song,
but it was not his alone, to own.
He had it, though, and kept it to himself
as we rowed-rowed-rowed the boat
through English country gardens
with all the whispering hope
we could muster, along with occasional
choruses of funiculi-funicula!

Weren't we a cheery lot—
comin' 'round the mountain
with Susanna, banjos on our knees,
rompin' through the leaves
of the third-grade music textbook.

Then Rayford Butler raised his hand.
For the first time, actually,
in all the weeks he had been in class,
and for the only time before he'd leave.
Yes, quiet Rayford, silent Rayford,
little Rayford, dark Rayford—
always in the same overalls—
that Rayford, Rayford Butler, raised his hand:

"Miss Gordon, ma'am—
we always singing your songs.
Could I sing one of my own?"

Pause. We looked at one another,
we looked at Rayford Butler,
we looked up at Miss Gordon, who said:

"Well, I suppose so, Rayford—
if you insist. Go ahead.
Just one song. Make it short."

And Rayford Butler stood up very straight,
and in his high voice, sang:

"*Suh-whing ah-loooow,*
suh-wheeet ah-charr-eee-oohh,
ah-comin' for to carr-eee
meee ah-hooooome . . . "

Pause. Classroom, school, schoolyard,
neighborhood, the whole world

focusing on that one song, one voice
which had a light to it, making even
Miss Gordon's white hair shine
in the glory of it, glowing
in the radiance of the song.

Pause. Rayford Butler sat down.
And while the rest of us
may have been spellbound,
on Miss Gordon's face
was something like a smile,
or perhaps a frown:

    "Very good, Rayford.
    However, I must correct you:
    the word is 'chari*ot*.'
    'Chari*ot*.' And there is no
    such thing as a 'chario.'
    Do you understand me?"

    "But Miss Gordon . . ."

    "I said 'chari*ot*, chari*ot*.'
    Can you pronounce that for me?"

    "Yes, Miss Gordon. Chari*ot*."

    "Very good, Rayford.
    Now, class, before we return
    to our book, would anyone else
    care to sing a song of their own?"

Our songs, our songs, were there—
on tips of tongues, but stuck
in throats—songs of love,
fun, animals, and valor, songs
of other lands, in other languages,
but they just wouldn't come out.
Where did our voices go?

Rayford's song was Rayford's song,
but it was not his alone, to own.

    "Well, then, class—
    let's turn our books to
    'Old Black Joe.'"

Lawson Inada

2. Preserving and Appreciating Various Dialects and Voices

Possible Procedures

1. Share with students the poem "Rayford's Song," by Lawson Inada (1993) (Figure A.11, p. 230). Discuss the issues and concerns it raises.

In Linda Christensen's article "Celebrating the Student's Voice" (1994a), she explains that Inada came to her classroom and gave the following background on this story:

> In "Rayford's Song," Inada remembers one of his classrooms in the 1930s in Fresno, a town in California's San Joaquin Valley where many people of African, Chinese, Filipino, Japanese, and Mexican descent worked in the fields and canneries. "Our classroom was filled with shades of brown," he recalls. "Our names were Rayford Butler, Consuela and Pedro Gonzales, Susie Chin, and Sam Shimabukuro. We were a mixture. The only white person in the room was our teacher. Our textbooks had pictures and stories about white kids named Dick and Jane and their dog, Spot. And the songs in our songbooks were about Old Susanah coming 'round the mountain and English gardens—songs we never heard in our neighborhood." (p. 109)

In discussing the language issues raised by "Rayford's Song," you might also discuss other poems or passages wherein the persona expresses a connection between identity and language:

> "Words," by Vern Rutsala (1992), which explains why students rejected the fancy words of the teacher and school.
> Letter to Nettie from Celie, on pp. 183–184 of Alice Walker's *The Color Purple* (1982).
> The poems "Learning English" and "English con Salsa," in *Cool Salsa: Bilingual Poems on Growing Up Latino in the United States* (Carlson, 1994).

2. Share different literary works in which the author has attempted to represent an ethnic, regional, or community dialect. Picture books often appeal to readers of all ages. In Figure A.12 are listed several books that represent the Appalachian dialect, other regional and ethnic dialects, and Black English Vernacular.

3. Invite students to write or "translate" a piece into an ethnic, regional, or community dialect. For example, here is a translation by Gayle Crittenden,

FIGURE A.12   References representing various dialects.

APPALACHIAN DIALECT IN PICTURE BOOKS

Birdseye, T., & Birdseye, D. H. (1994). *She'll be comin' round the mountain*. Illus. A. Glass. New York: Holiday House. An adaptation of the familiar song, which was originally a black spiritual called "When the Chariot Comes."

Compton, J. (1994). *Ashpet, an Appalachian tale*. Illus. K. Compton. New York: Holiday House. A retelling of the Appalachian version of the Cinderella story.

Turner, T. N. (1994). *Hillbilly night afore Christmas*. Illus. J. Rice. Gretna, LA: Pelican. An adaptation of the *The night before Christmas,* by Clement Moore.

Van Laan, N. (1990). *Possum come a-knockin*. Illus. G. Booth. New York: Alfred A. Knopf, Dragonfly Books.

OTHER REGIONAL AND ETHNIC DIALECTS IN PICTURE BOOKS

"Trosclair." (1992). *Cajun night before Christmas*. Illus. J. Rice, Ed. by Howard Jacobs. Gretna, LA: Pelican. The dust jacket mentions several other books written or illustrated by James Rice that may include regional dialect, including *Texas night before Christmas* (1986), *Cowboy night before Christmas* (1986), *A southern time Christmas* (Bernardini, 1991), and *Cajun Columbus* (Hughes, 1991).

BLACK ENGLISH VERNACULAR

Simmons, G. M., & Hutchinson, H. D. (Eds.). (1972). *Black culture: Reading and writing black*. New York: Holt, Rinehart. For adults and young adults, an anthology that includes some essays on Black English Vernacular, including some that employ features of the dialect.

---

an African American, who was a preservice teacher in one of my grammar classes. Read aloud by someone who speaks Black English Vernacular, the passage has a beauty, rhythm, and genuineness that preserves, for me at least, the reverence of the King James Version of the Bible, upon which it was based.

1 Corinthians of the Holy Bible: King James Version
Chapter 13
Black English Vernacular Translation

1. I could take languages that I ain't been taught, and be knowing every one in all of heaven and earth, but if I ain't got no love for nobody, I jus' be makin' noise.
2. If I be goin' round prophesyin' and knowin' all about what gon' to be happenin' in the future, and know everything 'bout *everything*, and (if

I) ain't got no love for folks, it still don't make no difference. I could be movin' mountains and I still wouldn't be nothin' without no love.

3. Peoples could be givin' everything dey got to po' folks, an' even get jacked for preachin' the Gospel. But if there ain't no love, they be jus' goin' round in circles.

4. Love be patient and kind. It ain't jealous or envious. It ain't boastful or proud.

5. And love ain't selfish or rude. It don't take its own way, or be ruffled easily. It don't hold a grudge and hardly even notice when folks do it wrong.

6. It never glad 'bout wrong things. It be happy when truth win out.

7. Love bear up under anything and everything that come. Love always believe the best of everybody, an' it stand everything an' not fade. It endure everything and stay strong.

8. Love go on forever and ever, when all the prophesyin', language and knowledge gone.

9. 'Cause we be knowin' so little, even with these things, and the preachin' of those who is gifted still don't be enough.

10. But when we be made perfect, then all these thing will come to an end, and they will disappear.

11. It like this: When I was a chile, I talk and thought and reasoned like a chile do. But when I became a man, I have did away with childish things.

12. 'Cause now it like we lookin' through blurry glass that we can't see through, and be knowin' a little: but when He comes we be knowin' things that only God know and I'll understand and know things the way God been understandin' and knowin' me.

3. Considering Dialect Appropriateness for Audience and Purpose

Possible Procedures

1. Invite students to consider the dialect patterns reflected in the following two essays. The first is from Geneva Smitherman's "English Teacher, Why You Be Doing the Thangs You Don't Do?" (1972). The second is from Suzette Elgin's "Don't No Revolutions Hardly *Ever* Come by Here" (1978). Discuss whether the use of dialect and informal speech patterns is appropriate to the writer's purpose and audience. Are there situations today where the use of ethnic, regional, or community dialect forms is particularly appropriate in writing, other than in poetry, drama, or fiction?

Let me say right from the bell, this piece is not to be taken as an indictment of *all* English teachers in inner-city Black schools, for there are, to be sure, a few brave, enlightened souls who are doing an excellent job in the ghetto. To them, I say: just keep on keepin' on. But to those others, that whole heap of English teachers who be castigating Black students for using a "nonstandard" dialect—I got to say: the question in the title is directed to you, and if the shoe fit, put it on.

In all fairness, I suppose, one must credit many such correctionist English teachers for the misguided notion that they are readying Black students for the world (read: white America). . . . As a daughter of the Black ghetto myself, don't seem like it's no reason the teacher be doin' none of that correctin' mess. (After all, what do you want—good grammar or good sense?) [Smitherman, 1972]

There were some other bothersome things I noticed at the time. Just for a for-instance, we know that the part of the brain that runs things when we talk and understand is a different part than the one we use for reading and writing. Seeing as how that's so, it's not unreasonable to think about that as being a need for a bridge from the one part to the other. We know that when somebody's convinced a student he'll do badly, and when he has a teacher that thinks the same, you can count on him to oblige by doing as near his worst as he can get. In my state of California a student can't hardly pick up a paper or turn on the TV news without getting told yet one more time how many dreadful things are wrong with her or him; it seems likely they'd take it for granted their teachers believe the news. And then my experience with students in linguistics has always been that—writing classes or no writing classes—somehow or tother they do learn how to write. Same as the professors, they may write stuff that's boring, or it sounds like a brand new preacher wrote it with his collar too tight at the time, or that has a whole lot of other things about it that could do with some rearranging; but one and all they learn College English, and they're right good at putting it to use. Finally, there's few creatures as crazy for finding out how things go together and what you do with them as people are. It seems no more than common sense that just taking advantage of that side of human nature would make a student work hard at learning things. [Elgin, 1978]

2. Compare the preceding Smitherman excerpt with the following excerpt from a language policy statement from the late 1980s, which Smitherman participated in drafting (Conference on College Composition and Communication, 1988). Consider whether this seems a reasonable language policy for the late twentieth and twenty-first centuries. (Item 1 is meant to include competence in a so-called standard dialect of English, at least for those who speak English as their native language.)

Be it resolved that CCCC members promote the National Language Policy adopted at the Executive Committee meeting on March 16, 1988. This policy has three inseparable parts:

1. To provide resources to enable native and nonnative speakers to achieve oral and literate competence in English, the language of wider communication.
2. To support programs that assert the legitimacy of native languages and dialects and ensure that proficiency in one's mother tongue will not be lost.
3. To foster the teaching of languages other than English so that native speakers of English can rediscover the language of their heritage or learn a second language.

Teaching Punctuation and Mechanics for Convention, Clarity, and Style

In this section, I have chosen to illustrate three lessons relevant to editing for the conventions of written English and one lesson on breaking those conventions for particular effects.

1. Using the Apostrophe in Possessives

GOAL   To heighten writers' awareness of how the apostrophe is used in possessives, along with the fact that it is not used in ordinary plurals or in ordinary verbs.

Possible Procedures

1. Choose some sentences from students' writing that use the apostrophe correctly in possessives. Demonstrate how these possessive nouns always modify (describe) a following noun. Figure A.13 shows some sentences from my own students' writing.

2. For a second lesson, choose sentences in which the apostrophe has been overgeneralized to an ordinary plural or an ordinary verb. Show how these constructions fail to meet the criterion just explained (see Figure A.14).

FIGURE A.13   Punctuating possessive nouns.

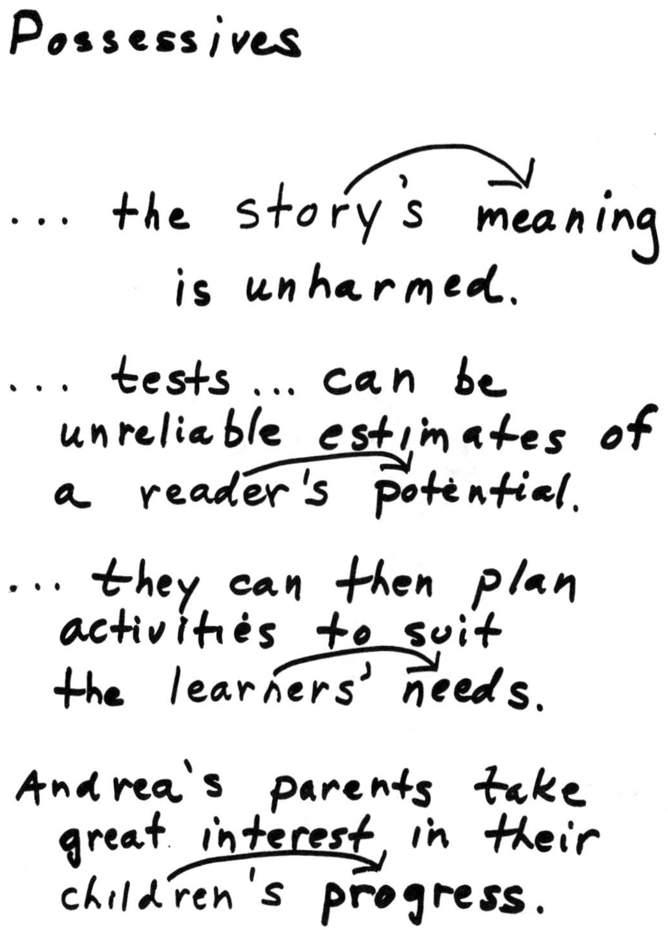

Possessives

... the story's meaning
is unharmed.

... tests ... can be
unreliable estimates of
a reader's potential.

... they can then plan
activities to suit
the learners' needs.

Andrea's parents take
great interest, in their
children's progress.

2. Using the Colon as an Announcer

GOAL   To clarify how the colon is used.

Possible Procedures

1. I compare the colon to a trumpet signaling an announcement. Most commonly, the colon is said to introduce a list of things. However, it is also

FIGURE A.14   Ordinary plurals versus possessives.

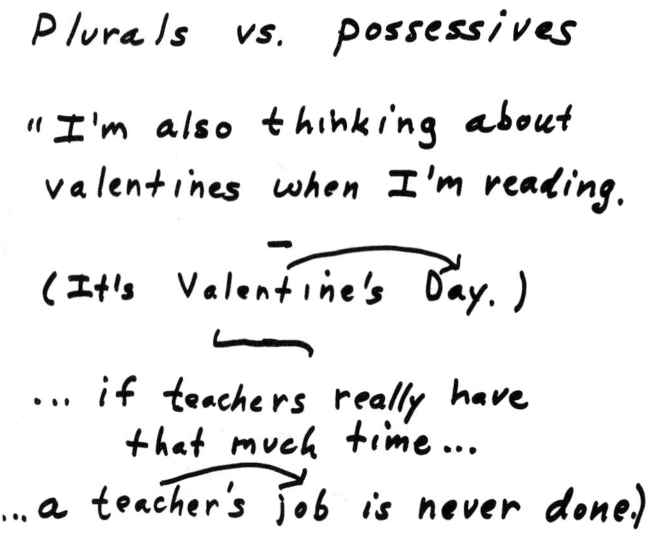

Plurals vs. possessives

"I'm also thinking about valentines when I'm reading.

(It's Valentine's Day.)

... if teachers really have that much time...

...a teacher's job is never done.)

used at the end of an independent clause to signal that the following clause or phrase in some way explains, clarifies, or summarizes the first. Examples that can be shared on transparencies:

> We brought lots of things back from Europe: some Austrian crystal, wax ornaments, two nutcrackers, and a beer stein.
>
> There are at least three reasons we can't go again this summer: it's too expensive, we have to work, and we promised ourselves to go to Hawaii first.
>
> Travel planners usually suggest trips that are way too expensive: my agent, for example, recommended a complete tour of Asia for several thousand dollars. [A semicolon could go here instead of a colon. But when a second sentence clarifies or gives an example relating to the first, a colon is at least an option. So is a period, of course.]
>
> This is what I really want: to go on safari in Africa.
>
> There was just one thing he wanted to do in Arizona: see the Grand Canyon.
>
> There was just one place he wanted to go: the Grand Canyon. [A dash could replace the colon in this sentence and the previous one.]

2. Three uses of the colon are commonly discouraged by the grammar handbooks. These could be shared in a follow-up mini-lesson.

> The six basic colors are: red, orange, yellow, green, blue, and purple. [delete colon after *am, is, are, was,* or *were* functioning as the verb]
>
> We wanted to go someplace warm, such as: Hawaii, Jamaica, or Cancun. [delete colon after *such as* or *for example*]
>
> The places where we could still get reservations consisted of: Las Vegas, Miami, and Phoenix. [delete colon between a preposition and its object]

3. Punctuating Restrictive and Nonrestrictive Clauses and Elements

As usual, a good way to present the information is via a transparency. I have sketched here the kind of information that might be presented in a sequence of mini-lessons (use of the grammatical terminology may be minimized or eliminated). This treatment, not usually found in the grammar handbooks, emphasizes the relationship between whole clauses and the phrases that can be viewed as reductions of them. For other explanations and examples, check a grammar handbook's treatment of restrictive and nonrestrictive clauses, participial phrases, appositives, and of course the uses of the comma.

Here are some of the points you may want to make, through a discussion of examples:

1. Restrictive and nonrestrictive clauses are adjective clauses; they modify nouns.
2. A restrictive clause (or a phrase or word derived from a deep structure clause) is one that the writer considers essential for identifying who or what is being discussed. Therefore, a restrictive clause may also be called an essential clause.
3. In contrast, a nonrestrictive or nonessential clause (or phrase or word) is one not considered essential for identifying who or what is being discussed. It adds details that are interesting, but not crucial for identification.
4. A restrictive or essential modifier is not set off by commas or other punctuation—precisely because it is essential.
5. A nonrestrictive or nonessential modifier is set off by commas from the rest of the sentence. That is, a comma comes both before it and

after it, unless the modifier occurs at the beginning or end of the sentence. (Sometimes, when a sentence contains commas for other reasons, a nonessential modifier will be set off with dashes or parentheses.)

6. The word *that* is ordinarily used to introduce restrictive clauses, the word *which* to introduce nonrestrictive clauses. *Who* can introduce either kind.

Examples

The kids *who broke into our garage* left tennis shoe prints on the oily floor. [The clause is essential to identify which kids. Therefore, it is not set off by commas.]

The riot *that occurred at Mt. Pleasant this weekend* should never have happened.

The riot *at Mt. Pleasant this weekend* should never have happened. [The clause or phrase is essential to clarify which riot. Therefore, it is not set off by commas.]

All triangles *that consist of three sides of equal length* are equilateral triangles.

All triangles *consisting of three sides of equal length* are equilateral triangles. [The clause or phrase is considered essential for identifying which triangles.]

She likes best my book that is called *Understanding Whole Language*.

She likes best my book *Understanding Whole Language*. [The title is essential for identifying which book, because I've written more than one. Notice that we would ordinarily reduce the underlying clause to just a phrase, the actual title of the book.]

My latest book, [which is] *Success At Last!*, deals with helping students who have an attention deficit disorder achieve success—in life, and in the classroom. [The word *latest* already clarifies which book. Therefore, the title would be considered nonessential.]

Our next-door neighbor, [who is] *Mr. Hawking*, teaches music at the middle school.

Mr. Hawking, [who is] *our next-door neighbor*, teaches music at the middle school. [The modifying clause or phrase is not considered essential to clarify who is being discussed. Therefore it is set off by commas.]

The rhythm method, *which is often mistakenly considered birth control*, is nearly 100% effective in producing parents. [The clause or phrase is nonessential.]

Often mistakenly considered birth control, the rhythm method is nearly 100% effective in producing parents.

Similarly, in each of the following instances the person is identified by name. Therefore, the modifying clause or phrase is considered nonessential and is set off by commas.

Old Mr. MacGregor, *who hated for rabbits to eat his carrots*, chased Peter with a hoe.

Hating for rabbits to eat his carrots, Old Mr. MacGregor chased Peter with a hoe.

Paul, *who wanted to be sure the rapids could be run safely*, went ahead to scout them.

Wanting to be sure the rapids could be run safely, Paul went ahead to scout them.

Paul went ahead to scout the rapids, *wanting to be sure they could be run safely*.

Carla, *who was involved in her book*, did not hear the emergency siren.

Involved in her book, Carla did not hear the emergency siren.

Charlie, *who was eager to see what might happen*, poured the chemicals together.

Eager to see what might happen, Charlie poured the chemicals together.

4. Using Punctuation and Orthography for Particular Effects

Many teachers familiar with the poetry of e.e. cummings have encouraged their students to experiment with using punctuation or orthography unconventionally, for particular effect. One such poem, which my son wrote in a high school creative writing class, follows:

CUMMINGNESS

is it a virus
a disease
is this (cummingness) catchy
cant i X-cape
h(l)pm(e)
pl-ease

John Weaver

Such playfulness with language does not, however, have to be confined to poetry. In fact, it can be employed with serious informative or persuasive intent.

One teacher in my grammar class, Martha Bay, became fascinated with the ideas in Tom Romano's article "Breaking the Rules in Style" (1988), ideas that came originally from Winston Weathers's *An Alternate Style: Options in Composition* (1980). Intrigued enough to try the ideas herself, Martha described her evolving philosophy of teaching grammar in the double voice mode, with one voice that of a traditional English teacher, and the other that of a teacher eager to try teaching grammar in the context of its use. Following are what read like journal entries from these two voices. In this excerpt, it is mostly orthography that is used unconventionally, not punctuation.

Mini-lessons; WOW. mini-LESSONS-WOW. No more diagramming of sentences. Discovery-exPloration of other writers will help to show different styles students can use in their own writing. EXPERimenting (EXPERience—EXPERt). If there is a need with a specific grammar problem it can be taken care of individually. Short LESSONS (mini) to whole class on concept. Let them find use for lesson in each others' writing.

FrrrrraGMENTS! not Here in my room. Dieagramming is the only way to learn the proper sentence structure for my students. Teachers from other classes are always complaining on the poor content and grammar of the students' writing so they must need more work, more dittos. more, more, More, mORe papers. Good writers, must know; at all times—what is cor retcht in grammar.

In our concern for correctness and teaching the conventions of Edited American English, let us be sure to still encourage such playfulness with language as that exhibited by Martha Bay.

GLOSSARY OF GRAMMATICAL TERMS

This glossary does not list all the grammatical or grammar-related terms used in the book, but it defines the the ones mentioned as most useful and describes or illustrates a few others that are used frequently or that teachers of writing might use incidentally in explaining how grammar determines punctuation. However, some of the more technical grammatical terms are illustrated and sometimes briefly defined within the main entries; for instance, the gerund is mentioned under **Verb,** and the direct object and predicate nominative are mentioned under **Noun.** The glossary mainly reflects traditional terminology with which teachers may be familiar, though I have also drawn upon insights from structural and transformational linguistics (see Chapter 3) in an attempt to improve upon the traditional explanations.

Among the most useful terms are **subject, verb, predicate; clause, independent clause,** and **dependent clause; sentence, grammatical sentence,** and **T-unit** (all three meaning the same); and **modifier** and **free modifier.** It is recommended that those with little background in grammar read these entries before reading others.

Absolute   An absolute construction functions as a free modifier within a sentence. Though technically a phrase, the absolute has a subject of sorts, and most of a verb phrase; therefore, it is sometimes characterized as a near-clause. In each of the following examples, the absolute could be made into an independent clause by adding a form of the verb BE (*am, is, are, was,* or *were*). This reveals its near-clause nature.

I shouldn't have been surprised that the flooding Pacuare rose while we slept beside it for the night, *its muddy waters picking up speed as it swelled its banks.*

My *protesting lungs ready to betray me,* I worked my way to the edge of the raft and popped out from under, gasping for air.

Once hauled in, for the longest time I lay in the raft like an overturned turtle, *my arms and legs useless.*

Other, less common examples of the absolute include the incomplete verb *being:*

Joe borrowed my car for Saturday night, *the deal being that I can use his CD player for the party Sunday.*

I won't be in class on Friday, *the reason being that the debate team is going to a tournament.*

While such absolute constructions are grammatical, they may be less effective than another alternative. In the second example, for instance, *the reason being that* could be changed to *because.*

Adjective   An adjective is a word used to describe or "modify" a noun. More generally, any word or group of words that modifies a noun can be called an adjectival. Basic adjectives can usually be compared for degree: *slow, slower, slowest; good, better, best; reasonable, more reasonable, most reasonable.* Other single words may function like adjectives, but they are not regular adjectives. For writers, what is most important is the adjectival *function*, not the niceties of what is and is not technically an adjective. In the following examples, the adjectivals are italicized, and the actual adjectives are underlined. (However, I have not marked as adjectivals the articles *a*, *an*, and *the*, or other determiners like *this* and *these* when they function adjectivally.)

The raft had been swept over a <u>modest</u> waterfall.

The *most <u>frightening</u>* part was a <u>long</u> rapids *on a river called the Général.* [Notice that *on a river called the Général* describes what rapids, and within that modifier the phrase *called the Général* describes what river. The first of these two modifiers is called a prepositional phrase, while the second is a participial phrase.]

But then, <u>*another*</u> wave engulfed me. [*Another* is an adjectival here, though it can also function as a pronoun.]

I was game, despite our <u>little</u> adventure in the Nantahala at <u>high</u> *flood* stage the <u>previous</u> summer. [This sentence contains three regular adjectives, plus a noun functioning as an adjectival: *flood*. A noun modifying another noun is more technically called a noun adjunct.]

Getting thrown into the *raging* river was <u>scary.</u> [The first adjectival is a present participle. The second one, *scary*, functions as a predicate adjective: it occurs in the predicate part of the sentence but modifies the subject, *Getting thrown into the raging river*.]

And Rollie, *a water lover since childhood*, had been warned not to "go out too far." [This adjectival is more technically called an appositive construction.]

The wall *of water* momentarily crushed me, *pushing me toward the bottom of the river.* [*Of water* is a prepositional phrase modifying the noun *wall*. The other adjectival modifies the same noun; it is a participial phrase telling what the wall of water did.]

The rush *of fear* had left me absolutely <u>limp</u>, *my arms and legs useless.* [The prepositional phrase *of fear* describes *rush*. *Limp* describes *me*, and so does the absolute phrase *my arms and legs useless*.]

Adverb Traditionally, an adverb is said to describe and modify a verb, an adjective, or another adverb. More generally, any word or group of words that functions like an adverb can be called an adverbial. Many adverbials seem to describe the action of the sentence (or clause), so they have therefore been said to modify the verb. However, many adverbials seem to modify the entire clause: the agent and the action together, the entire subject-verb unit. Adverbs and other adverbials often tell how, when, where, or why, with respect to the action (see, for instance, the subordinating conjunctions listed in Figure A.5, which make independent clauses into adverbial clauses). Like regular adjectives, regular adverbs can be compared: *slow, slower, slowest; rapidly, more rapidly, most rapidly.* However, many other words and groups of words can work adverbially. For writers, what is most important is the adverbial *function*, particularly the function of modifying an entire clause. In the following examples, adverbs and adverbials are italicized, with no further distinction made.

The *most* frightening part was . . . [*Most* modifies the adjective *frightening*.]

I seemed to be ascending *all too slowly* through the murky water. [The adverbial phrase *all too slowly* modifies the verb phrase *seemed to be ascending*. Within the adverbial, *too* is an adverb modifying *slowly*, and *all* is an adverb modifying *too*.]

Early in the summer, it had seemed a great idea to sign up for a whitewater rafting trip in Costa Rica. [The adverbial phrase seems to modify the entire main clause.]

The friendly salesgirl was eager *to help me* / *when I mentioned that we'd signed up for an Adventure trip in Costa Rica.* [The infinitive phrase *to help me* seems to modify the adjective *eager*. The subordinate clause beginning with *when* seems to modify the entire main clause—and indeed, the adverbial clause can be placed in front of the entire main clause.]

The words *barely* had time to flit *through my mind / before the raft capsized for a second time, / throwing me unceremoniously into the raging water.* [*Barely* modifies the verb *had,* and *through my mind* seems to modify the verb form *flit* (actually the infinitive, *to flit*). The clause beginning with *before* seems to modify everything that precedes it, the entire main clause. The participial phrase *throwing me unceremoniously into the raging water* seems to modify the entire preceding clause, a subordinate adverbial clause.]

Appositive An appositive is a noun or nominal that functions adjectivally, to modify a noun that (ordinarily) immediately precedes the appositive. The appositive functions to rename or categorize the noun or nominal. Serving as free modifiers, normal appositives are set off from the rest of the sentence by commas.

The friendliest guide, *Miti,* was the one who led us to near-disaster.
The one who led us to near-disaster was the friendliest guide, *Miti.*
The Paçuare, *one of the rivers that we ran,* had two falls named "The Indians' Graveyard."
One of the oldest rivers that we ran, *the Paçuare,* had two falls named "The Indians' Graveyard."
Rollie, *a water lover since childhood,* had been warned not to "go out too far."
A water lover since childhood, Rollie had nevertheless been warned not to "go out too far."

Auxiliary verb An auxiliary verb is a helper that comes before the main verb. A main verb may have more than one helper before it. See in the Appendix the lesson emphasizing auxiliaries. In the following examples, the auxiliaries are italicized.

was leaving
has left
might leave
should be leaving
must have been leaving
ought to have left

Clause A clause consists of a subject and a predicate (that is, a subject and a verb plus anything that may come after it to complete or modify it). An independent, or main, clause is one that can stand alone as a sentence, grammatically speaking. A dependent, or subordinate, clause is one that cannot stand alone, grammatically speaking: it depends upon the meaning expressed in the main clause. There are three kinds of subordinate clauses: noun clauses, which function as nominals; adjective clauses, which function as adjectivals; and adverb clauses, which function as adverbials. In the following sentences, the main clause is italicized; the subordinate clause (if there is one) is underlined and labeled as to function.

Then flying home from North Carolina, *I read parts of the book on Costa Rican rivers.* [The italicized part is the main clause. The remainder is a free modifier that relates to the main clause. Although it contains a verb form, *flying*, it is not a complete clause because it does not have a subject.]

True, we had to sign up for the advanced kayak and rafter's trip, <u>because I couldn't go any other time</u>. [main clause plus adverb clause]

I can see <u>if there's anything we need for the Costa Rica trip</u>. [Within the main clause, this noun clause functions as the direct object of *see*.]

She showed me a book on Costa Rican rivers <u>that I bought to take home to Rollie</u>. [main clause with adjective clause modifying *book*]

Comma splice   When two independent clauses are joined by just a comma (with no conjoining word), the resulting sentence is called a comma splice. (Or, a comma used in this way can itself be called a comma splice.) Comma splices are usually prohibited by the grammar handbooks, but short comma splice sentences can be quite effective (see the discussion in Chapter 4, including Figure 4.10). Following are a longer, ineffective comma splice sentence and a shorter, more effective one.

Early in the summer, it had seemed a great idea to sign up for a whitewater rafting trip in Costa Rica, Rollie had been wanting to go there. [The second comma is the comma splice, between the two independent clauses.]

I gasped for air, I couldn't wait. [This shorter comma splice sentence is more effective because the absence of a conjoining word propels the reader through the sentence, reflecting the inability to wait.]

Conjunction   A conjunction is a word or phrase that joins words and constructions. There are two basic kinds of conjunctions, coordinating conjunctions and subordinating conjunctions. Correlative conjunctions are pairs of conjunctions working like coordinators. For lists of

Coordinating conjunctions, Correlative conjunctions, and **Subordinating conjunctions** see Figures A.4 and A.5.

Conjunctive adverb Conjunctive adverbs are words or phrases that have an adverbial sense to them but that join two independent clauses in the same way that coordinating conjunctions do. Figure A.6 lists common conjunctive adverbs, including words and phrases like *hence, thus,* and *then; however, furthermore,* and *moreover; for example, as a result,* and *on the other hand.* Usually a semicolon is used between the independent clauses, but a period may be used instead. In the following examples, notice that most conjunctive adverbs are set off by commas. (Reading the sentence aloud can usually help the writer decide whether to set off a conjunctive adverb with the comma.)

I was only free in October; *hence* we had to take the advanced kayaking trip.

I wanted to go whitewater rafting; *however,* we never should have taken the advanced trip.

I wanted to go whitewater rafting; the truth, *however,* is that the video of rafting on the Général scared me to death.

To this day, Rollie believes he nearly drowned in the Paçuare; *as a result,* we have not gone whitewater rafting since then.

We've used every excuse and ruse we can think of; *for example,* we've made sure to avoid the part of North Carolina where the Nantahala River runs.

Construction This is simply a term for more than one word functioning together as a unit.

Coordinating conjunction Coordinating conjunctions (see Figure A.4) join constructions that are of equal grammatical weight; the constructions should be the same kind of units grammatically. The coordinating conjunctions are *and, but, or, yet, so, nor.* These conjunctions can be used to join words, phrases, or clauses. When used to connect independent clauses, they may stand at the beginning of the second clause; published writers occasionally use them this way, despite what the grammar handbooks say.

True, we had to sign up for the advanced kayak *and* rafter's trip, because I couldn't go any other time. *But* we cheerfully sent in our $1,000 deposit to the Nantahala Outdoor Center.

Correlative conjunction   Correlative conjunctions (see Figure A.4) are pairs that link grammatically equal elements in the same way coordinating conjunctions do. The correlative conjunctions are *either . . . or, neither . . . nor, not only . . . but also, both . . . and, whether . . . or.* Examples:

We'd *either* finish the rafting trip *or* hike through the rain forest, up the mountain.

Neither Rollie *nor* I wanted to hike out alone.

We had to keep rafting, *whether* we liked it *or* not. [*Not* seems to stand for "whether we didn't like it"; the underlying structure is parallel.]

Dependent clause   See **Clause.**

Direct object   See **Noun.**

Fragment   A fragment is something punctuated as a sentence that is not grammatically complete (does not consist of or contain an independent clause). Dependent clauses and phrases are fragments when punctuated as sentences. Grammar handbooks typically warn against fragments. However, they can be quite effective when used judiciously, and they occur with increasing frequency in published writing. Subordinate clauses punctuated as sentences seem to bother more people than phrases so punctuated.

We went whitewater rafting in Colorado. *Because it sounded like fun.* [an example of a fragment I would <u>not</u> actually use]

Then, with a thwack, I hit the surface—the surface of the raft, that is: the underneath surface. *Safe, and not safe.* [a fragment I used in "The Graveyard" narrative]

Most of the time, a fragment can be connected to the sentence that comes before it. Notice, however, that this is not true with the second example, which I consider stylistically effective. This is an instance of the independent fragment, as characterized by Kline and Memering (1977). See Chapter 4 and particularly Figure 4.10 for more details about the effective use of fragments as punctuated sentences. These are so common among published writers that Kline and Memering call them minor sentences.

Free modifier   As described by Francis Christensen (1967), the free modifier is an optional modifier that meets at least one of the following criteria, and often both: (1) it can be moved to at least one other position in the sentence; (2) it is set off by commas (or could be and possibly should be). One frequent kind of free modifier is the adverbial, including the adverb clause. (See **Adverb, Clause, Subordinating conjunction.**) The other kind is the adjectival, including appositives, participial phrases, and adjective clauses that are set off by commas (but the adjective clauses are not movable, unlike most free modifiers). (See **Appositive, Participle.**) Adjective clauses are described in the Appendix in the lesson on punctuating restrictive and nonrestrictive clauses and elements. The absolute construction is a free modifier popularized by Christensen (1967). Being a modifier, the absolute has to have an adjectival or adverbial function, but sometimes it is difficult to decide what, exactly, a particular absolute modifies. (See **Absolute.**)

Early in the summer, it had seemed a great idea to sign up for a whitewater rafting trip in Costa Rica. [adverbial phrase modifying the verb *seemed*]

I read parts of the book on Costa Rican rivers *during the flight home from North Carolina.* [adverbial prepositional phrase that can be moved to the front of the sentence, where it would typically be set off by a comma]

And she offered to show me a video on whitewatering in Costa Rica, *as soon as some guys were finished looking at rafting on the Colorado.* [adverb clause]

Rollie, *a water lover since childhood,* had been warned not to "go out too far." [appositive]

I drove to the Nantahala Outdoor Center, *conveniently arriving, after a full day's drive across the state, just too late for the last rafting trip.* [participial phrase, containing an adverbial prepositional phrase within it]

I shouldn't have been surprised that the flooding Paçuare rose while we slept beside it for the night, *its muddy waters picking up speed as it swelled its banks.* [absolute]

My *protesting lungs ready to betray me,* I worked my way to the edge of the raft and popped out from under, *gasping for air.* [first an absolute, then a participial phrase]

The video, *which showed people whitewater rafting in Costa Rica,* scared me to death. [A restrictive clause, which is conventionally set off by commas. This example demonstrates the typical awkwardness of such unmovable modifiers when they modify the simple subject of the clause.]

Fused sentence   See **Run-on.**

Gerund   See **Verb.**

Grammar   The term *grammar* has several meanings. For example, it means a description of the syntactic structures and "rules" of a language, as well as the actual structures and patterns themselves. It also means a functional command of these structures and patterns, that is, the ability to understand and use a language and its structures. *Grammar* can also refer to the study of the structures of a language. It can mean the rhetorically effective use of syntactic structures (see **Rhetoric** and **Syntax, Syntactic**). It is commonly used to refer to prescriptions for using certain grammatical constructions and forms, and avoiding others: in other words, prescriptions for using the language according to socially determined norms. It can be used to refer to a book that reflects a description of the language or contains prescriptions for using it. Sometimes the term *grammar* includes spelling, the mechanics of punctuation, and so forth (though in this book, spelling is excluded). Typically the context will make the relevant meaning(s) of *grammar* clear.

Grammatical sentence   An independent clause plus the dependent clause(s) or phrase(s) (if any) that are attached to it or embedded within it. In research studies, the grammatical sentence has often been called a minimum terminable unit, or T-unit. See **T-unit.**

Independent clause   See **Clause.**

Indirect object   See **Noun.**

Infinitive   See **Verb.**

Interjection   In traditional grammar, the interjection is typically considered the eighth part of speech. However, it is not really a grammatical construction. Rather, the interjection is a word or phrase that expresses emotion and that is not grammatically part of a clause: an expression like *Yikes!* or *Darn it!* or *Well,* when it occurs at the beginning of a sentence.

Main clause   See **Clause.**

Main verb   See **Verb.**

Minor sentence   A grammatical fragment punctuated as a sentence. Kline and Memering (1977) introduced the term *minor sentence* to describe kinds of fragments that are punctuated as sentences in published writing.

Modifier   A modifier is a word or construction that describes or limits something. In English, there are two kinds of modifiers: adjectival and adverbial. See **Adjective, Adverb, Free modifier.**

M-unit   A grammatically incomplete group of words that can be reconstructed as a T-unit. This term was developed for research in analyzing young children's utterances and writings. It contrasts with *garble*, a group of words that cannot reasonably be reconstructed as a T-unit. See **T-unit.**

Near-clause   See **Absolute.**

Nominal   See **Noun.**

Noun   Traditionally, a noun is said to be the name of a person, place, thing, or idea. A noun is a word that takes an ending for plural or possessive, and usually both: *boy, boys, boy's, boys'*; *deer, deer's*; *oatmeal, oatmeal's*; *scissors, scissors'*; *Mary, Mary's*. More generally, any word or group of words that works like a noun can be called a nominal. Within sentences, there are five basic noun functions: subject, direct object, indirect object, predicate nominative, and object of preposition. Several kinds of constructions can serve in direct object position, and most of these can serve in other positions as well; however, the variety is illustrated below only in direct object position. For writers, what is probably most important is the nominal *function*. Thus in the following examples, the nominals are italicized, with no further distinction made between regular nouns and other kinds of nominals. Furthermore, the different noun functions are illustrated and different nominal constructions are named, but with no further explanation. One way to identify a nominal is to see whether the word *something* or the word *someone* can be substituted for the construction. If the answer is yes, the construction is functioning like a noun.

The *raft* had been swept over a modest *waterfall*. [*The raft* is the subject. *Waterfall* is the object of the preposition *over.*]
The most frightening part was *a long rapids*. [*The most frightening part* is the subject. *A long rapids* is a predicate nominative: a nominal in the

predicate part of the sentence that categorizes or renames the subject.]

I watched horrified as a *raft* tackled *the rapid*. [*I* is the subject of *watched*; *raft* is the subject of *tackled*; *the rapid* is the direct object of *tackled*.]

One of the guides gave *me* *the paddle he'd retrieved*. [*One* is the subject of *gave*, and *the guides* is the object of the preposition *of*. The direct object of *gave* is *the paddle he'd retrieved* (which has nominals within it). The indirect object of *gave*, the recipient of the paddle, is *me*.]

I didn't know *how much deeper he had been pushed by the second wave*. [*I* is the subject of *know*, and its direct object is *how much deeper he had been pushed by the second wave*. There are other nominals within this nominal, of course.]

I really wanted

- *a vacation.* [nominal]
- *not to go whitewater rafting in Costa Rica.* [infinitive nominal]
- *for him to say we didn't have to go.* [infinitive nominal that has a nominal clause within it]
- *what I knew was impossible.* [WH word nominal]

[Each of these nominals is serving as the direct object of *wanted*.]

Object   See **Noun.**

Object of preposition   See **Noun, Preposition.**

Participial phrase   See **Participle.**

Participle   Two of a verb's forms are participial. The *-ing* form of a verb is the present participle form, while the form that we would use after *has, have,* or *had* is the past participle form (for our dialect, whatever it may be). These verb forms may be used as adjectivals, to modify nouns. The participles may occur as single-word modifiers (usually before the noun), but they may also occur as the head word in a participle phrase, also called a participial phrase. See also **Verb.**

There were 500 *exciting* miles of whitewater.

I shouldn't have been surprised that the *flooding* Pacuare rose.

The paddle *floating downstream* was Rollie's. [participial phrase]

The authors talked about flash floods in the rainy season, *describing an incident when a film crew was making a commercial*. [participial phrase]

Our *scheduled* trip was for October, the rainy season.

Scheduled for October, our trip would surely occur during the rainy season. [participial phrase]

We went on a trip *scheduled during the rainy season.* [participial phrase]

Parts of speech   In English, there are said to be eight parts of speech. Four of these convey the unique meanings of the sentence: nouns, verbs, adjectives, and adverbs. Pronouns take the place of nouns. Two parts of speech serve as connecting words: prepositions and conjunctions. The eighth part of speech, the interjection, is not really a grammatical unit at all, but a word or phrase that expresses emotion and that is not grammatically part of a clause.

Phrase   A phrase is a group of words that functions as one construction. Unlike a clause, a phrase does not have both a subject and a complete verb. In some of the following examples, the phrase has a verb form, but not a complete verb. Each example illustrates a kind of phrase that is discussed separately under its own heading, but there are other kinds of phrases too. Some of the labeled phrases are free modifiers, while others are not. See **Free modifier.**)

The raft had been swept *over a modest waterfall,* landing off-balance *in a hole.* [prepositional phrases]

Rollie, *a water lover since childhood,* had been warned not to "go out too far." [appositive]

One *of the oldest rivers that we ran,* the Paçuare, had two falls *named "The Indians' Graveyard."* [*Of the oldest rivers that we ran* is a prepositional phrase that includes an adjective clause within it; *the Paçuare* is an appositive, and *named "The Indians' Graveyard"* is a past participle phrase.]

Unnerved by our second swim in the Paçuare, we nevertheless continued downstream. [past participle phrase]

The paddle *floating downstream* was Rollie's. [present participle phrase]

Eileen ferried me to the passenger raft, *dipping her paddle with sure skilled strokes, keeping us from continuing downstream.* [two present participle phrases]

I went under again, *my struggles useless against the powerful wave.* [absolute]

Predicate   The predicate is one of two obligatory parts of a clause, along with the subject. The predicate part of a clause includes the verb (verb phrase) plus anything that completes or modifies it. In the following simple sentences, everything that is not part of the subject is part of the predicate.

She *showed me a book on Costa Rican rivers*.
The raft *had been swept over a modest waterfall*.
The wall of water *momentarily crushed me*.
I *wasn't really scared*.
The book on Costa Rican rivers *scares me*.

Predicate nominative   See **Noun**.

Preposition   A preposition (see Figure A.3) is a word that comes before a noun or other nominal (hence *pre*-position). The preposition and the nominal, its object, together constitute a prepositional phrase. A prepositional phrase often modifies a noun that comes before it, and hence functions as an adjectival. Alternatively, a prepositional phrase may function as an adverbial, to modify the verb or the entire clause. The prepositional phrases are italicized in the following sentences.

The wall *of water* momentarily crushed me. [functions adjectivally]
The raft had been swept *over a modest waterfall*, landing off-balance *in a hole*. [function adverbially]
I was game, *despite our little adventure in the Nantahala at high flood stage the previous summer*. [Here, we have prepositional phrases within prepositional phrases. The levels of structure can be indicated like this:
(1) *I was game* [main clause];
  (2) *despite our little adventure the previous summer* [prepositional phrase];
    (3) *in the Nantahala* [prepositional phrase modifying *adventure*];
      (4) *at high flood stage* [prepositional phrase modifying *Nantahala*].

Prepositional phrase   See **Preposition**.

Pronoun   A pronoun is a word that stands for a noun (hence the name: *pro*, 'for,' and *noun*). The following list includes most pronouns. Pronouns have traditionally been defined in terms of their function: they stand for a noun or nominal. However, many of these words can also function as adjectivals.

I	me	my	mine	myself
we	us	our	ours	ourself, ourselves
you		your	yours	yourself
he	him	his		himself
she	her		hers	herself
it		its		itself
they	them	their	theirs	themselves

this	each	none	no one	who
that	one	any	nobody	whom
these	few	every	anyone	whose
those	both	some	anybody	which
	several		everyone	what
	many		everybody	
	all		someone	
	either		somebody	
	neither			

Punctuated sentence   Whatever occurs between an initial capital (upper-case) letter and the end mark of punctuation (period, question mark, exclamation point). A punctuated sentence may consist of one T-unit, more than one T-unit, or less than a T-unit. In the last sentence, the punctuated sentence would be called a fragment (also a minor sentence). (See **Fragment** and **Minor sentence.**) The following punctuated sentences illustrate these different relationships.

I wanted to go whitewater rafting in Costa Rica. [one T-unit]

I wanted to go whitewater rafting in Costa Rica but not to go during the rainy season. [still just one independent clause and therefore one T-unit]

I wanted to go whitewater rafting in Costa Rica, but after I saw the video about it I was scared. [two T-units]

No way! [a fragment (minor sentence); we might imagine this punctuated sentence following a sentence like "Did I want to go rafting during the rainy season?"]

Rhetoric   Rhetoric is the art of using language effectively, to achieve the speaker's or writer's purpose. Often, rhetoric is thought of as persuasive in nature. While rhetoric is not a part of grammar or vice versa, the two are related. As Christensen (1967) said, "Grammar maps out the possible; rhetoric narrows the possible down to the desirable or effective" (p. 39).

Run-on Two (or more) independent clauses with no connecting word or punctuation between them. A run-on sentence is sometimes called a *fused sentence*. Example: *Rollie didn't dare breathe he was still underwater.* Published writers avoid run-on sentences except for special effects, such as when they want to portray a character's thoughts as run-on and perhaps chaotic.

Semantics, semantic *Semantics* refers to meaning, particularly to the meanings within language. The term is often contrasted with *syntax*, which refers to structure. See **Syntax.**

Sentence In this book, the term *sentence* usually refers to a grammatical sentence. But when context seems likely to clarify, the term *sentence* may be used to refer to something punctuated as a sentence, with a beginning capital (uppercase) letter and an end mark of punctuation. See **Grammatical sentence, Punctuated sentence.**

Subject A subject is one of the two obligatory parts of every clause, which must have both a subject and a predicate. The predicate must at least have a complete verb, which is said to show action or a state of being. The subject tells *who* or *what* is doing the action or existing in the state of being. Essentially the subject names who or what the clause is about. Often, the easiest way to identify a subject is to locate the verb (or verb phrase) and then ask *who?* or *what?* with respect to the verb, or the verb plus the rest of the predicate. See the Appendix for two lessons on subject-verb agreement. See also **Verb.**

> *The book on whitewater rafting in Costa Rica scared me.* [The verb is *scared.* What scared me? *The book on whitewater rafting in Costa Rica,* which is the subject. Notice that the verb "agrees with" the first noun, *book*—the noun that does not occur after a preposition. This first noun is said to be the simple subject, the one with which the verb should agree.]

Subordinate clause See **Clause.**

Subordinating conjunction A subordinating conjunction is a word that introduces an adverb clause. Or to express it differently, when a subordinating conjunction is put in front of an independent clause, it reduces the clause to a subordinate (dependent) clause. Words that commonly function as subordinating conjunctions include *before, after, since; until, when, while; though, although, even though; because, since; if, unless.* (Some of these words function as prepositions, too.) A more complete list is given in the Appendix as Figure A.5.

The words barely had time to flit through my mind *before* the raft capsized for a second time.

I wasn't really scared *until* I actually drove to the Nantahala Outdoor Center in North Carolina.

And she offered to show me a video on whitewatering in Costa Rica, *as soon as* some guys were finished looking at rafting on the Colorado.

Syntax, syntactic   *Syntax* refers to structure, particularly to the structure or structures within language, or to the rules that describe such structure(s). Thus *syntax* is synonymous with certain meanings of *grammar.* See also **Grammar.**

T-unit   A T-unit consists of one independent clause, plus the dependent clause(s) or phrase(s) (if any) that are attached to it or embedded within it. T-units are the smallest units into which a piece of writing can be divided, grammatically speaking, without fragments of sentences being left over. Hence the full name, minimum terminable unit. In this book, the term *grammatical sentence* is synonymous with *T-unit.* The concept of a T-unit may be clarified by demonstrating how a paragraph can be divided into T-units. Brackets are used to identify the T-units in the following paragraph.

[I'm not sure I should ever have watched that video.][The most frightening part was a long rapids on a river called the Général.][I've repressed the rapids' exact name,][but it was something like "Hell's Run."][And believe me, that's what it looked like!][I watched horrified as a raft tackled the rapid, only to be buried among the waves.][Could the raft still be there somewhere, invisible, as wave after wave crashed over it?][More to the point, could the rafters still be in the raft?][All I could think of was how would they ever get you back into the raft if you got thrown out?]

Verb   Traditionally, a verb is said to show action or a state of being. All verbs except the modal auxiliaries have four or five distinct forms: *go, goes, went, going, gone; watch, watches, watched, watching; has, have,* *having, had.* (The *be* verb has eight forms: *be, am, is, are, was, were, being, been.*) A verb is the one essential part of the predicate of a clause. Main verbs may stand alone or be preceded by one or more auxiliary verbs:

laughs
is laughing
have laughed
must be laughing
has been laughing

Any group of words that functions like a verb (one or more auxiliaries plus the main verb) can be called a verbal; however, it is more common to call such a combination a verb phrase. A verb phrase is sometimes called a simple predicate.

Different forms of the verb can perform nonverb functions in a sentence. For example, the infinitive—*to* plus the base form—can function as a noun, adverb, or adjective, as in the following examples:

To quit would have been sensible. [works as a noun, the subject]

To rest, I lay in the raft instead of paddling. [adverbial, telling why I *lay* in the raft]

The thing *to do*, I thought, was stop running rivers. [adjectival, describing *thing*]

The *-ing* form of a verb can also function as a noun, in which case it is called a gerund. The second of the preceding sentences contains the gerund *paddling*, which functions as the object of the preposition *of*; the third sentence contains the gerund phrase *running rivers*, which functions as the object of *stop*.

When the *-ing* form of the verb functions as an adjectival, it is said to be a participle: a present participle. When the so-called past participle form of the verb (the one we would use after the auxiliary *has, have,* or *had*) functions as an adjectival, it is also a participle: a past participle. These participles may function alone or as the head word in a phrase. In each of the following examples, the participial word or phrase is functioning as an adjectival, even though the participle itself is a verb in the underlying structure.

There were 500 *exciting* miles of whitewater.

I shouldn't have been surprised that the *flooding* Paçuare rose.

The paddle *floating downstream* was Rollie's.

The authors talked about flash floods in the rainy season, *describing an incident when a film crew was making a commercial.*

Our *scheduled* trip was for October, the rainy season.

Scheduled for October, our trip would surely occur during the rainy season.

We went on a trip *scheduled during the rainy season.*

REFERENCES

Altwerger, B. (1991). Whole language teachers: Empowered professionals. In J. Hydrick (Ed.), *Whole language: Empowerment at the chalk face* (pp. 15–29). New York: Scholastic.

Arches and vaults in the Ancient Near East. (1989). *Scientific American* (July).

Atwell, N. (1987). *In the middle: Writing, reading, and learning with adolescents.* Portsmouth, NH: Heinemann.

Avery, C. (1993). . . . *And with a light touch: Learning about reading, writing, and teaching with first graders.* Portsmouth, NH: Heinemann.

Bartholomae, D. (1980). The study of error. *College Composition and Communication, 31,* 253–269.

Barzun, J. (1975). *Simple and direct.* Chicago: University of Chicago Press.

Base, Graeme. (1986). *Animalia.* New York: Harry N. Abrams.

Bateman, D., & Zidonis, F. (1966). *The effect of a study of transformational grammar on the writing of ninth and tenth graders* (Research Report No. 6). Urbana, IL: National Council of Teachers of English.

Belanoff, P., Rorschach, B., & Oberlink, M. (1993). *The right handbook: Grammar and usage in context* (2nd ed.). Portsmouth, NH: Boynton/Cook.

Berenstain, S., & Berenstain, J. (1971). *Bears in the night.* New York: Random House.

Bernardini, R. *(1991). A southern time Christmas.* Illus. J. Rice. Gretna, LA: Pelican.

Birdseye, T., & Birdseye, D. H. (1994). *She'll be comin' round the mountain.* Illus. A. Glass. New York: Holiday House.

Bissex, G. (1980). GNYS AT WRK: *A child learns to write and read.* Cambridge, MA: Harvard University Press.

Bloomfield, L. (1933). *Language.* New York: Holt, Rinehart.

Bloomfield, L. (1942). Linguistics and reading. *The Elementary English Review, 19,* 125–130, 183–186.

Bradbury, R. (1950). *The Martian chronicles.* New York: Bantam Books.

Braddock, R. (1969). English composition. In R. L. Ebel, V. H. Noll, & R. M. Bauer (Eds.), *Encyclopedia of educational research* (4th ed., pp. 443–461). London: Macmillan.

Braddock, R., Lloyd-Jones, R., & Schoer, L. (1963). *Research in written composition.* Urbana, IL: National Council of Teachers of English.

Bridwell, N. (1966). *Clifford takes a trip.* New York: Scholastic.

Brosnahan, I. T. (1976). A few good words for the comma splice. *College English, 38,* 184–188.

Brown, R. (1988). *A dark, dark tale.* Toronto: Stoddart.

Brown, R. W. (1957). Linguistic determinism and part of speech. *Journal of Abnormal and Social Psychology, 55,* 1–5.

Brown, R. W. (1973). *A first language: The early stages*. Cambridge, MA: Harvard University Press.

Bruner, J. (1983). *Child's talk: Learning to use language*. Oxford: Oxford University Press.

Bruner, J. (1986). *Actual minds, possible worlds*. Cambridge: Harvard University Press.

Caine, R. N., & Caine, G. (1994). *Making connections: Teaching and the human brain* (2nd ed.). Menlo Park, CA: Innovative Learning Publications.

Calkins, L. M. (1980). When children want to punctuate: Basic skills belong in context. *Language Arts, 57*, 567–573.

Calkins, L. M. (1983). *Lessons from a child*. Portsmouth, NH: Heinemann.

Calkins, L. M. (1986). *The art of teaching writing*. Portsmouth, NH: Heinemann.

Calkins, L. M. (1994). *The art of teaching writing* (new edition). Portsmouth, NH: Heinemann.

Calkins, L. M., & Harwayne, S. (1987). *The writing workshop: A world of difference*. Portsmouth, NH: Heinemann.

Calkins, L. M., with Harwayne, S. (1993). *Living between the lines*. Portsmouth, NH: Heinemann.

Cambourne, B. (1988). *The whole story: Natural learning and the acquisition of literacy in the classroom*. Auckland, New Zealand: Scholastic.

Carlson, L. M. (Ed.). (1994). *Cool salsa: Bilingual poems on growing up Latino in the United States*. New York: Henry Holt.

Carroll, L. (n.d.) *The complete works of Lewis Carroll*. New York: Modern Library, 1979.

Cazden, C. B. (1972). *Child language and education*. New York: Holt, Rinehart and Winston.

Chomsky, C. (1978). Approaching reading through invented spelling. In L. B. Resnick & P. A. Weaver (Eds.), *Theory and practice of early reading* (Vol. 2, pp. 43–65). Hillsdale, NJ: Erlbaum.

Chomsky, N. (1957). *Syntactic structures*. The Hague: Mouton.

Chomsky, N. (1965). *Aspects of the theory of syntax*. Cambridge, MA: MIT Press.

Chomsky, N. (1968a). *Language and mind*. New York: Harcourt Brace Jovanovich.

Chomsky, N. (1968b). Language and the mind. *Psychology Today, 1* (February), 48, 50–51, 66–68.

Christensen, F. (1967). *Notes toward a new rhetoric: Six essays for teachers*. New York: Harper & Row.

Christensen, F. (1968a). *The Christensen rhetoric program: The sentence and the paragraph*. New York: Harper & Row.

Christensen, F. (1968b). The problem of defining a mature style. *English Journal, 57*, 572–579.

Christensen, F., & Christensen, B. (1978). *Notes toward a new rhetoric: Nine essays for teachers* (2nd ed.). New York: Harper & Row. (Earlier edition published 1967)

Christensen, L. (1994a). Celebrating the student's voice. In B. Bigelow, L. Christensen, S. Karp, B. Miner, & B. Peterson (Eds.), *Rethinking our* classrooms: *Teaching for equity and justice* (p. 109). Milwaukee, WI: Rethinking Schools.

Christensen, L. (1994b). Whose standard? Teaching standard English. In B. Bigelow, L. Christensen, S. Karp, B. Miner, & B. Peterson (Eds.), *Rethinking our classrooms: Teaching for equity and justice* (pp. 142–145). Milwaukee, WI: Rethinking Schools.

Clarke, L. K. (1988). Invented versus traditional spelling in first graders' writings: Effects on learning to spell and read. *Research in the Teaching of English, 22,* 281–309.

Clay, M. M. (1987). *Writing begins at home.* Portsmouth, NH: Heinemann.

Cochrane, O., Cochrane, D., Scalena, S., & Buchanan, E. (1984). *Reading, writing, and caring.* Winnipeg: Whole Language Consultants. Distributed in the United States by Richard C. Owen.

Collerson, J. (1994). *English grammar: A functional approach.* Newtown NSW, Australia: Primary English Teaching Association.

Compton, J. (1994). *Ashpet, an Appalachian tale.* Illus. K. Compton. New York: Holiday House.

Conference on College Composition and Communication. (1988). *The national language policy* (position statement). Urbana, IL: National Council of Teachers of English.

Connors, R. J., & Lunsford, A. A. (1988). Frequency of formal errors in current college writing, or Ma and Pa Kettle do research. *College Composition and Communication, 39,* 395–409.

Cordeiro, P. (1988). Children's punctuation: An analysis of errors in period placement. *Research in the Teaching of English, 22,* 62–74.

Cordeiro, P., Giacobbe, M. E., & Cazden, C. (1983). Apostrophes, quotation marks, and periods: Learning punctuation in the first grade. *Language Arts, 60,* 323–332.

Cowley, J. (1983). *The bicycle.* Illus. D. Britten. Bothell, WA: The Wright Group.

Cowley, J. (1986). *Huggles goes away.* Illus. E. Fuller. Bothell, WA: The Wright Group.

Cowley, J. (1987). *Ratty-tatty.* Illus. A. Matijasevic. Bothell, WA: The Wright Group.

Crowhurst, M. (1979). On the misinterpretation of syntactic complexity data. *English Education, 11,* 91–97.

Crowhurst, M. (1981). *The effect of syntactic complexity on writing quality: A review of research.* (ERIC Document Reproduction Service No. ED 202 024).

Crowhurst, M., & Piche, G. L. (1979). Audience and mode of discourse effects on syntactic complexity in writing at two grade levels. *Research in the Teaching of English, 13,* 101–109.

Cupery, D. (1992). *Syntactic growth of ESL writers in a reading-writing intensive class.* Unpublished paper. Kalamazoo, MI: Western Michigan University.

Cutting, J. (1988). *Look.* Bothell, WA: The Wright Group.

Dahl, K. L., & Freppon, P. A. (1992). *Learning to read and write in inner-city schools: A comparison of children's sense-making in skills-based and whole language classrooms*. Final Report to the Office of Educational Research and Improvement. Washington, DC: U.S. Department of Education (Grant No. R117E00134).

Daiker, D. A., Kerek, A., & Morenberg, M. (1990). *The writer's options: Combining to composing* (4th ed). New York: Harper & Row.

Dale, P. S. (1976). *Language development: Structure and function* (2nd ed.). Hindsdale, IL: Dryden Press.

DeBeaugrande, R. (1984). Forward to the basics: Getting down to grammar. *College Composition and Communication, 35*, 358–367.

DeBoer, J. J. (1959). Grammar in language teaching. *Elementary English, 36*, 413–421.

D'Eloia, S. (1981). The uses—and limits—of grammar. In G. Tate & E. P. J. Corbett (Eds.), *The writing teacher's sourcebook* (pp. 225–243). New York: Oxford University Press. (Reprinted from *Journal of Basic Writing*, 1977, *1*(Spring/Summer), 1–20)

Delpit, L. D. (1992). Acquisition of literate discourse: Bowing before the master? *Theory into Practice, 31*, 296–302.

De Villiers, J. (1980). The process of rule learning in child speech: A new look. In K. E. Nelson (Ed.), *Children's language* (Vol. 2, pp. 1–44). New York: Gardner Press.

De Villiers, J., & De Villiers, P. (1973). A cross-sectional study of the acquisition of grammatical morphemes in child speech. *Journal of Psycholinguistic Research, 2*, 267–278.

De Villiers, J., & De Villiers, P. (1979). *Early language*. Cambridge, MA: Harvard University Press.

Dickens, C. (1859). *A tale of two cities*. Cutchogue, NY: Buccaneer Books, 1987.

DiStefano, P., & Howie, S. (1979). Sentence weights: An alternative to the T-unit. *English Education, 11*, 98–101.

DiStefano, P., & Killion, J. (1984). Assessing writing skills through a process approach. *English Education, 16*, 203–207.

Dove, R. (1983). "Parsley." From *Museum: Poems*. Pittsburgh: Carnegie Mellon University Press. Reprinted in N. Baym et al. (Eds.), *The Norton anthology of American literature* (4th ed., Vol. 2). New York: W. W. Norton Co.

Dream of the wild horses. (1982). *The writing process*. Book 9. Boston: Allyn & Bacon.

Dunn, R., & Dunn, K. (1978). *Teaching students through their individual learning styles: A practical approach*. Reston, VA: Reston Publishing Company.

Dykema, K. W. (1961). Where our grammar came from. *College English, 22*, 455–465.

Ebbitt, W. R., & Ebbitt, D. R. (1990). *Index to English* (8th ed). New York: Oxford University Press.

Edelsky, C. (1983). Segmentation and punctuation: Developmental data from young writers in a bilingual program. *Research in the Teaching of English, 17*, 135–156.

Edelsky, C., & Draper, K. (1989). Reading/"reading"; writing/"writing"; text/"text." *Reading-Canada-Lecture, 7*, 201–216.

Eeds, M., & Wells, D. (1989). Grand conversations: An exploration of meaning construction in literature study groups. *Research in the Teaching of English, 23,* 4–29.

Elbow, P. (1985). The challenge for sentence combining. In D. Daiker, A. Kerek, & M. Morenberg (Eds.), *Sentence combining: A rhetorical perspective* (pp. 232–245). Carbondale, IL: Southern Illinois University Press.

Elgin, S. H. (1978). Don't no revolutions hardly *ever* come by here. *College English, 39,* 784–789.

Elley, W. B. (1989). Vocabulary acquisition from listening to stories. *Reading Research Quarterly, 24,* 174–187.

Elley, W. B. (1991). Acquiring literacy in a second language: The effect of book-based programs. *Language Learning, 41,* 375–411.

Elley, W. B., Barham, I. H., Lamb, H., & Wyllie, M. (1976). The role of grammar in a secondary English curriculum. *Research in the Teaching of English, 10,* 5–21. (Reprinted from *New Zealand Journal of Educational Studies,* May 1975, *10,* 26–42).

Elley, W. B., & Mangubhai, F. (1983). The impact of reading on second language learning. *Reading Research Quarterly, 19,* 53–67.

Ellison, R. (1952). *Invisible man.* New York: New American Library.

Emig, J. (1983). Non-magical thinking: Presenting writing developmentally in schools. In *The web of meaning: Essays on writing, teaching, learning, and thinking* (pp. 133–144). Portsmouth, NH: Boynton/Cook.

Engelmann, S., & Bruner, E. C. (1988). *Reading mastery: DISTAR.* Blacklick, OH: SRA.

Engelmann, S., & Osborn, J. (1987). *DISTAR language.* Blacklick, OH: SRA.

Erskine, J. (1946). *Twentieth century English.* A later edition, edited by W. Knickerbocker, is published by Ayer, Salem, NH.

Faigley, L. (1980). Names in search of a concept: Maturity, fluency, complexity, and growth in written syntax. *College Composition and Communication, 31,* 291–300.

Falk, J. S. (1979). Language acquisition and the teaching and learning of writing. *College English, 41,* 436–447.

Farr, M., & Daniels, H. (1986). *Language diversity and writing instruction.* Urbana, IL: ERIC Institute for Urban and Minority Education and the National Council of Teachers of English.

Farrell, E. J. (1971). *Deciding the future: A forecast of responsibilities of secondary teachers of English, 1970–2000 A.D.* (Research Report No. 12). Urbana, IL: National Council of Teachers of English.

Ferreiro, E., & Teberosky, A. (1982). *Literacy before schooling* (K. G. Castro, Trans.). Portsmouth, NH: Heinemann.

Fillmore, C. (1968). The case for case. In E. Bach & R. T. Harms (Eds.), *Universals in linguistic theory* (pp. 1–90). New York: Holt, Rinehart.

Fitzgerald, S. (1984). Beginning reading and writing through singing: A natural approach. *Highway One, 7* (ii), 6–12.

Five, C. L. (1991). *Special voices.* Portsmouth, NH: Heinemann.

Flower, L., & Hayes, J. R. (1981). A cognitive process theory of writing. *College Composition and Communication, 32*, 365–387.

Foster, H. M. (1994). *Crossing over: Whole language for secondary English teachers.* Orlando, FL: Harcourt Brace Jovanovich.

Francis, W. N. (1954). Revolution in grammar. *Quarterly Journal of Speech, 40*, 299–312.

Francis, W. N. (1958). *The structure of American English.* New York: Ronald Press.

Freeman, Y., & Freeman, D. (1994). Whole language learning and teaching for second language learners. In C. Weaver, *Reading process and practice: From socio-psycholinguistics to whole language* (2nd ed., pp. 558–629). Portsmouth, NH: Heinemann.

Fries, C. C. (1952). *The structure of English.* New York: Harcourt, Brace.

Frogner, E. (1939). Grammar approach versus thought approach in teaching sentence structure. *English Journal, 28*, 518–526. [as cited in Searles & Carlson, 1960, and more recent sources]

Fulwiler, L. (1992). The constructivist culture of language-centered classrooms. In C. Weaver & L. Henke (Eds.), *Supporting whole language: Stories of teacher and institutional change.* Portsmouth, NH: Heinemann.

Gage, N. L. (1963). *Handbook of research on teaching.* Chicago: Rand McNally.

Genishi, C., & Dyson, A. (1984). *Language assessment in the early years.* Norwood, NJ: Ablex.

Gentry, J. R., & Wallace, J. (1993). *Teaching kids to spell.* Portsmouth, NH: Heinemann.

Giacobbe, M. E. (1984). Helping children become more responsible for their own writing. *LiveWire, 1* (1), 7–9. (Reprinted in *The best of LiveWire*, 1989, by the National Council of Teachers of English).

Gibson, W. (1966). *Tough, sweet and stuffy: An essay on modern American prose styles.* Bloomington: Indiana University Press.

Gibson, W. (1969). *Persona: A style study for readers and writers.* New York: Random House.

Glatthorn, A. A. (1981). *Writing in the schools: Improvement through effective leadership.* Reston, VA: National Association of Secondary School Principals.

Glazier, T. F. (1994). *The least you should know about English writing skills* (Form B, 5th ed.). Fort Worth: Harcourt.

Goodman, K. S. (1965). A linguistic study of cues and miscues in reading. *Elementary English, 42*, 639–643.

Goodman, K. S. (1986). *What's whole in whole language?* Richmond Hill, Ontario: Scholastic. Distributed in the United States by Heinemann.

Goodman, K. S., Shannon, P., Freeman, Y., & Murphy, S. (1988). *The report card on basal readers.* Katonah, NY: Richard C. Owen.

Goodman, Y. (1978). Kid watching: An alternative to testing. *The National Elementary Principal, 57* (June), 41–45.

Gordon, K. E. (1993a). *The deluxe transitive vampire: The ultimate handbook of grammar for the innocent, the eager, and the doomed* (2nd ed.). New York: Pantheon Books.

Gordon, K. E. (1993b). *The new well-tempered sentence: A punctuation handbook for the innocent, the eager, and the doomed* (expanded and revised ed.). New York: Ticknor & Fields.

Gradman, H. L., & Hanania, E. (1991). Language learning background factors and ESL proficiency. *Modern Language Journal, 75,* 39–51.

Graves, D. H. (1975). An examination of the writing processes of seven year old children. *Research in the Teaching of English, 9,* 227–241.

Graves, D. H. (1983). *Writing: Teachers and children at work.* Portsmouth, NH: Heinemann.

Graves, D. H. (1994). *A fresh look at writing.* Portsmouth, NH: Heinemann.

Gray, P. (1991). A fight over liquid gold. *Time,* July 22.

Green, J. L. (1969). Acrobats, plowmen, and the healthy sentence. *English Journal, 58,* 892–899.

Greenbaum, S., & Quirk, R. (1990). *A student's grammar of the English language.* London: Longman.

Greene, H. A. (1950). English—language, grammar, and composition. In W. S. Monroe (Ed.), *Encyclopedia of educational research* (revised ed., pp. 383–396). New York: Macmillan.

Greene, S. S. (1854). *Treatise on the structure of the English language.* Philadelphia: Cowperthwaite.

Greene, S. S. (1874). *An analysis of the English language.* Philadelphia: Cowperthwaite.

Greenfield, E. (1978). *Honey, I love, and other love poems.* New York: Harper & Row.

Hacker, D. (1991). *The Bedford handbook for writers* (3rd ed.). Boston: Bedford Books of St. Martin's Press.

Hacker, D. (1995). *A writer's reference* (3rd ed.). New York: St. Martin's Press.

Hairston, M. (1981). Not all errors are created equal: Nonacademic readers in the professions respond to lapses in usage. *College English, 43,* 794–806.

Hairston, M. (1982). The winds of change: Thomas Kuhn and the revolution in the teaching of writing. *College Composition and Communication, 33,* 76–88.

Halliday, M. A. K. (1985). *An introduction to functional grammar.* London: Edward Arnold.

Halliday, M. A. K., & Hasan, R. (1976). *Cohesion in English.* London: Longman.

Harris, M. (1994). *Prentice Hall reference guide to grammar and usage* (2nd ed.). Englewood Cliffs, NJ: Prentice Hall.

Harris, M., & Rowan, K. E. (1989). Explaining grammatical concepts. *Journal of basic writing, 8* (2), 21–41.

Harris, R. J. (1962). *An experimental inquiry into the functions and value of formal grammar in the teaching of written English to children aged twelve to fourteen.* Unpublished doctoral dissertation, University of London. (Summarized in R. Braddock, R. Lloyd-Jones, and L. Schoer, *Research in written composition* [Urbana, IL: National Council of Teachers of English, 1963], pp. 70–83.)

Hartwell, P. (1980). Dialect interference in writing: A critical view. *Research in the Teaching of English, 14,* 101–118.

Hartwell, P. (1985). Grammar, grammars, and the teaching of grammar. *College English, 47,* 105–127.

Hartwell, P., & LoPresti, G. (1985). Sentence combining as kid-watching. In D. A. Daiker, A. Kerek, & M. Morenberg (Eds.), *Sentence combining: A rhetorical perspective* (pp. 107–126). Carbondale, IL: Southern Illinois University Press.

Harwayne, S. (1992). *Lasting impressions: Weaving literature into the writing workshop.* Portsmouth, NH: Heinemann.

Heller, R. (1988). *Kites sail high: A book about verbs.* New York: Putnam Publishing Group.

Heller, R. (1989a). *A cache of jewels and other collective nouns.* New York: Putnam Publishing Group.

Heller, R. (1989b). *Many luscious lollipops: A book about adjectives.* New York: Putnam Publishing Group.

Heller, R. (1990). *Merry-go-round: A book about nouns.* New York: Putnam Publishing Group.

Hemingway, E. (1926). *The sun also rises.* New York: Modern Library.

Hillocks, G., Jr. (1986). *Research on written composition: New directions for teaching.* Urbana, IL: ERIC Clearinghouse on Reading and Composition Skills and the National Conference on Research in English. Distributed by the National Council of Teachers of English.

Hillocks, G., Jr., & Anderson, E. (1992). Grammar. In M. C. Alkin, M. Linden, J. Noel, & K. Ray (Eds.), *Encyclopedia of educational research,* 6th ed. (Vol. 2, pp. 560–561). New York: Macmillan.

Hillocks, G., Jr., & Mavrogenes, N. (1986). Sentence combining. In G. Hillocks, Jr., *Research on written composition: New directions for teaching* (pp. 142–146). Urbana, IL: ERIC Clearinghouse on Reading and Composition Skills and the National Conference on Research in English. Distributed by the National Council of Teachers of English.

Hillocks, G., Jr., & Smith, M. W. (1991). Grammar and usage. In J. Flood, J. M. Jensen, D. Lapp, & J. R. Squire (Eds.), *Handbook of research on teaching the English language arts* (pp. 591–603). New York: Macmillan.

Holdaway, D. (1979). *The foundations of literacy.* Sydney: Ashton Scholastic. Distributed in the United States by Heinemann.

Holdaway, D. (1986). The structure of natural learning as a basis for literacy instruction. In M. R. Sampson (Ed.), *The pursuit of literacy: Early reading and writing* (pp. 56–72). Dubuque, IA: Kendall Hunt.

Holzman, M. (1983). Scientism and sentence-combining. *College Composition and Communication, 34,* 73–79.

Hughes, A. H. (1991). *Cajun Columbus* (rev. ed.). Gretna, LA: Pelican.

Hughes, T. O. (1975). *Sentence combining: A means of increasing reading comprehension.* (ERIC Document Reproduction Service No. ED 112 421).

Hunt, K. W. (1965a). *Grammatical structures written at three grade levels* (Research Report No. 3). Urbana, IL: National Council of Teachers of English.

Hunt, K. W. (1965b). A synopsis of clause-to-sentence length factors. *English Journal, 54,* 300–309.

Hunt, K. W. (1966). Recent measures in syntactic development. *Elementary English, 43,* 732–739.

Hunt, K. W. (1970). *Syntactic maturity in schoolchildren and adults* (Monographs of the Society for Research in Child Development, No. 134). Chicago: University of Chicago Press.

Hunt, K. W. (1977). Early blooming and late blooming syntactic structures. In C. R. Cooper & L. Odell (Eds.), *Evaluating writing: Describing, measuring, judging* (pp. 94–104). Urbana, IL: National Council of Teachers of English.

Hunter, M. (1982). *Mastery teaching.* El Segundo, CA: TIP Publications.

Hunter, M., & Wallace, R. (Eds.). (1995). *The place of grammar in writing instruction: Past, present, future.* Portsmouth, NH: Boynton/Cook.

Huntsman, J. F. (1983). Grammar. In D. L. Wagner (Ed.), *The seven liberal arts in the Middle Ages* (pp. 58–95). Bloomington: Indiana University Press.

Hutchins, P. (1968). *Rosie's walk.* New York: Macmillan.

Inada, L. F. (1993). *Legends from camp.* Minneapolis: Coffee House Press.

Ingram, D. (1989). *First language acquisition: Method, description, and explanation.* Cambridge: Cambridge University Press.

Johnson, D. W., & Johnson, R. T. (1985). *Structuring cooperative learning: Lesson plans for teachers.* Edina, MN: Interaction Book Company.

Johnson, D. W., Johnson, R. T., & Holubec, E. J. (1984). *Circles of learning: Cooperation in the classroom* (revised). Alexandria, VA: Association for Supervision and Curriculum Development.

Jones, H. (Ed.) (1993). *The trees stand shining.* Illus. R. A. Parker. New York: Dial. [Earlier edition, 1971]

Jones, R. L. (1994). What's wrong with Black English? In P. Eschholz, A. Rosa, & V. Clark (Eds.), *Language awareness* (pp. 131–134). New York: St. Martin's Press.

Kafka, F. (n.d.). The great wall of China. In *Shorter works,* Vol. 1. (M. Pasley, Trans.). London: Secker & Warburg, 1973.

Kagan, D. M. (1980). Run-on and fragment sentences: An error analysis. *Research in the Teaching of English, 14,* 127–138.

Kaster, R. A. (1988). *The guardians of language: The grammarian and society in late antiquity.* Berkeley: University of California Press.

Katz, J. J. (1964). Mentalism in linguistics. *Language, 40* (April–June), 124–137.

Kemper, D., Nathan, R., & Sebranek, P. (1995). *Writers express: A handbook for young writers, thinkers, and learners.* Burlington, WI: Write Source.

Kerek, A., Daiker, D., & Morenberg, M. (1980). Sentence combining and college composition. *Perceptual and motor skills, 51,* 1059–1157.

Killgallon, D. (1984). *Sentence composing: Grade 10* and *Sentence composing: Grade 11.* Porstmouth, NH: Boynton/Cook.

Killgallon, D. (1987). *Sentence composing: The complete course.* Portsmouth, NH: Boynton/Cook.

Kitzhaber, A. R. (Ed.). (1970). *The Oregon Curriculum: A sequential program in English.* New York: Holt, Rinehart.

Klima, E. S., & Bellugi-Klima, U. (1966). Syntactic regularities in the speech of children. In J. Lyons & R. J. Wales (Eds.), *Psycholinguistic papers* (pp. 183–208). Edinburgh: Edinburgh University Press.

Kline, C. R., Jr., & Memering, W. D. (1977). Formal fragments: The English minor sentence. *Research in the Teaching of English, 11,* 97–110.

Kolln, M. (1981). Closing the books on alchemy. *College Composition and Communication, 32,* 139–151.

Kolln, M. (1991). *Rhetorical grammar: Grammatical choices, rhetorical effects.* New York: Macmillan.

Krashen, S. D. (1981). *Second language acquisition and second language learning.* Oxford: Pergamon Press.

Krashen, S. D. (1982). *Principles and practice in second language acquisition.* New York: Pergamon Press.

Krashen, S. D. (1985). *The input hypothesis: Issues and implications.* New York: Longman.

Krashen, S. D. (1993). *The power of reading: Insights from the research.* Englewood, CO: Libraries Unlimited.

Kroll, B., & Schafer, J. (1978). Error analysis and the teaching of composition. *College Composition and Communication, 29,* 242–248.

Labov, W. (1969). The logic of non-standard English. In A. C. Aarons et al. (Eds.) *Linguistic-cultural differences and American education* (pp. 60–74, 169). (A special anthology issue of *The Florida FL Reporter,* 7:1.) Reprinted in *Georgetown Monograph Series on Languages and Linguistics* No. 22, 1–43. Washington, DC: Georgetown University Press, 1970.

Labov, W., Cohen, P., Robins, C., & Lewis, J. (1968). A *study of the non-standard English of Negro and Puerto Rican speakers in New York City.* 2 vols. Washington, DC: Educational Resources Information Center. (ED 028 423 and ED 028 424).

Lakoff, R. (1975). *Language and woman's place.* New York: Harper & Row.

Laminack, L. (1991). *Learning with Zachary.* Richmond Hill, Ontario: Scholastic.

Lindfors, J. W. (1987). *Children's language and learning* (2nd ed.). Englewood Cliffs, NJ: Prentice Hall.

Little, V. (1994). Coming of age: Working with older ADHD student populations. In C. Weaver (Ed.), *Success at last! Helping students with Attention Deficit (Hyperactivity) Disorders achieve their potential* (pp. 102–114). Portsmouth, NH: Heinemann.

Loban, W. D. (1970). The limitless possibilities for increasing knowledge about language. *Elementary English, 47,* 624–630.

Loban, W. D. (1976). *Language development: Kindergarten through grade twelve* (Research Report No. 18). Urbana, IL: National Council of Teachers of English.

Love, G. A., & Payne, M. (Eds.). (1969). *Contemporary essays on style: Rhetoric, linguistics, and criticism.* Glenview, IL: Scott, Foresman.

Macauley, W. J. (1947). The difficulty of grammar. *British Journal of Educational Psychology, 17,* 153–162.

MacGowan-Gilhooly, A. (1991a). Fluency before correctness: A whole language experiment in college ESL. *College ESL, 1*(1), 37–47.

MacGowan-Gilhooly, A. (1991b). Fluency first: Reversing the traditional ESL sequence. *Journal of Basic Writing, 10*(1), 73–87.

MacGowan-Gilhooly, A. (1993). *Achieving fluency in English: A whole-language book* (2nd ed.). Dubuque: Kendall/Hunt.

MacGowan-Gilhooly, A. (1995). *Achieving clarity in English: A whole-language book* (2nd ed.). Dubuque: Kendall/Hunt.

MacKenzie, T. (Ed.). (1992). *Readers' workshops: Bridging literature and literacy.* Toronto: Irwin.

Malmstrom J., & Weaver, C. (1973). *Transgrammar: English structure, style, and dialects.* Glenview, IL: Scott, Foresman.

Manning, M., Manning, G., & Long, R. (1994). *Theme immersion: Inquiry-based curriculum in elementary and middle schools.* Portsmouth, NH: Heinemann.

Master, D. (1977). Build a skill, step by step. In O. Clapp (Ed.), *Classroom practices in teaching English 1977–1978: Teaching the basics—really!* (pp. 90–92). Urbana, IL: National Council of Teachers of English.

Mayher, J. S. (1990). *Uncommon sense: Theoretical practice in language education.* Portsmouth, NH: Boynton/Cook.

Mayher, J. S., Lester, N., & Pradl, G. (1983). *Writing to learn: Learning to write.* Portsmouth, NH: Boynton/Cook.

McCaig, R. A. (1972). *The writing of elementary school children: A model for evaluation.* Grosse Pointe, MI: Grosse Pointe Public School System.

McCaig, R. A. (1977). What research and evaluation tell us about teaching written expression in the elementary school. In C. Weaver & R. Douma (Eds.), *The language arts teacher in action* (pp. 46–56). Kalamazoo, MI: Western Michigan University. Distributed by the National Council of Teachers of English.

McGee, L. M., & Richgels, D. J. (1990). *Literacy's beginnings: Supporting young readers and writers.* Boston: Allyn & Bacon.

McQuade, F. (1980). Examining a grammar course: The rationale and the result. *English Journal, 69,* 26–30.

Meckel, H. C. (1963). Research on teaching composition and literature. In N. L. Gage (Ed.), *Handbook of research on teaching* (pp. 966–1006). Chicago: Rand McNally. [see pp. 981–982 especially]

Mellon, J. C. (1969). *Transformational sentence-combining* (Research Report No. 10). Urbana, IL: National Council of Teachers of English.

Mellon, J. C. (1975). *National assessment and the teaching of English.* Urbana, IL: National Council of Teachers of English.

Mellon, J. C. (1976). Round two of the national writing assessment—interpreting the apparent decline of writing ability: A review. *Research in the Teaching of English, 10,* 66–74.

Memering, D. (1978). Forward to the basics. *College English, 39,* 553–561.

Mendez, P. (1989). *The black snowman.* Illus. C. Byard. New York: Scholastic.

Michigan State Board of Education. (1994). *Assessment Frameworks for the Michigan High School Proficiency Test in Communication Arts. Part I: Writing.* Prepared by the Michigan Council of Teachers of English. E. H. Brinkley, Project Manager. Lansing. (Printed in the *Michigan English Teacher* [May 1993], a publication of the MCTE.)

Morenberg, M., Daiker, D., & Kerek, A. (1978). Sentence combining at the college level: An experimental study. *Research in the Teaching of English, 12,* 245–256.

Morrison, K. F. (1983). Incentives for studying the liberal arts. In D. L. Wagner (Ed.), *The seven liberal arts in the Middle Ages* (pp. 32–57). Bloomington: Indiana University Press.

Most, B. (1978). *If the dinosaurs came back.* San Diego: Harcourt Brace Jovanovich.

Murray, D. M. (1985). *A writer teaches writing.* Boston: Houghton Mifflin. (Earlier edition published 1968)

Nelson, N. W. (1988). The nature of literacy. In M. A. Nippold (Ed.), *Later language development: Ages nine through nineteen* (pp. 11–28). Boston: College Hill Press.

Newman, J. M. (1984). *The craft of children's writings.* Richmond Hill, Ontario: Scholastic. Distributed in the United States by Heinemann.

Ninio, A., & Bruner, J. (1978). The achievement and antecedents of labelling. *Journal of Child Language, 5,* 1–15.

Nippold, M. A. (Ed.). (1988). *Later language development: Ages nine through nineteen.* Boston: College Hill Press.

Noguchi, R. R. (1991). *Grammar and the teaching of writing: Limits and possibilities.* Urbana, IL: National Council of Teachers of English.

O'Donnell, R. C., Griffin, W. J., & Norris, R. C. (1967). *Syntax of kindergarten and elementary school children: A transformational analysis* (Research Report No. 8). Urbana, IL: National Council of Teachers of English.

O'Hare, F. (1973). *Sentence combining: Improving student writing without formal grammar instruction* (Research Report No. 15). Urbana, IL: National Council of Teachers of English.

PAT reading comprehension and reading vocabulary tests. (1969). Wellington: New Zealand Council for Educational Research.

Paulsen, G. (1988). *The island.* New York: Dell.

Paulsen, G. (1991). *The river.* New York: Dell.

Perera, K. (1984). *Children's writing and reading.* London: Blackwell.

Perera, K. (1986). *Language acquisition as a continuing process: The role of the English teacher.* Paper presented at the Fourth International Conference on the Teaching of English, Ottawa, Ontario, May.

Porter, W. S. (1936). *The complete works of O. Henry.* Garden City, NJ: Doubleday, Doran.

Postman, N., & Weingartner, C. (1966). *Linguistics: A revolution in teaching.* New York: Dell.

Quintilian [Marcus Fabius Quintilianus]. (n.d.). *Institutes of oratory.* 12 vols. (J. S. Watson, Trans.). London: George Bell and Sons, 1887.

Quirk, R., Greenbaum, S., Leech, G., & Svartvik, J. (1985). *A comprehensive grammar of the English language.* London: Longman.

Read, C. (1975). *Children's categorization of speech sounds in English.* (Research Report No. 17). Urbana, IL: National Council of Teachers of English.

Reed, A., & Kellogg, B. (1909). *Higher lessons in English: A work on English grammar and composition, in which the science of the language is made tributary to the art of expression.* New York: Charles E. Merrill. (First edition published 1872.)

Reed, H. (1946). Naming of parts. In *A map of Verona.* London: Jonathan Cape.

Rice, J. (1986a). *Cowboy night before Christmas.* Gretna, LA: Pelican.

Rice, J. (1986b). *Texas night before Christmas.* Gretna, LA: Pelican.

Rice, S. (1993). *Right words, right places.* Belmont, CA: Wadsworth.

Richards, J. C. (1971). A non-contrastive approach to error analysis. *English Language Teaching, 25,* 204–219.

Rief, L. (1991). *Seeking diversity: Language arts with adolescents.* Portsmouth, NH: Heinemann.

Roberts, P. (1956). *Patterns of English.* New York: Harcourt Brace Jovanovich.

Romano, T. (1987). *Clearing the way: Working with teenage writers.* Portsmouth, NH: Heinemann.

Romano, T. (1988). Breaking the rules in style. *English Journal, 77,* 58–62.

Romano, T. (1995). *Writing with passion: Life stories, multiple genres.* Portsmouth, NH: Heinemann.

Rosen, L. M. (1987). Developing correctness in student writing: Alternatives to the error-hunt. *English Journal, 76,* 62–69.

Routman, R. (1991). *Invitations: Changing as teachers and learners K–12.* Portsmouth, NH: Heinemann.

Rutherford, W. E. (1973). *Sentence sense.* New York: Harcourt Brace Jovanovich.

Rutsala, V. (1992). Words. In J. Nims (Ed.), *Western wind: An introduction to poetry* (3rd ed.). New York: McGraw-Hill.

Safire, W. (1993). *Quoth the maven.* New York: Random House.

Sanborn, J. (1986). Grammar: Good wine before its time. *English Journal, 75,* 72–80.

Scardamalia, M., Bereiter, C., & Goelman, H. (1982). The role of production factors in writing ability. In M. Nystrand (Ed.), *What writers know: The language, process and structure of written discourse* (pp. 173–210). New York: Academic Press.

Schumann, J. H. (1974). Implications of pidginization and creolization for the study of adult second language acquisition. In J. H. Schumann & N. Stenson (Eds.), *New frontiers in second language learning* (pp. 137–151). Rowley, MA: Newbury House.

Scott, C. M. (1988). Spoken and written syntax. In M. A. Nippold (Ed.), *Later language development: Ages nine through nineteen* (pp. 49–95). Boston: College Hill Press.

Searles, J. R., & Carlson, G. R. (1960). Language, grammar, and composition. In C. W. Harris (Ed.), *Encyclopedia of educational research* (3rd ed., pp. 454–470). New York: Macmillan.

Sebranek, P., Meyer, V., & Kemper, D. (1990). *Writers Inc.* (2nd ed.). Burlington, WI: Write Source.

Sebranek, P., Meyer, V., & Kemper, D. (1995). *Write source 2000: A guide to writing, thinking, and learning* (3rd ed.). Burlington, WI: Write Source.

Sedgwick, E. (1989). Alternatives to teaching formal, analytical grammar. *Journal of Developmental Education, 12* (3), 8–10, 12, 14, 20.

Semple, C., & Tuer, J. (1988). *Mom's haircut*. Bothell, WA: The Wright Group.

Seymour, D. Z. (1971). Black children, black speech. *Commonweal Magazine*, November 19. Reprinted in P. Eschholz, A. Rosa, & V. Clark (Eds.), *Language awareness* (6th ed., pp. 122–130). New York: St. Martin's Press, 1994.

Shaughnessy, M. P. (1977). *Errors and expectations: A guide for the teacher of basic writing*. New York: Oxford University Press.

Shook, R. (1983). Response to Martha Kolln, "Closing the Books on Alchemy," CCC 32 (May, 1981), 139–151. *College Composition and Communication, 34*, 491–495.

Shuman, R. B. (1995). Grammar for writers: How much is enough? In S. Hunter & R. Wallace (Eds.), *The place of grammar in writing instruction: Past, present, future* (pp. 114–128). Portsmouth, NH: Boynton/Cook.

Simmons, G. M., & Hutchinson, H. D. (Eds.). (1972). *Black culture: Reading and writing black*. New York: Holt, Rinehart.

Sledd, J. H. (1959). *A short introduction to English grammar*. Chicago: Scott, Foresman.

Sledd, J. H. (1969). Bi-dialectalism: The linguistics of white supremacy. *English Journal, 58*, 1307–1315.

Slobin, D. I. (1972). *They learn the same way all around the world*. Psychology Today, 6 (July), 72–74, 82.

Smart, P. R. (1969). *Let's learn English in the 70's*. Wellington, New Zealand: A. H. & A. W. Reed.

Smith, B. K. (1966). *Dictionary of English word-roots*. Savage, MD: Littlefield Adams.

Smith, F. (1975). *Comprehension and learning: A conceptual framework for teachers*. Katonah, NY: Richard C. Owen.

Smith, F. (1981a). Demonstrations, engagement, and sensitivity: A revised approach to language learning. *Language Arts, 58*, 103–112.

Smith, F. (1981b). Demonstrations, engagement, and sensitivity: The choice between people and programs. *Language Arts, 58*, 634–642.

Smith, F. (1990). *To think*. New York: Teachers College Press.

Smith, H. L., Dugdale, K., Steele, B. F., & McElhinney, R. S. (1946). *One hundred fifty years of grammar textbooks*. Bloomington: Indiana University, Division of Research and Field Services.

Smith, W. L., & Hull, G. A. (1985). Differential effects of sentence combining on college students who use particular structures with high and low frequencies. In D. A. Daiker, A. Kerek, & M. Morenberg (Eds.), *Sentence combining: A rhetorical perspective* (pp. 17–32). Carbondale, IL: Southern Illinois University Press.

Smitherman, G. (1972). English teacher, why you be doing the thangs you don't do? *English Journal, 61*, 59–65.

Smitherman, G. (1992). Black English, diverging or converging? The view from the National Assessment of Educational Progress. *Language and education, 6* (1), 47–61.

Snow, C. E. (1986). Conversations with children. In P. Fletcher & M. Garman

(Eds.), *Language acquisition: Studies in first language development* (2nd ed., pp. 69–89). New York: Cambridge University Press.

Snow, C. E., Dubber, C., & De Blauw, A. (1982). Routines in mother-child interaction. In L. Feagans & D. C. Farran (Eds.), *The language of children reared in poverty: Implications for evaluation and intervention.* New York: Academic Press.

Sommers, N. (1980). Revision strategies of student writers and experienced adult writers. *College Composition and Communication, 31,* 378–388.

Stephens, D. (1991). *Research on whole language: Support for a new curriculum.* Katonah, NY: Richard C. Owen.

Stires, S. (Ed.). (1991). *With promise: Redefining reading and writing needs for special students.* Portsmouth, NH: Heinemann.

Strickland, K., & Strickland, J. (1993). *UN-covering the curriculum: Whole language in secondary and postsecondary classrooms.* Portsmouth, NH: Boynton/Cook.

Strong, W. (1981). *Sentence combining and paragraph building.* New York: McGraw-Hill.

Strong, W. (1984a). *Crafting cumulative sentences.* New York: McGraw-Hill.

Strong, W. (1984b). *Practicing sentence options.* New York: McGraw-Hill.

Strong, W. (1986). *Creative approaches to sentence combining.* Urbana, IL: ERIC/RCS and the National Council of Teachers of English.

Strong, W. (1991). *Writing incisively: Do it yourself prose surgery.* New York: McGraw-Hill.

Strong, W. (1993). *Sentence combining: A composing book* (3rd ed.). New York: McGraw-Hill.

Stull, W. L. (1983). *Combining and creating: Sentence combining and generative rhetoric.* New York: Holt, Rinehart.

Tan, A. (1992). *The moon lady.* New York: Macmillan.

Taylor, D. (1989). Toward a unified theory of literacy learning and instructional practices. *Phi Delta Kappan, 71,* 184–193.

Temple, C., Nathan, R., Temple, F., & Burris, N. (1993). *The beginnings of writing* (3rd ed.). Boston: Allyn & Bacon.

Terrell, T. D. (1991). The role of grammar instruction in a communicative approach. *Modern Language Journal, 75,* 52–63.

Thomas, O. (1965). *Transformational grammar and the teacher of English.* New York: Holt, Rinehart.

Thomas, O., & Kintgen, E. R. (1974). *Transformational grammar and the teacher of English* (2nd ed.). New York: Holt, Rinehart.

"Trosclair." (1992). *Cajun night before Christmas.* Illus. J. Rice, Ed. by Howard Jacobs. Gretna, LA: Pelican.

Troyka, L. Q., with Dobie, A. B., & Gordon, E. R. (1992). *Simon & Schuster handbook for writers* (3rd ed.). Englewood Cliffs, NJ: Prentice Hall.

Tunnell, M. O., & Jacobs, J. S. (1989). Using "real" books: Research findings on literature based reading instruction. *The Reading Teacher, 42,* 470–477.

Turner, T. N. (1994). *Hillbilly night afore Christmas.* Illus. J. Rice. Gretna, LA: Pelican.

Vail, N. J., & Papenfuss, J. F. (1989–1990). *Daily oral language*. Levels 1–12. Evanston, IL: McDougal, Littell.

Van Laan, N. (1990). *Possum come a-knockin*. Illus. G. Booth. New York: Alfred A. Knopf, Dragonfly Books.

Vaura, E. (1994). *Teaching grammar as a liberating art*. Williamsport, PA: Rose Parisella Productions.

Villiers, U. (1989). *Luk mume dade I kan rite*. New York: Scholastic. (Spanish version also available)

Vygotsky, L. S. (1986). *Thought and language*. (A. Kozulin, Trans.). Cambridge, MA: MIT Press. (Earlier edition published 1962)

Vygotsky, L. S. (1978). *Mind in society: The development of higher psychological processes*. (M. Cole, V. John-Steiner, S. Scribner, & E. Souberman, Eds.). Cambridge, MA: Harvard University Press.

Walker, A. (1982). *The color purple*. New York: Harcourt Brace Jovanovich.

Warriner, J. E. (1986). *Warriner's English grammar and composition* series (Liberty ed.). New York: Harcourt Brace Jovanovich. (First edition published 1951)

Warriner's high school handbook. (1992). Orlando, FL: Holt, Rinehart.

Weathers, W. (1980). *An alternate style: Options in composition*. Portsmouth, NH: Boynton/Cook.

Weaver, C. (1979). *Grammar for teachers: Perspectives and definitions*. Urbana, IL: National Council of Teachers of English.

Weaver, C. (1982). Welcoming errors as signs of growth. *Language Arts, 59*, 438–444.

Weaver, C. (1990). *Understanding whole language*. Portsmouth, NH: Heinemann.

Weaver, C. (1994). *Reading process and practice: From socio-psycholinguistics to whole language* (2nd ed.). Portsmouth, NH: Heinemann. (First edition published 1988)

Weaver, C. (1996). Understanding and helping Jaime with language: A psycholinguistic and constructivist perspective. In E. R. Silliman, L. C. Wilkinson, & L. P. Hoffman (Eds.), *Children's journeys through school: Assessing competence in language and literacy*. San Diego, CA: Singular Publishing Group.

Whitehall, H. (1956). *Structural essentials of English*. New York: Harcourt, Brace.

Wilde, S. (1992). *You kan red this! Spelling and punctuation for whole language classrooms, K–6*. Portsmouth, NH: Heinemann.

Williams, J. M. (1981). The phenomenology of error. *College Composition and Communication, 32*, 152–168.

Williams, J. M. (1990). *Style: Toward clarity and grace*. Chicago: University of Chicago Press.

Woods, W. F. (1986). The evolution of nineteenth-century grammar teaching. *Rhetoric Review, 5* (1), 4–20.

Wright, R. (1935). *White man, listen!* New York: Paul R. Reynolds.

Wright, R. (1937). *Black boy*. New York: Harper & Row, 1966.

Yeats, W. B. (1924). Leda and the swan. In P. Allt & R. K. Alspach (Eds.), *The variorum edition of the poems of W. B. Yeats*. New York: Macmillan, 1957.

Zemelman, S., & Daniels, H. (1988). *A community of writers: Teaching writing in the junior and senior high school*. Portsmouth, NH: Boynton/Cook.

Index

Dionysios of Thrace, 3
direct methods of instruction, 175–76
Donatus, 3
"Don't No Revolutions Hardly *Ever* Come By Here," 234–35
Dove, Rita, 228
drawings of children, errors in, 60–62

Early Language, 45
editing
   copyedited manuscript, sample, 92
   of final revision, teaching, 87–101
   living with errors in final draft, 97
   peer editing/proofreading, use of, 95, 96, 97
   resources useful for, developing, 88, 91
   sample lessons for teaching concepts used in, 190–213
   selected errors in final draft, responding only to, 97, 100
   teacher as copyeditor, technique of, 100
   teacher comments during editing process, 94, 96
   teachers helping students edit/proof own writing, 84–85
   teaching concepts for, 142
Editorial Skills course, effects of, 22–23
Elgin, Suzette, 234
Elley, Warwick, 20–21, 50–52
Ellison, Ralph, 214, 221
empowerment, in constructivist learning model, 159, 161
Encyclopedia of Educational Research, 9–10, 152
English as second language. *See also* second language acquisition
   review of research on, 50–55
"English Teacher, Why You Be Doing the Thangs You Don't Do?," 234–35
errors
   behavioral and constructivist approaches to, contrast between, 63
   in children's drawings, analyzing, 60–62
   culture, errors as products of, 114, 115
   effects of varied emphasis on, in ESL college instruction, 53, 54
   in final drafts, 87–100
   frequency of different types of, 117
   handbooks prohibitions and stylistic effectiveness, 75–82
   living with, in final draft, 97
   more sophisticated, replacing less sophisticated, 72–74
   as necessary for growth, 59–62, 63
   as necessary result of instruction, 69–72
   overreacting to, 81–82
   as part of learning, 62, 64–69
   proofreading, teaching, 87–100
   in published writing, treatment of, 74–75
   ranking of errors, research concerning, 105–15
   rate of, analyzing, 72–74
   reconsidering what counts as error, 74–75, 104–15
   responding to, constructively, 81–82
   selected errors in final draft, responding only to, 97, 100
   spelling, as part of learning, 62, 64–69
   stylistic effectiveness in writing, error analysis and, 75–82
Errors and Expectations, 70, 140
"Errorwocky," 100
Erskine, John, 131
examples, used as alternative to grammar instruction, 26
expectation, 169
"Explaining Grammatical Concepts," 148
explanations, in constructivist learning model, 158–59
extended mini-lessons, 171

"Fight over Liquid Gold, A," 215
first language acquisition. *See also* language acquisition
   process of, 56–57
"Fluency Before Correctness: A Whole Language Experiment in College ESL," 52
"Fluency First: Reversing the Traditional ESL Sequence," 52
formal grammar instruction
   alternatives to, 26–28
   based on behaviorist learning theory, 148, 152–53
   learning theory basis for, 148, 152–53
   reasons for, 7–9, 23–25
   reconceptualizing grammar instruction. (*see* reconceptualizing grammar instruction)
   references for and against, 8

formal grammar instruction (continued)
  research studies, 9–16, 16–20, 20–21,
    22–23, 26
  transference to students' writing, 27–28,
    102–4
  transmission model of education and,
    148–50
fragments
  as basic grammatical concept, 116
  defined, 122, 249
  judicious use of, 76–77, 78–81
  sample lessons, 201–9
Francis, W. Nelson, 30
free modifiers, 116
  defined, 121, 249–51
  examples of writing using, 132–33
  illustration of, 118–20
  sample lessons, 217, 222–23
Frogner, Ellen, 174
functional grammar, 14
functional linguistics, 146
function words, grammatical competence
    and, 42
fused sentences
  basic grammatical concepts and, 116
  defined, 121–22
  sample lessons, 207–9

generative rhetoric, 131–33
Gordon, Michael, 223
grammar. *See also* syntax
  basic grammatical concepts that need to
    be understood, 115–23
  competence with. (*see* grammatical
    competence)
  defined, 1–2, 251
  formal teaching of. (*see* formal grammar
    instruction)
  historical overview of grammar
    instruction, 3–6
  reconceptualizing grammar instruction.
    (*see* reconceptualizing grammar
    instruction)
  sample lessons for teaching, 187–242
  scope and sequence in the teaching of,
    138–47
  senses of, 2
  teaching of. (*see* formal grammar
    instruction; teaching grammar)

Grammar and the Teaching of Writing, 104
Grammar for Teachers, 82
"grammar" schools, 4
grammatical competence
  acquisition of, 38
  adult utterances and, 40, 42, 56
  increased representation of surface
    structure, 40–43
  initial stages of, 39–40
  in kindergarteners, 43–45
  in language acquisition process, 56
  miscue patterns in development of,
    45–48
  in second language acquisition, 48–50
grammatical sentence
  defined, 120–21, 251
  illustration of, 118
  punctuated sentence and, 32
"Graveyard, The," 118–20
Gray, Paul, 215
"Great Wall of China, The," 227
Greece, grammar instruction and ancient,
    3, 6
Greene, H.A., 152

Hacker, Diana, 185
Harris, Roland, 175–76
Heller, Ruth, 189
Hemingway, Ernest, 226
Hillocks, George, 11, 13–14
historical overview of grammar
    instruction, 3–6
Holy Bible (Black English Vernacular
    Translation), 233–34
Hunt, Kellogg
  minimum terminable unit research, 32
  syntactic maturity research, 12, 123–31
Hunter, Madeline, 151, 152

"I am" poems, writing, 216–17
"if" clause, sample lesson for teaching
    hypothetical, 190
If the Dinosaurs Came Back, 190
Immediate Constituent Analysis (ICA), 30
immersion, 168
Inada, Lawson, 230–31, 232
incidental lessons, 166–69, 188–90
independent clauses
  as basic grammatical concept, 115–16

McQuade, F., 22–23
meaning units (M-units), 39
mechanics, teaching, 144
Meckel, Henry C., 15–16
Mellon, John, 12, 72
Mendez, Phil, 215
Minehart, Tom, 215
mini-conferences, teaching
    editing/proofreading during, 87,
    93
mini-lessons
  as basis for effective teaching of
    grammatical concepts, 150–51,
    171
  characteristics of effective, 150–51
  commercially produced, 172
  description of, 171
  sample, 185–242
  technique compared to ITIP procedures,
    156–57
minor sentence, defined, 252
miscue
  defined, 45
  patterns, and grammar acquisition,
    45–48
modeling the editing/proofreading process,
    87, 93
modifier, defined, 121, 252
monitor, language, 50
Moon Lady, The, 214
Most, Bernard, 190
motivation, in constructivist learning
    model, 158, 159, 161
M-unit, defined, 252
"My Brothers," 192

National Assessment of Educational
    Progress, 73
negative sentences, skill acquisition in
    constructing, 37–38
New Zealand, research on grammar
    instruction in, 20–21
Noguchi, Rei, 104–5, 228
nonrestrictive clauses, sample lessons,
    239–42
Notes Toward a New Rhetoric, 75
noun
  defined, 252–53
  importance of teaching concept,
    122

incidental lessons for teaching, sample,
    188–90

O'Hare, Frank, 12
"On Top of Mount Fuji, People Hope for
    Change," 215
options, in constructivist learning model,
    159

parents, pressure to teach formal grammar
    and, 25
"Parsley," 228
Parsons, Joel, 217
participial phrases
  errors in use of, 71–72
  importance of teaching concept, 123
  sample lessons, 189, 214–20
participle, defined, 253–54
parts of speech
  defined, 254
  lessons for, 168–69, 188–90
past tense of verbs, skill acquisition in
    forming, 36, 37–38
*PAT Reading Comprehension and Reading
    Vocabulary Tests,* 20
Paulsen, Gary, 191
phrase
  defined, 121, 254
  teaching concept of, 142
possessives
  errors concerning, 70, 71, 117
  sample lessons, 236
Power of Reading, The, 56, 225
predicate, defined, 255
preposition, defined, 255
prepositional phrase, sample lessons,
    189–90, 199–200
Priestley, J.B., 225
Priscian, 3
pronoun, defined, 255–56
proofreading. *See* editing
propositions, 31, 33
  combining, in children, 42
  syntactic maturity and, 129–30
published writing
  helping students use same process as
    published writers, 82–86
  stylistic effectiveness in, analysis of,
    75–82
punctuated sentence, defined, 32, 256

punctuation
"dos and dont's," 212–13
sample lessons, 211–13, 236–42
teaching, 144

Quintilian, 4
quotation marks, sample lesson on,
164–65

"Rayford's Song," 230–31, 232
*Reading Mastery: DISTAR and DISTAR
Language,* 162
Reading Process and Practice, 225
reading workshops, references for
instituting, 86
reconceptualizing grammar instruction
basic grammatical concepts that need to
be understood, 115–23
focus, narrowing the, 104–23
promoting growth in syntactic
complexity, 134–37
ranking of errors, research into, 105–15
suggestions on how to, 181–83
terminology, limiting the, 104–23
reductionist learning theory. *See also*
transmission model of education
constructivist learning theory compared
to, 149, 162–63
Reeves, Pat, 217
references
dialects
on dialects versus Language of Wider
Communication, 229
representing various dialects, 233
on early development of spelling and
writing, 70
grammar as style, for teaching, 80
grammar texts and reference books,
89–91
on sentence combining and sentence
generating, 135
teaching formal grammar, references for
and against, 8
on whole language as constructivist
learning, 163
writers' and readers' workshops,
references for instituting, 86
research
constructivist learning theory, in
support of, 174–79

English as second language, review of,
50–56
errors
professional people, Hairston study of
errors and, 105, 108–15
students' errors, Connors and
Lunsford study of, 105, 106–8, 111,
115
on formal grammar instruction, 9–16,
16–20, 20–21, 22–23, 26
on structural linguistics, 11
on transformational grammar, 11–14
Research in Written Composition, 10
response, 169
responsibility, 169
rhetoric
defined, 256–57
generative rhetoric, 131–33
stylistic effectiveness in writing, analysis
of, 75–82
Rhetorical Grammar, 16
Rice, Scott, 185, 221, 227
*Right Handbook, The: Grammar and Usage
in Context,* 185
Right Words, Right Places, 185, 221, 227
Romano, Tom, 242
Rosie's Walk, 169, 190
run-on sentences
basic grammatical concepts and,
116
defined, 121–22, 257
sample lessons, 203–4
Rutsala, Vern, 232

Safire, William, 74
scaffolding, 160
Schoer, Lowell, 10
scope and sequence in the teaching of
grammar, 138–47
Scotland, research on grammar instruction
in, 16–20
second language acquisition
knowledge of grammar and, 9, 51–52
process of, 48–50, 57
research on, 50–55, 57
semantics, defined, 257
senses of grammar, 2
sentence combining
sample lessons for teaching style
through, 214–22

traditional teaching of grammar. (*see* formal grammar instruction)

via mini-lessons. (*see* mini-lessons)

whole language as constructivist learning and teaching, references on, 163

teaching strategies, constructivist, 165–74

terminology, narrowing the, 104–23, 144, 145

texts

examination of, as alternative to grammar instruction, 27

historical perspective, 3–6

Thorndike, Edward, 152

To Think, 153

traditional teaching of grammar. *See* formal grammar instruction

transactional model of education

constructivism as basis for, 148, 153–55

transmission model of education compared to, 149

transductional learning theory. *See also* constructivist learning theory

transmission learning theory compared to, 149

transformational grammar

development of, 30–32

in Elley, et. al. study, 20–21

sample lessons, 224–27

value of studying grammar through, 11–14

transformational linguistics, 146

development of, 30–32

transmission model of education

as basis for formal grammar instruction, 148

behavioralism as basis for, 148, 152–53

constructivist model contrasted with the, 149

transactional model of education compared to, 149

transparencies, teachers' use of, 185

Trees Stand Shining, The, 215

trivium, 3

Trujillo, Rafael, 228

T-unit

defined, 32, 120–21, 124, 258

illustration of, 118

in syntactic maturity, 124–25, 129

verbs

auxiliary, skill acquisition in ordering, 34, 35–36

defined, 258–60

importance of teaching concept, 122

past tense, skill acquistion in forming, 36, 37–38

sample lessons, 188–90, 190–200

teaching concept of, 142

Walker, Alice, 232

Warriner's English Grammar and Composition series, 2

Warriner's High School Handbook, 2

Weathers, Winston, 242

Weaver, Constance, 82, 100, 217, 225

whole language education as constructivist learning, references on, 163

Williams, Joseph, 74–75

word endings, grammatical competence and, 42

word order, grammatical competence and, 42

"Words," 232

words, sample lesson for teaching meaningful parts of, 187–88

workshops

editing, 93

for writers, 83, 84, 86

Wright, Richard, 215, 227

Writer's Reference, A, 185

writers' workshops, 83, 84, 86

writing

editing. (*see* editing)

engaging students in writing across curriculum, importance of, 141, 144

errors. (*see* errors)

final drafts, editing, 87–100

handbook rules and stylistic effectiveness, comparing, 75–81

mini-lessons as basis for teaching. (*see* mini-lessons)

process of published writers, helping students use, 82–86

proofreading. (*see* editing)

published

students use same process as published writers, helping, 82–86

stylistic effectivenes in, analysis of, 75–81

The author and publisher thank those who granted permission to reprint borrowed material:

Excerpt from "The Role of Grammar in a Secondary English Curriculum" by W. B. Elley, I. H. Barham, H. Lamb, and M. Wyllie. From New Zealand *Journal of Educational Studies* 10, May 1975. Reprinted by permission of the New Zealand Council for Educational Research.

Excerpt from "Fluency First: Reversing the Traditional ESL Sequence" by Adele MacGowan-Gilhooly. From *Journal of Basic Writing* 10(1), Spring 1991. Reprinted by permission of the City University of New York, Instructional Resource Center.

Excerpts from *Huggles Goes Away* (© 1986), *The Bicycle* (© 1983), and *Ratty-Tatty* (© 1987) by J. Cowley; *Mom's Haircut* (© 1988) by C. Semple and J. Tuer; and *Look* (© 1988) by J. Cutting. Published by The Wright Group, Bothell, Washington. Reprinted by permission of The Wright Group.

Excerpt from *Clifford Takes a Trip* by Norman Bridwell. Copyright © 1966 by Norman Bridwell. Reprinted by permission of Scholastic Inc. *Clifford* and *Clifford the Big Red Dog* are registered trademarks of Norman Bridwell.

Figure 4.3 from "Error and Analysis and the Teaching of Composition" by Barry M. Kroll and John C. Schafer. From *College Composition and Communication* 29, 1978. Reprinted by permission of the National Council of Teachers of English.

Figure 4.5a from "Beginning Reading and Writing Through Singing: A Natural Approach" by Sheila Fitzgerald in *Highway One* 7(ii), Spring 1984. Reprinted by permission of the author and the Canadian Council of Teachers of English.

Figure 4.5b from *Reading, Writing and Caring* by Cochrane, Cochrane, Scalena, and Buchanan. Copyright 1984. Reprinted by permission.

Figure 4.10 from "A Few Good Words for the Comma Splice" by Irene Brosnahan. From *College English* 38, 1976. Reprinted by permission of the National Council of Teachers of English.

Figure 4.11 from "Formal Fragments: The English Minor Sentence" by C. R. Kline and W. D. Memering. From *Research in the Teaching of English* 11, 1977. Reprinted by permission of the National Council of Teachers of English.

Figure 4.16 from "Helping Children Become More Responsible for Their Own Writing" by Mary Ellen Giacobbe. From *LiveWire* 1(i), 1984. Reprinted by permission of the National Council of Teachers of English.

Excerpts and Figure 5.1 from "Frequency of Formal Errors in Current College Writing, or Ma and Pa Kettle Do Research" by Robert Connors and Andrea Lunsford. From *College Composition and Communication* 39, 1988. Reprinted by permission of the National Council of Teachers of English.

Figures 5.2 and 5.3 from "Not All Errors Are Created Equal: Nonacademic Readers in the Professions Respond to Lapses of Usage" by Maxine Hairston. From *College English* 43, 1981. Reprinted by permission of the National Council of Teachers of English.

Figure 5.6 from "Syntactic Maturity in Schoolchildren and Adults" by Kellogg Hunt. From *Monographs of the Society for Research in Child Development* (134), 1970. Reprinted by permission of the Society for Research in Child Development.

Excerpt from "Build a Skill, Step by Step" by Doris Master. From *Classroom Practices in Teaching English, 1977–1978: Teaching the Basics—Really!*, edited by O. Clapp. Copyright © 1977. Reprinted by permission of the National Council of Teachers of English.

Excerpt from "Between the World and Me" by Richard Wright. Copyright © 1935 by Richard Wright. Reprinted by permission of John Hawkins & Associates, Inc.

Excerpt from "Leda and the Swan" by W. B. Yeats. From *The Poems of W. B. Yeats: A New Edition*, edited by Richard J. Finneran. Copyright 1928 by Macmillan Publishing Company, renewed 1956 by Georgie Yeats. Reprinted with the permission of Simon & Schuster, Inc.

"Rayford's Song" by Lawson Fusao Inada. From *Legends from Camp* by Lawson Fusao Inada. Copyright 1993. Reprinted by permission of Coffee House Press.

Figure A.1 from "Explaining Grammatical Concepts" by Muriel Harris and Katherine E. Rowan. From *Journal of Basic Writing* 8(2), Fall 1991. Reprinted by permission of The City University of New York, Instructional Resource Center.